Waltham Forest Libraries

Please return this item by the last date stamped. The loan may be
renewed unless required by ~~~~~~~~~~~

AUG 2015		

Need to renew your books?
http://www.londonlibraries.gov.uk/walthamforest or
Dial 0115 929 3388 for Callpoint – our 24/7 automated telephone renewal
line. You will need your library card number and your PIN. If you do not
know your PIN, contact your local library.

ANY OTHER BUSINESS

ANY OTHER BUSINESS

LIFE IN AND OUT OF THE CITY

COLLECTED WRITINGS FROM
THE SPECTATOR AND ELSEWHERE

MARTIN VANDER WEYER

FOREWORD BY FRASER NELSON

First published 2014 by
Elliott and Thompson Limited
27 John Street
London WC1N 2BX
www.eandtbooks.com

ISBN: 978-1-78396-016-3

All articles are from *The Spectator* unless otherwise indicated.
Article on page 179 reprinted with permission from *Country Life*.

9 8 7 6 5 4 3 2 1

A catalogue record for this book is available from the British Library.

Jacket illustrations: Morten Morland
Typesetting: Marie Doherty
Printed in the UK by TJ International Ltd

Contents

Foreword

When I started out as a business journalist, there was an unwritten rule separating my colleagues and I from the general news reporters. They regarded us as being unable to write, and we regarded them as unable to understand anything more complex than a lunch receipt. It was part of the strange tension that has long existed in British journalism between those who do numbers and those who do words – and, underlying it, the notion that the term 'financial writer' is a contradiction in terms.

I'd like to say that this was all senseless bigotry, but then I can't think of a financial writer as good as Martin Vander Weyer. His columns have been informing and entertaining *Spectator* readers for more than two decades, and are still without equal. He routinely exposes the humour and absurdity behind much of what passes for high finance. He can see and describe the personalities behind the businesses and the clashing egos which power the City – and then jump on the train and talk about life in the country.

Crucially, he did not start out a journalist. The son of a banker, he was in the trade himself before he started to write about it for fun – his starting point was knowing all about the City. This is far better than those who, like me, went straight from journalism school to the financial pages, tried to work out what the hell was going on and vainly searched for stories through the footnotes of company reports. It was the devil's own job to try to get to know the people behind business: an army of public relations men made it their job to see that you never got close. And that the press was fed nothing but dull stories: about the Interim Results of Widgets Plc, and its EBITDA edging higher.

Martin has never had any involvement in this world. His contacts book was full when he entered journalism, and he has fished in different (and deeper) waters than his rivals. In short, he has only ever been interested in the fun stuff. What started as a distraction became a profession as demand for his writing grew. It was not just the quality of his prose, but the depth of his insight – and his ability to explain, in just a few paragraphs, what the businesses pages say in a thousand words that no one can bring themselves to read.

The Spectator has only had a few business columnists – three, in fact, over the last six decades – all of them sharing knowledge, wit, flair and a knack for exposition. The longest serving was Nicholas Davenport, who started in 1953, survived nine editors and was asking for more space than usual in the week's issue of his death in 1979. Next came Christopher Fildes, whose City & Suburban column in *The Spectator* was as legendary as the man himself. He and Martin first met in the City in 1976; the two kept in touch and eventually he converted Martin from a *Spectator* subscriber to a *Spectator* writer.

So, like many of our columnists – from Matthew Parris to Rod Liddle – Martin came to writing as a second career. And, like them, he's a natural: incapable of writing a dull sentence, as was clear from his very first pieces for the magazine. In 1992, the year he left banking, he wrote a prescient warning about the mega-bank mergers then in vogue (Midland Bank had just been gobbled up by HSBC). He is too modest to include the piece in this collection, but some of it does bear repeating.

'It is a safe piece of advice for a new chairman of a large international bank that at any given moment somebody, somewhere in your group, will be doing something utterly disastrous,' he wrote. 'Your Swiss foreign exchange manager is a fraudster; half the board want you to bid for Standard Chartered; someone else just recruited forty equity analysts in New York.' Making banks bigger would only increase the risk, he wrote: they would have mind-boggling diversity 'coupled with the complexity of the market risks involved and a fatal lack of comprehension between colleagues'. Result? 'A recipe for things to go awry.'

So it was to prove. But there have been plenty of histories of the crash, and not enough good writing about the business life outside it. And nowhere near enough writing that you actually want to read. This book is, like Martin's column, a collection of tales from Britain's financial front line with the fun bits left in. A romp through the City, its characters and their foibles, then into Yorkshire, with occasional diversions to violin competitions in Kazakhstan, the cuisine of the Dordogne and the lagoons of Bora Bora. The world of business is mad, sometimes bad and always thrillingly unpredictable – but, as *Spectator* readers know, there is no better guide.

Fraser Nelson

Introduction

I think myself lucky. Not in every aspect of life, to be sure, and not without making mistakes and wrong turnings – but in the way in which my second career as a journalist and financial commentator was born out of the demise of my first career as a banker and made space for what I think of as my third and fourth careers, in the performing arts and as an active, even hyperactive, citizen of my Yorkshire town of Helmsley.

I decided at the age of seventeen that I wanted to be a writer, and specifically that I wanted to write for *The Spectator*, which I had begun reading at home and at school during the editorship of Nigel Lawson in the late 1960s. At Oxford in the mid 1970s I somehow forgot that aspiration and decided to follow my father into the banking world, where I stayed for a decade and a half. I didn't hate it but I never loved it and it only ever engaged my brain fully when I was working abroad, in postings to Brussels, Kuala Lumpur, Tokyo and Hong Kong, and on assignments that took me to exotic spots from Bangkok to Budapest. In London I was habitually bored – and troubled by the thought that I had chosen the wrong career, or allowed it to choose me.

So my survival strategy was to jump on aeroplanes at every opportunity, and if you had met me in Hong Kong at my first-career zenith you might have thought me a caricature of the globe-trotting 1980s merchant banker: well tailored, wreathed in cigar smoke, with a chauffeured Mercedes at my disposal and a card that said 'managing director'.

I was undeservedly lucky to have got that far, given my lack of zest for the deal-making that marks out banking's real high-fliers, but I was even luckier in June 1989 to find myself – on a flight to Taipei – staring at a picture in *Country Life* of the house in Helmsley that I decided should become my home. It was, literally, a life-changing moment. I've always had a feeling that if I had not invested so much energy in that house over the following two years after I returned to a disagreeable City job – by now the card said 'chief operating officer' – my banking career might not have petered out when it did. And I might not have found the garden gate into journalism that opened for me so magically at the age of thirty-six.

But that's what happened next. One cold, sunny morning in January 1992 I was summarily sacked, and when a friend happened to telephone me a few minutes later I said, 'Well, maybe now I can start writing for *The Spectator*.' With a little help from Christopher Fildes, doyen of City commentators, and under the patronage of the magazine's then editor Dominic Lawson, I achieved that ambition a few weeks later – beginning with the first piece in this collection, 'The Phantom of the Gravy Train'.

I am lucky to be writing for it still, despite many changes of editorial regime. I eventually succeeded Christopher as *The Spectator*'s weekly financial columnist, and I can honestly say that to have been a member of the extended *Spectator* family all these years, to have experienced the last boozy breath of literary bohemia in its old house in Bloomsbury and the electric buzz of political intrigue in its new house in Westminster, has been the happiest passage of my life.

Meanwhile, under the tutelage of the incomparable Hugh Massingberd, I found another congenial niche as the author of the *Daily Telegraph*'s obituaries of businesspeople – a collection of which was published in 2006 as *Closing Balances*. I wrote comment, features and reviews for the *Telegraph* and many other parts of the national press. And because I was pigeonholed as that chap who broke out of the City and knew from the inside how the money world works, editors encouraged me to draw parables from personal experience – allowing me the luxury of telling my own life story in anecdotal episodes.

I thought it would be fun to collect some of those pieces (mostly from *The Spectator*, but from other sources where indicated) into a kind of autobiographical jigsaw puzzle, interspersed with travelogue and samples of my poetry. I hope this isn't just an exercise in vanity, and that the selection conveys a mischievous enjoyment of everything I do and observe – but also a set of underlying principles, including a belief in the positive power of capitalism, an admiration for entrepreneurship, and a fear that the financial sector in which I once worked is permanently prone to greed and delusion.

This selection also records other evolutions of my post-banking life, as an amateur actor, an occasional playwright, a promoter of arts projects, an elected town councillor, and briefly as a would-be MP. People often ask me how I fitted all this in. I don't really know the answer, except that I might have done some things better if I had not done so many other things, and that I abide by one more guiding principle – never have a dull day.

And looking back on what I might pompously call my body of work, written and otherwise, I can see that if there has been a consistent fault it is probably a consequence of thinking myself lucky: I have tended to err on the side of cheerfulness. Except for a bleak moment of financial crisis in 2008 when I recommended readers to take a shotgun and a bottle of whisky into the woods, I have always seen the light at the end of the tunnel and looked forward to the bounce that follows the crash. The cyclical nature of economic life is such that both the doomsters and the diehard optimists are always right in the end – but if I aimed a bit high or called the recovery a bit early, it's not a fault of which I'm particularly ashamed.

Besides Dominic Lawson at *The Spectator* and later at the *Sunday Telegraph*, there are many other editors and their deputies whom I must thank for giving me these opportunities to say what I wanted to say: notably Boris Johnson, who appointed me as his business editor, followed by Matthew d'Ancona and Fraser Nelson, at *The Spectator*; Sir Max Hastings and Charles Moore at the *Daily Telegraph*; Mark Law at both *Telegraph* titles; Sir Max again at the *Evening Standard*. I salute all my friends on the staff of those papers, past and present.

It was in my *Telegraph* obituary work that I came across a phrase which became yet another guiding principle, and which I have rec-ommended to many other people including the school prize-giving audiences I have occasionally been asked to address. I found it in an interview with the late Lord King of Wartnaby, a self-made grandee best known for his battling chairmanship of British Airways, who had started out as a car salesman and was not someone I would have cited as a role model except for this one remark: 'I am now what I always imagined myself to be.' I'm extraordinarily lucky – I sincerely hope this doesn't sound smug – to be able to say that too.

CHAPTER 1

In the City

THE PHANTOM OF THE GRAVY TRAIN

Merchant banking was the ultimate eighties career. It found its time in the middle of that decade in a great blaze of swaggering hubris, just as membership of the Soviet Communist Party had peaked as a lifestyle choice a few years earlier. How appropriate, for me, that it should come to an abrupt end just ahead of a general election which, whatever the outcome, completes the postscript to the Thatcher era.

For times change. An occupation which had once been the most luxurious of international gravy trains had transmuted itself into something more like British Rail's new InterCity 225: high-tech but unstable, full of disgruntled and ill-matched people for whom, even though their numbers were shrinking, there were somehow never quite enough seats. It was certainly time to get off. One January morning I arrived to find the decision had been taken for me.

The feeling is one of rage mixed with relief, and nostalgia for the heyday of a few years ago. And what a heyday it was, for this was a job which offered practically everything: glamorous travel, an ecstasy of name-dropping, a gold Mercedes with a chauffeur, a key to the executive toilet and the opportunity to blunder like Flashman into every boudoir and battlefield of the financial world.

1

One of the merchant banker defendants in the Guinness trials,* Lord Spens, was described as a noted stamp collector. Many merchant bankers have that particular mentality, but, rather than postage stamps, we tended to treasure the sort of stamps you get in your passport, and the names of the most obscure and exotic airports en route: Gdansk, Penang, Misawa and Memphis spring to mind. We collected book matches from every restaurant and nightclub, casually displaying them in large glass bowls all over south-west London. An almost random handful gives me The Good Time Club of Roppongi, Iberia Airways, the Palace Hotel in Prague, the Tahiti Beachcomber, Annabel's, the Ginza karaoke in Albemarle Street, Delmonico's off Wall Street, the Lai Lai Sheraton in Taipei and the Auberge des Trois Bonheurs in the rue Saint-Honoré.

And on the way through, I recall, I shook the silken hand of Asil Nadir and was shaken by the granite fist of Gerald Ronson. I had my elbow grasped by the soon-to-be-disgraced Ronald Li of the Hong Kong stock exchange muttering 'We can do deals together' and I actually employed the Recruit Company of Japanese scandal fame to recruit someone. I exchanged pleasantries with President Iliescu of Romania and I bumped into Richard Nixon in a lift lobby. I went backstage to meet a starlet of the Royal Ballet, played pool with a cowboy in the Fort Worth stockyards, carried a briefcase through the bazaar in Kathmandu, got sprayed with holy water by Thailand's highest priest and held a meeting stark naked in the Riverside Sauna in Seoul.

I could fill pages with these lists, but there was a day in May 1989 which, looking back, seems to have been the zenith (perhaps it was two days, but memory condenses them). Did I really try to gain access to the hotel bedroom of Taiwan's Finance Minister, Mrs Shirley Kuo, in the company of a knighted fellow of All Souls? Did I attend a meeting in Beijing's Great Hall of the People addressed by President

---

* The criminal trials relating to an illegal 'share support scheme' deployed in Guinness's takeover bid for The Distillers Company in 1986. The real-estate tycoon Gerald Ronson, also mentioned, was one of those convicted.

Yang Shangkun, witness the first of the great student demonstrations in Tiananmen Square, and take afternoon tea with a minister of the Papua New Guinea government who was high as a kite? Did I then go on, posing uncomfortably as the All Souls knight's wife, to crash Merrill Lynch's invitation-only cocktail party in a closed pavilion of the Forbidden City? Yes I did, and at the time it seemed as normal a way to spend the day as the dentist at his chair or the potter at his wheel.

But what did I actually do, you may well ask. What is a merchant banker anyway, apart from a man who avoids rhyming slang? Well, at the beginning of the eighties, for instance, I could have told you how to price syndicated loans to Brazil and Mexico; the pricing didn't really matter in the long run because, as everybody knows, practically none of those loans ever came back. Late 1982 found me writing papers on the legality of British local authority interest rate swaps. Whoops; eight years later a judge found that some London boroughs had used this particular piece of arithmetic to gamble themselves into perdition. He told us to our grief and amazement that we couldn't make them pay us back, because it had been illegal (for them, not us) all the time. Somewhere in the mid eighties we discovered cross-border mergers and acquisitions, which meant spending years trying to persuade giant Japanese corporations to buy every famous European brand name from Aquascutum to Zeiss. The end of the decade found us in liberated Eastern Europe, taking tea with ministers and selling them Mrs Thatcher's great gift to merchant bankers, better than any tax cut, the concept of privatisation.

In parallel with all this there was Big Bang, the revolution of the London securities market which put us in bed with the brokers and traders, the 'big swinging dicks' of Michael Lewis's *Liar's Poker* (1989), who apparently thought we were pussies. Of course we looked down on them. They were coarse, shallow and greedy (greedier even than we were) and they didn't know how to take tea with the Minister. But they had fun, and sometimes we got to join in. A big international share placing may be the most exciting half-hour you will ever spend in business: the adrenalin of a huge risk taken for a very short time; the stadium clamour of a roomful of salesmen who've all seen *Wall Street* in the cinema; the cash-register ring of a colossal profit materialising before your very eyes.

Of course, as always, it can go horribly wrong, now or later. I spent an exhilarating night on a London trading floor selling many millions of dollars' worth of paper called Perpetual Floating Rate Notes to investors in Japan. Now, thanks to obscure changes in international regulations on bank capital, they will show a substantial loss on them forever. There was another long and memorable night in October 1987 when we watched the Hong Kong stock market drop like a Korean airliner over Kamchatka. It was a night which included, in the Far Eastern lunch-hour, a pre-dawn break for beer, darts and fried breakfast (but sadly no bookmatches) in the Fox & Anchor in Smithfield. The meat porters probably thought we were pussies too, but we thought we were tremendous.

How was it, you may well also ask, for our employers? More pertinently, how was it for their shareholders, footing the bill for this ten-year ego-trip? It wasn't all bad: collectively we got into and out of all kinds of booms as well as busts, we broke new ground, we were ahead of the game, in some instances we even invented the game. We were proud of what we built but it never looked anything like the three-year plan said it should, and stable growth was not a feature; this was the roller-coaster gravy train. When we were not making enough money for them we thought of ourselves as the go-faster stripes on the livery, adding the lustre their rolling-stock lacked, and we asked for bigger bonuses. When we were making enough money for them, which was not often but sometimes, we asked for bigger bonuses still, lest we go and do all this for some other company.

At its best it was so much fun that we should have been paying them, but they didn't know that. Often they did give us bigger bonuses. Sometimes they gave us phantom ones as well, as an incentive to stay, artificial share options which couldn't be cashed in for several years. And what a grim world the survivors found themselves in by the time the day arrived to encash the phantom options, like coming out of your bunker after the bomb to find the banknotes of some obliterated state wafting in the nuclear wind.

Gone is the iconic figure of the eighties, whisked for the last time from the Hong Kong Mandarin to Kai Tak airport in the back of a white Rolls Royce. If he's still got a job at all, he's stuck at Frankfurt on his way back from Warsaw with a Eurotraveller Economy ticket, a ham roll and a bout of flu. He may recover: markets and bank proprietors have short memories, the gravy train may roll again in all its glory. But not for a while. For now perhaps, the iconic figure of the nineties, the one who's ahead of the game, is the former merchant banker cultivating his garden and relishing his memories: been there, done that, met the Minister, got the bookmatches.

April 1992

— ✳ —

NICE WORK IF YOU CAN GET IT

When I talk about my office in the City, I no longer mean to imply that I have a job there. Like many professionals and business people, I have not had one of those for some time.

What I mean is that I enjoy a co-operative office arrangement that is a model of survival for middle-class victims of the recession. An elegant building within a stone's throw of the Bank of England, much of it has been 'To Let' for as long as I can remember. On the floors that are occupied, only one small company is still fully operational.

Perhaps half a dozen people in the building actually draw salaries. The rest of us are 'between jobs', 'looking at new ventures', 'doing a bit of consultancy work' or just passing the time of day. I gather that one or two have not got around to telling their wives that their employment circumstances have changed. It is sociable, convenient and discreetly impressive if you bump into former colleagues in the street outside.

Such set-ups are increasingly common as the rate of executive job losses rises. In the financial sector, that rate has reached 30,000 per year – with the greatest concentration among the overpaid young bucks of the City. Even lawyers and accountants are feeling the chill breeze up their striped trouser-legs.

Worst hit of all are the professions caught by the property slump. According to the RIBA, more than a third of all salaried architects have been axed; many scratch along doing loft conversions, some run sandwich bars or draw cartoons. For surveyors, so little activity is in prospect, so many young people are still seeking to qualify, that middle-aged job-losers may never find work in the profession again.

Computer programmers, advertising executives, fine art specialists, all feature on the casualty lists. Overall, the carnage is more severe than at any time since the early 1930s, when the number of 'black-coated' unemployed passed 300,000.

The social consequences include unpaid school fees and respectable wives driven to pyramid selling. I am not about to mock the distress of redundancy. It is traumatic, whoever you are. But it is surely much worse for a miner than a merchant banker, who may be more susceptive to a dent in the ego but is almost certainly better cushioned financially. What it does present to him is a test of personality – a rare opportunity to show true grit, to rise to the difficult occasion.

Perhaps, in the spirit of 'Dear Mary', I can offer some useful tips, starting with how to conduct yourself when the chopper falls. The time allowed to you may be a matter of weeks or it may be no longer than it takes to fill a bin-liner with personal belongings and depart under the eyes of a security guard. They may even bar you from the building when you've gone out to lunch.

Conventional minor-public-school advice, to retreat in silent dignity, is best ignored. This is a rare opportunity for a short burst of cathartic rage of the sort which you might otherwise pay $10,000 to an exclusive Arizona clinic to induce. The perpetrators of your redundancy should be made to feel absolutely rotten, to provoke them to pay maximum compensation.

Social embarrassment, however, is no longer something you have to feel, now that so many of your confrères are occupationally challenged. The P45 form is this year's fashion accessory, a lifetime office career is 'as eighties as a Filofax'; or so you can tell your friends. Nonchalance on your part will make it easier for them to look you in the eye, and will make you feel better: the dice have rolled, so many other things to be done, so much demand for your kind of wisdom; the world is your oyster.

The best display of this I saw came from a senior banker in New York, whose departure 'by mutual agreement' had just been announced. Still entitled to the privileges of rank, he entertained me in a panelled Wall Street dining room. 'I may go and do political work in Washington, on foreign policy issues,' he drawled, casually ringing for the butler, 'or get together with some friends and make another fortune.'

But, however you behave, getting fired is irrevocable. You cannot get unfired, and you have to work out what to do next.

My own response was, as it happens, a good example of what sensible career advisers urge people not to do. I gathered suggestions as varied as joining the Foreign Office and buying a motorcycle repair business in Clapham, and took a series of holidays. Then I listed the choices which appealed: find some consultancy work until something more exciting comes along; write; dabble in politics; or look for a serious job. I decided to do all of them, except the last.

As a stopgap, 'consultancy' is nice work if you can get it. Several of my friends have successfully resorted to it. One of them even invented the title 'Leisure Consultant' for his business card. Daily fees are attuned to the rates charged by big firms with all the usual office overheads, so if you operate from a briefcase, the money looks quite good.

Other areas of keeping busy are equally crowded with involuntary non-executives. Local politics is a haven for slightly downtrodden men in their fifties who used to be 'big in knitwear' or 'something at ICI'. In the literary world, itself hard hit by falling sales, new manuscripts arrive by every post. 'My dear,' an agent told me breezily, 'all the unemployed are writing novels.'

For some sufferers from executive joblessness, treatment is available in the form of 'outplacement'. This sounds nasty, like colonic irrigation, and I was curious to find out what it actually is: counselling paid for by the ex-employer (or 'sponsor', as he now becomes) to assist the ex-employee (the 'prospect') to cross the 'employment gap'. It is, you may guess, an American invention. I visited Coutts Career Consultants, the first British firm to offer the service.

The first thing that happened, as I waited for a lift, was that a man from a different company sprang out of his office and said that if I was going to see Coutts I should come to see him as well, as he was in 'executive search' and had lots of opportunities to offer. It seemed possible that this is staged as part of the therapy, to cheer the new prospect as he arrives.

Colin Walkinshaw, a reassuringly ex-naval Coutts director, told me that new prospects often need 'picking up off the floor', especially those who have been dismissed with particular abruptness. Counselling aims not to restore self-respect, but to combat complacency in those who expect a new job just to turn up; or in others, the irrational urge to 'go self-employed' or drop out of the rat race for ever. The key to the treatment is momentum and focus, making people work at finding a viable new future, rather than sloping off to the bookies after a quick browse through the Sits Vac.

But outplacement, which costs the 'sponsor' several thousand pounds a time, is not offered to everyone. For many others, the last resort is the Jobcentre, and with it the dole. The middle-class unjobbed don't usually admit to claiming – a notable exception being Kevin Maxwell,* whose weekly handout was detailed to the penny in the national press. Proud ignorance of the various entitlements is probably a more typical attitude.

One friend of mine said, 'I went into one of those benefits offices but I came straight out again, it just wasn't for me. It seemed somehow, you know, unethical to claim.' 'But you've paid plenty of tax in the past,'

---

* Youngest son of Robert Maxwell, the disgraced publishing tycoon, and one of history's biggest bankrupts after the collapse of the Mirror Group.

I suggested. 'Why shouldn't you claim something back when you need it?' 'Oh sure,' he agreed, rather spoiling the effect. 'But the thing is I've got this consultancy contract . . .'*

Hunched into a raincoat for fear of meeting anyone I knew, I set off to sample the experience at my local small-town Jobcentre. The ground-floor shopfront had been abandoned, its display stands forlornly empty on the day that the number of vacancies across the country slumped to an eleven-year low. An arrow directed me up linoleum stairs. I anticipated a long wait, passively smoking among hostile ex-cons, punks and new-age travellers. I could not have been more wrong.

It looked exactly like a travel agency, and a good deal smarter than my last real office in the City; just like Coutts Career Consultants, in fact. The only other 'client' – which is what Jobcentres now call their prospects – was a respectable middle-aged man in a suit. On the wall was the Jobseeker's Charter ('If you have an appointment, we aim to start on time. If you do not, we aim to see you within ten minutes . . .').

I had no appointment, but a matronly woman labelled 'Reception' saw me immediately. She showed me a copy of *New Executive Post*, a mixture of vacancy ads and features on 'opportunities in franchising', 'coping with stress', 'It'll never happen to me!' and 'Why you need financial planning'. I learned about Executive Job Clubs, now to be found in most big cities, providing office facilities and 'networking opportunities' for managerial job-hunters.

And how much dole would I get, if it came to the crunch? The answer was £43.10p per week, plus up to £30 on Income Support. In the tradition of this sort of journalism, I made an excuse and left. But (for job-seeking rather than benefit-claiming) the experience was not an unpleasant one. Whoever has redesigned the Employment Service is to be congratulated. If you have, as it were, nothing better to do, it may be worth a visit.

---

* Having reinvented himself as a successful investment banker, he now manages the fortune of a billionaire Russian oligarch.

There is, however, an alternative last resort (some would place it higher up the order) and that is the 'on yer bike' solution, going abroad to find new fortune. Hong Kong, always a mobile job market, is still a good bet for the last boom before the Union Jack comes down; and an all-in expatriate package will solve most financial problems. For the really bold, Eastern Europe offers long odds for all kinds of otherwise redundant skills and enterprise.

In Poland last year, for example, I came across Alan Bond's ex-finance director, shaking off his former boss's business crash and trying to re-launch a local brewery. Prague was full of young chancers 'bored with the City', looking at 'leisure opportunities'. Albanian contacts report that the irrepressible Peter Earl, a 1980s City takeover merchant fallen on tough times, has been spotted in Tirana.

Earl is also, I hear, planning to climb Everest, and I take my hat off to him. If your job or your business has gone, there's no point in repining. It may be a ghastly shock, but it is also a moment of what Clinton-speakers now call empowerment – of taking responsibility for your own destiny, of making things happen. If that means trying to achieve your wildest fantasy, why not?

Those who need an inspirational role model should remember how Jalal ud Din, youthful ruler of Bokhara and Samarkand, faced his employment gap. Having lost the day against the Mongol hordes, he galloped his horse over a cliff, swam the Kabul river and went on to conquer another splendid kingdom.* Go for it, is the moral of the story; you cannot go back.

December 1992

—— ✳ ——

---

* I borrowed the reference to Jalal ud Din from Eric Newby's *A Short Walk in the Hindu Kush* (1958).

THE GENERATION THAT FAILED

I am looking at a group photograph of the Oxford University Gridiron Club in the summer of 1976. There I am in the second row, with big lapels and hair like Starsky's.

'The Grid' was an enclave for public-school undergraduates, housed above a menswear shop in Queen Street in rooms which were regularly vandalised by the club's own members. Though it was disreputable, its denizens were unusually pleased with themselves. The line-up of jutting jaws and buttoned blazers speaks across the years of an assumption of God-given advantage, a belief that the future would offer effortless success wherever they might go – including the City. What is interesting about them now is not what prats they were then, but how insignificant, in City terms, they became. I am looking at a portrait of the generation that failed.

There are seventy of us in that picture, and I do not exclude myself from this analysis; on the contrary, I am a prime example. We can, however, leave out the two distinguished senior members, Warden Sparrow of All Souls and the historian Richard Cobb, as well as the long-suffering steward Mr Tippler – whose eventual successor is said to have resigned in protest at being addressed as 'Tippler'. And we might as well omit the half-dozen leaders of the pack who were too rich and dangerous for any sort of serious career.

Of the remainder, at least half ended up in the Square Mile, in banking, stockbroking, investment, accountancy or insurance. Among those who took other paths, I can pick out a former Tory minister, a general and a prominent QC. But among the City boys, I can see only one person who could unequivocally be said to have made it to the top:* the impeccable John Varley, a close colleague during my own banking

---

* Perhaps I should also have mentioned Johnny Cameron, who became head of investment banking at Royal Bank of Scotland but was later banned, after an FSA investigation, from holding senior jobs in the financial sector; and James (now Lord) Sassoon, a vice-chairman of UBS Warburg who became a Treasury minister.

days, who is due to become chief executive of Barclays at the end of this year. The rest have either (like me) changed career altogether, or achieved nothing more than well-heeled obscurity.

The Bollinger-fuelled hooligans of the Grid can hardly be held up as a cross-section of a whole generation. But if, in the summer of 1986, ten years after that picture was taken and a few months before the Big Bang reform which changed the City for ever, I had labelled it with the names of the employers of those smart young men, it would have included a roll call of historic houses – Hambro, Kleinwort, Baring, Montagu, Rothschild – and the London branches of several powerful foreign firms besides. And I would have felt safe to predict that a fair proportion of us would end up running the whole show before we were fifty.

But apart from Varley (and the hereditary Roddie Fleming of Flemings), none of us did, and even if I stretch my survey to include everyone else I can think of who entered the City as a conventional Oxbridge graduate between 1974 and 1979, my assertion still holds good. Almost all failed the Darwinian test: somehow we lacked the stamina, aggression, adaptability or luck that was needed to reach the summit of the seething anthill that the money world became. I think I know why, and it is not a problem of worn-out genes: we were the product of our times, and we were peculiarly ill-adapted for the times that came afterwards.

The Grid photograph was taken a few weeks after the accession as prime minister of James Callaghan, whose administration our editor has recently declared the worst in modern times. For four years prior to that, since the industrial crises of 1972, the country had passed through economic hell: the three-day week, the OPEC oil-price hike, the collapse of property and stock markets, high inflation, high interest rates and crippling taxes.

I took my A levels in 1972; it was probably also the year in which I first began to form a view about Britain's, and my own, prospects. It was hard to grow up thinking positive; despite the bizarre claim by the New Economics Foundation last week that 1976 was the best year we ever had, my recollection is that things seemed only to get worse and worse.

By the time I started as a £54-a-week graduate trainee at Schroder Wagg – one of the elite merchant banks known as Accepting Houses – in August that year, the outlook was as bleak as ever and the public finances in total disarray. In November, I took part in a training course at the Bank of England for all the Accepting Houses' graduate intake (among whom, if memory serves, the only one to achieve any sort of fame was Peter Norris, the chief executive of Barings at the time of its crash). In that very same week, Chancellor Denis Healey was eyeball-to-eyeball with the men from the IMF, who had arrived to demand huge cuts in public spending as a precondition for a humiliating bail-out.

No wonder my lot lacked in the sort of drive that was later encapsulated by Michael Lewis in *Liar's Poker*, quoting one the chiefs of Salomon Brothers' trading floor in New York, as the readiness to 'bite the ass off a bear'. No wonder that for the duration of the Callaghan era, the most exciting part of our day was the hour we spent on *The Times* crossword at lunchtime – though we must have struggled with words like 'enterprise' and 'incentive', which barely entered our vocabulary.

It was not that there was no one around who would eventually go on to glory. In my first months I worked for Nicholas Roditi, a hard-edged investment expert who became George Soros's man in London; as a junior clerk I sat alongside a prankster called Piers Pottinger, who became one of the City's most successful PR men. We were lectured on how computers worked (being arts graduates, we could barely be bothered to listen) by an unusually self-assured back-office manager called Chris Gent, who went on to build Vodafone into one of the world's most successful companies.* But thrusters like them were not what pompous Grid men would have called 'people like us' – not so much in the class sense as in the sense that, had we but known it, they were the vanguard of the share-price-driven, media-conscious, technology-literate, bear's-ass-biting business world of the eighties – whereas we were the rearguard of the City's gentleman-amateur past.

---

* Sir Chris Gent went on to become chairman of GlaxoSmithKline.

Ironically, the generation that started work a decade before us fared better. That was partly because they had a longer run before the script was rewritten in the mid eighties by deregulation, ownership changes and American competition; and partly because they had more to get their teeth into in their early years. The sixties City stood on its nineteenth-century dignity, but was also, in some respects, very progressive. Eurobond issues and contested takeovers were the new fashion, and some financiers who learned their skills back then are still around as veterans today. They were battle-hardened by the early-seventies boom and bust, and when the crunch came again twenty years later, they turned out tougher and more resilient than we were. 'It's not as if we didn't offer to take over from them,' lamented one ex-stockbroker contemporary of mine, now running holiday cottages in the West Country, 'but they just didn't trust us.'

In a sense they were probably right. On the other hand, it was they rather than we who took the disastrous decisions which eventually destroyed so many of those historic City houses, or turned them into departments of American and German conglomerates – and, in the process, derailed the careers of so many of my peers. 'If the City hadn't gone and bloody well changed,' said another, an ex-banker now importing Chinese silk scarves, 'we'd have been great.'

So a big bouquet to John Varley of Barclays, last standard-bearer of the Gridiron class of '76 and the man described to me by one of our bosses long ago as 'the best I've worked with in thirty years in the City'. As for the rest of us, we might as well relax and enjoy our second careers as booksellers, bar owners, poets, parish councillors and (in my case) pantomime dames. If it's any consolation, chaps, I hear the tree-hugging, trustafarian, post-Thatcher generation of the nineties is even limper than we were.

March 2004

——※——

THE SCANDINAVIAN SOLUTION

At the historic moment when the House of Representatives passed Hank Paulson's bail-out bill last Friday night – thus, we must hope despite early indications to the contrary, significantly improving the world's chances of avoiding economic cataclysm – I was conducting some research into the Scandinavian solution.

I don't mean the policies followed by the Swedish government to steer its banking sector through a near-terminal crisis in the early 1990s, of which more in a moment. I mean I was sitting in the back row of a packed cinema watching *Mamma Mia!*, the Abba-singalong movie, and observing the impact of a mass inoculation of feel-good on a crowd that had been battered with bad news all week. I can only describe the effect as a euphoric group high – and it occurred to me that if only the global financial community could be persuaded to take half a day off, head for their nearest multiplex and lose themselves in this cheerful, escapist fantasy, maybe the panic would start to subside.

That may sound flippant, especially if you are one of the 300,000 British savers whose cash is currently locked up in Icesave, the internet-based subsidiary of the probably insolvent Landsbanki of Iceland. But there is a serious point here. What we have been witnessing is a bankers' and traders' nervous breakdown, a collapse of confidence so overwhelming that it has temporarily lost all touch with rationality.

I don't mean, I'm afraid, that the economic damage can still be limited to a short downturn if only the City would unclench its collective sphincter and return to something like business as usual. That is what I thought a month ago, but we have passed into unknown territory since then. As every day goes by in which banks decline to lend, traumatised consumers decide not to buy new cars and houses, and businesses of all kinds contemplate their strangulated cash flows and the redundancies they will have to make this winter, the depth of the coming recession becomes more apparent.

What I do mean is that gibbering fear on the part of the people who move markets is now driving this crisis towards consequences that no one could seriously have foreseen. Tired of listening to financial pundits on Tuesday night, I asked a psychotherapist what she thought was the root cause: 'This isn't a fashionable word in my profession these days,' she replied, 'but it's pure hysteria.'

And the measures needed to restore sanity, we agreed, have more to do with mass psychology than with any textbook of central banking practice. What matters is what works, not what reinforces the principle of moral hazard or follows any particular ideology. To accuse politicians of dithering is unfair when the condition they are trying to treat mutates wildly day by day. There are precedents for this situation, but they are not the most talked-about ones of 1973 and 1929. To me (because I happened to be there at the time) it feels more like post-Soviet Eastern Europe, in the early months when bankers like me, as I was then, and economists and newly elected politicians, were thrashing around trying to invent innovative ways of kick-starting moribund economies and giving citizens a stake in them. Often you would hear the old joke about an Irishman who is asked for directions by a tourist and replies, 'Well, if I was you I wouldn't start from here.'

Right now, the free world's banking industry is in much more urgent need of kick-starting than, say, the Czech steel industry in 1991. But the similarity is that you wouldn't want to start from here, that any positive idea is worth considering, that big, bold schemes are more likely to work than small, footling ones, and that well-phrased, comforting speeches make no difference at all. That line of argument has led experts latterly to reconsider a more direct precedent – which was the muscular, hands-on solution to the early 1990s Scandinavian banking crisis. There the Swedish government issued a blanket guarantee on deposits, nationalised some banks and injected capital into others, and swept bad loans into a special-purpose bank which gradually realised the underlying assets and minimised the loss to Swedish taxpayers. Banks which recovered were eventually returned to the private sector. It worked so well that many people forgot it ever happened.

In the first half of this week, all this came sharply into focus. The conventional nineteenth- and twentieth-century remedy of injecting 'abundant' liquidity through central banks wasn't working. Banks continued to refuse to lend to each other, and rumours of near-insolvency blew from the canyons of Canary Wharf to the capitals of Europe, where a series of banks with very large balance sheets but unfamiliar names – Fortis, Dexia, Hypo Real Estate – suddenly went into intensive care. Even the Paulson bail-out in its revised form made no difference to market sentiment: in this mood of madness, there were those who were prepared to declare it a failure even before the ink was dry.

And so, on this side of the pond, bank shares started to collapse – particularly those of Royal Bank of Scotland, until last year the aggressive front-runner of British commercial banking, and the ailing HBOS, whose forced merger with Lloyds TSB looked in doubt. On Monday night, we heard that the major high-street banks were in conclave with the Chancellor. On Tuesday, Robert Peston of the BBC – now the nation's town crier – announced that a capital injection by the government was imminent; Barclays, for one, responded that it had not asked for capital and did not need it. Then we woke on Wednesday morning to find that Gordon Brown and Alistair Darling had decided to do something really bold and in Brown's word, 'far-reaching': to inject up to £50 billion of taxpayers' money in the form of new equity for British banks and up to £200 billion of additional liquidity to free up interbank lending markets. RBS and HBOS looked certain to take up the new capital on offer. For fear of further attacks on their shares and credit ratings, others may follow. Only HSBC looked strong enough to stand aside from the scheme.

Meanwhile, it was not in the least surprising that the grossly overextended Icelandic banking system had descended into frozen chaos: that was the one feature of the week's drama we could all have seen coming – and the Chancellor was right to say he would guarantee Icesave's depositors rather than leave them to find out whether there's any cash in Reykjavik to pay them out. Likewise, it was predictable that the artificial construct of a single European monetary regime would be swept aside in a rush by national governments – the Irish, Danes, Germans and Greeks so far – to reassure their own citizens that their bank deposits are safe.

The lesson so far, at least on this side of the Atlantic, is that citizens still have some faith in national governments, despite the fact that national governments are at least as prone to folly as commercial bankers. But the European Central Bank, without political traction or the support of a European fiscal authority, turns out to carry hardly any psychological clout at all. Ardent eurosceptics leapt on these developments as evidence that the euro is doomed (like the now forgotten late nineteenth-century monetary union between France, Belgium, Switzerland, Italy and Greece) for want of political underpinning. Objective observers might agree that its survival chances are now less good than those of our high street banks.

And if you want my opinion, our high street banks will survive. To have the government as a shareholder for a few years will be an uncomfortable but useful discipline, and no worse than having sovereign wealth funds from China or the Middle East breathing down their necks. The ultimate cost to the taxpayer, when all is worked out, will be much smaller than this week's headline figures. And there is now a lot more reason than there was a week ago for markets to stabilise; in the short term they may not, but sometime soon they will surely pause for thought. Which brings me back to my own remedy for mass hysteria, *Mamma Mia!* See it as often as you need to, until you start to feel calmer. Sing along to all its familiar refrains, except perhaps the one that goes: 'Money, money, money/ Always sunny/ In the rich man's world.' Not any more it isn't, but we'll get through this nevertheless.

September 2008

———✳———

THE OLD GREEN MAN

Robert Swannell, the veteran Citigroup financier, has been named as Sir Stuart Rose's likely successor as chairman of Marks & Spencer. Swannell is an old-style, safe pair of City hands, of a breed whose presence in any boardroom is as reassuring to institutional shareholders as it is disappointing to journalists in search of colour. What's more, reports suggest he will do the M&S job for a smaller pay package than Rose's, dousing any possible controversy on that front. Indeed, the only downside I can see to Swannell's appointment is that it scotches my own chance of a non-executive directorship of the great retailer, since I must have made such a bad impression when we last met. It was long ago when he had just joined Schroders, where I was a very junior banker. He was on an induction tour to learn what we all did (in my case, very little) and came to see me immediately after lunch – which in my case had been a very liquid lunch in a dank Victorian pub, now gone, called The Green Man in Bucklersbury. I can still see the clean-cut young Swannell, who had trained both as an accountant and a barrister and was clearly going to go far, glinting at me as I tried to form a coherent sentence without falling off my chair. Was there, in that encounter, a glimpse of how our future career paths would diverge? I fear there was.

August 2010

— ❋ —

ULTIMATE SOLUTION

Worried that banks such as HSBC might leave these shores altogether if new capital requirements crush their shareholder returns, David Cameron is said to be keen that the ring-fencing of their retail operations 'is of a "light-touch" variety'. All I can say is that we tried that with my golden retriever Douglas as his hormonal urges began to get the better of him, but matters came to a head at Easter when the scent of the local hairdresser's spaniel drove him to bust repeatedly through inadequate harnesses and hedges like the bulldog in the 'Tom and Jerry' cartoons – or a banker with a sniff of a seven-digit bonus. The ultimate solution (one which Vince Cable would no doubt advocate for the whole City if he could) was to castrate the poor chap. If you're going to ring-fence, do it properly or not at all.

September 2011

---※---

FORM-FILLING

My recent remarks item about the diminished state of the Court of the Bank of England, of which my father was a member, elicited an explanation of the problem from a distinguished City gent. 'Some years ago I applied to join the Court,' he told me. 'In the modern way, a vacancy had been advertised, and applicants were required to complete a twenty-page questionnaire. The process was handled, no doubt at great cost, by a leading headhunter on behalf of the Treasury. As the deadline approached I was told there would be a delay – probably because no suitable grandees could be bothered to fill a form of such length and crassness. Months later I was informed that my application had been unsuccessful, but the message came by an email sent to all losing candidates, accidentally revealing our names to each other. This produced several enjoyable lunches and, we may hope, the sacking of the headhunter.' In short, the old boys' network and the traditional tap on the shoulder was a much more reliable recruitment method.

June 2011

---※---

WHAT ARE MY ODDS?

C urious that the Treasury chose to advertise for the next governor of the Bank of England in *The Economist* but not in *The Spectator*. Given the embarrassing paucity of obvious candidates – so many having been knocked back in the Paddy Power odds by their proximity to money-laundering, sanctions-busting and Libor scandals – it might prove more fruitful to appeal to the sort of sophisticated dark-horse who spends Sunday afternoons browsing the small ads at the back of this paper. Tuscan farmhouse, tantric massage, 'advanced understanding of financial markets . . . strong communicator . . . good interpersonal skills': it all fits the image of *Spectator* Renaissance man.

Indeed, perhaps I should shake off my natural modesty and whack in an application myself. Here's a first draft. In my previous globe-trotting career as an investment banker, I spent plenty of time hanging around the lobbies of exotic central banks and freeloading on the international conference circuit, plus I'm on nodding terms with the present governor's butler, so I think I've got a fair idea what's involved. In terms of the technicalities of monetary management, I'm sure I could press 'Print' on the Quantitative Easing machine in the Threadneedle Street basement. Unlike other names in the frame, I combine an appetite for a big City lunch with a close view of provincial, small-business life. As an economic forecaster, I could hardly be more wrong than the Bank itself has been these past few years. And I certainly have the attribute that was missing from the ad but must be essential in a job whose incumbent is blamed for all economic ills and financial failures but rarely praised for disasters averted and corners turned: a good sense of humour.

September 2012

— ✳ —

THE INFLATION GAME

'I don't know how it is for you,' my friend the ambassador complained over supper, 'but for the things I have to spend money on, the idea that inflation is running at only 2.5 per cent is absolutely ludicrous. I'd say more like ten.' Trying to put a number on your personal inflation rate is the new game in town, and credit for inventing it must go to George Trefgarne, who pointed out in the *Daily Telegraph* the other day that the official Consumer Price Index is based on a basket of goods which is all very well for those whose spending priorities include cheap clothing, electronic gadgets and fast food, but bears very little relation to the commitments of the middle-class homeowner and parent.

I set out to find just how fast the cost of living is rising for the typical *Spectator* reader. Fuel bills and train fares are the most blatant inflation-busters, followed by Council Tax and household insurance. In London, plumbers, electricians and babysitters have all jacked their rates up. A bursar tells me school-fee inflation is currently '5 or 6 per cent, after a couple of years at 7 or 8', driven by rising salaries, heating bills and the cost of compliance with Ofsted and the Criminal Records Bureau. A Yorkshire quantity surveyor says that domestic contract prices in the building trade – for a barn conversion, say, or a granny flat – are also officially rising at 5 to 6 per cent, but in practice, because demand for decent builders far exceeds supply despite the influx of Polish trades-men, estimates tend to come in at 10 or 12 per cent more than last year. My friend the psychotherapist says that an hour on her couch costs 9.5 per cent more than it did last year but 'I'm worth it' – and that her own reflexologist recently put her fees up by 20 per cent.

It looks as if the ambassador has got it about right. For confirma-tion, I raised the question in the *Spectator* editorial conference – but I'm not sure how much reliance to put on the data offered. One participant claimed 'teenage friends' had told her that certain hallucinogenic drugs – she was, of course, vague about the precise substances involved – are a lot dearer than they used to be, reflecting disruption of supply from the war zones. And Rod Liddle said he'd heard 'Hoare's are charging a lot more this summer', what with so many wealthy Middle Easterners taking refuge in London. Maybe I misheard him, but I can find no evidence that the exclusive private bank in Fleet Street is doing any such thing.

August 2006

— ✳ —

CURSED WHARF

The death of the real estate tycoon Paul Reichmann reminded me of my first visit to his ultra-high-risk development at Canary Wharf. My diary tells me it was on 25 March 1992, in a week when Reichmann was grappling with his bankers over the £10 billion of debt that would sink his company Olympia & York just two months later. I wasn't there to witness that struggle but to meet the great Hugh Massingberd, who was about to recruit me as a *Daily Telegraph* obituarist. As Hugh later wrote, 'we lunched on a rather ropey boat' – the only eaterie available, alongside a desolate canyon of empty new offices. The Telegraph Group had just moved into the central tower, the paper's then proprietor Conrad Black having (his biographer Tom Bower tells us) 'made about £20 million' out of a lease deal with his friend and fellow Canadian Reichmann.

It was an auspicious day for me – and by no means the end for Reichmann, who regained control of the project three years later with new backers and drove it to completion against the odds. But for all its later opulence and buzz, the place has always made me shiver. That's why in March 2004 I published a piece by Damien McCrystal titled 'The Curse of Canary Wharf', cataloguing the misfortunes associated with what he called 'this monstrous folly'. As if to prove the point, Gordon Brown visited the Wharf a week later to make a speech at the opening of Lehman Brothers' gleaming European headquarters, congratulating the doomed investment bank on 'the contribution you make to the prosperity of Britain'.

RBS bought two blocks for a billion pounds; Bear Stearns was there and Bob Diamond of Barclays too, and the FSA pen-pushers who failed to see the storm coming. Those marbled towers became the falling dominoes of the financial crisis. As for Paul Reichmann, he died rich and righteous, having remade the skylines of New York, Toronto and London and given millions to Jewish causes. But he didn't escape the curse: his residual shareholding in Canary Wharf, pledged as collateral for a loan that went bad, was repossessed by Commerzbank of Germany in 2009.

October 2013

— ✳ —

THE TICKING PARCEL

Last week's panic on Wall Street was in part provoked by fear of gigantic losses yet to be realised in the arena of 'credit default swaps', which are a form of derivative contract – or 'weapon of financial mass destruction', as Warren Buffett once put it – akin to debt insurance. A ticking parcel of more than $400 billion worth of these arcane instruments relates to bonds issued by Lehman Brothers before it went bust. Since Lehman paper is now priced at only 8 cents on the dollar, enormous claims are likely to emerge against the parties to the swaps. The trouble is, as New York State's insurance superintendent Eric Dinallo observed, 'No one knows who owes this money, how much each counterparty owes, or whether any of these counterparties will now be in trouble themselves.'

As I read that, I recalled a misty day in April 2005 when I lunched in the private restaurant at the top of Norman Foster's Gherkin, the London headquarters of the Swiss Re insurance group, with three masters of the money universe, traders of thirty years' experience apiece.

This credit derivatives market is getting out of hand, they agreed, as we savoured the recommendation of Swiss Re's sommelier. No one knows how much paper has been issued, or who's holding it, or what it's really worth; fortunes are being made trading it, but one day it will blow up in our faces. That was three and a half years ago. I thought little more about it until Lehman went down. It was a huge story and I missed it. But then so did Swiss Re: the Gherkin was sold last year for £630 million, but that sum covered less than half of Swiss Re's losses so far on credit default swaps.*

October 2008

—— ✳ ——

EXCHANGE OF IDEAS

The classical frontage of the Royal Exchange above Bank tube station is a friendly landmark to anyone who has ever worked in the City, but I have held back from assembling a *Spectator* bid for the building because I think it may be cursed. Once the home of Lloyd's insurance market, its atrium is these days occupied by a fancy restaurant surrounded by luxury boutiques, and a 104-year lease on the whole place is about to be sold for around £80 million.

At its foundation by the financier Sir Thomas Gresham in 1571, the first bourse on the site had the noble purpose of reclaiming for English merchants a portion of the power over London's import-export trade held by the 'Lombardy men' and 'Alemanes' who would now be referred to as our European partners. But Gresham's building burned down in the Great Fire and its successor went the same way in January 1838, on 'a

---

* The purchase of the Gherkin by German investors in 2007 was funded by a loan in Swiss francs which appreciated against the pound until the loan was worth much more than the building; the borrower went into receivership in 2014.

night of so hard a frost that the very water from the fire engines froze in mid-air'. The dignified replacement designed by William Tite survived the Blitz but lost its mercantile purpose after Lloyd's moved to Lime Street, and eventually became a plaything of real-estate speculators: the sellers this time round include the Irish Bank Resolution Corporation, the vehicle that holds the remains of the failed Anglo Irish Bank and the Irish Nationwide building society.

So there's troubled history here, but still it would be good to see the trading floor of the Royal Exchange reclaimed from bland consumerism and restored to the buzz it must have had in Gresham's day. Given the rising popularity of live debate as entertainment, perhaps it could become the City's Speakers' Corner, with wild-eyed commentators shouting towards the Bank of England across the road, 'A pox on your forward guidance, Mr Governor Carney! Rates must rise!' and such like. My soapbox awaits.

November 2013

———✳———

CLOSE TO THE SUN

To Majorca, for the first time in thirty years, to attend a wedding party. Among the guests I find an old friend from the City. We discuss a mutual acquaintance, first encountered as a young man in the 1980s, who neither of us would have tipped to rise as high as he did in the banking world before suffering an Icarus-like fall. 'How much would you guess he made for himself?' I asked. 'About a hundred.' 'That would be millions?' 'Of course.' 'And how much do you think he lost for shareholders when it all went pear-shaped?' 'About twenty.' 'And that would be billions?' 'Of course, do keep up.' 'Any idea what he's doing these days?' 'I hear he's running another bank.'

June 2013

Who's to blame for the financial crisis?

Who's to blame for financial crisis,
Falling prospects, rising prices?
Europe's follies or bankers' vices?
You want to know what my advice is?

Banks lent too much, you spent too much –
Brits, Irish, Greek or French or Dutch –
And now at fragile straws we clutch
As growth retreats at Osborne's touch.

So who's the perp, to name and shame
And sentence to infernal flame –
The bankers in their high-stakes game
Or Gordon Brown's excuses lame?

Or was the culprit Mervyn King
Who really didn't do a thing
To halt the bankers' greedy fling
Or stimulate a new upswing?

Or are the villains continental,
Our own faults coincidental –
Excesses relatively gentle
Problems not so monumental

As those of Italy and Greece
Whose citizens refuse to cease
Habits that made their debts increase
And state-paid fat cats more obese?

Now everyone must share the pain.
Pensions? Savings? Down the drain.

Embrace austerity, don't complain,
Be thankful you don't live in Spain.

When inflation's three, four, five per cent
Why chant the mantra of discontent
Or rage at capitalism to repent?
What use is protest in a tent?

You spent last winter at St Paul's
But the bankers all ignored your calls,
They're more afraid of market falls
And the rise of Miliband and Balls.

But still we have this urge to curse
The financier who made things worse,
The bonus he won't reimburse,
The mugger who stole the public purse.

And self-regarding Euro-cronies
Sarkozys, Merkels, Berlusconis,
All those other friends of Tony's,
Economic quacks and phoneys.

By all means tell them they betrayed us
And calculate how poor they've made us
These speculators, spivs and traders,
These rich, uncaring hedge-fund raiders.

A culture of unfettered greed
Small change at best for those in need ...
But let's be honest, let's concede
We were all caught up in this stampede.

And cursing won't reverse the trend
That we must strive to comprehend.
If money's cheap we'll spend, spend, spend,
It's human nature in the end.

So now we've hit the triple dip,
An icebound, bleak *Titanic* trip,
But stay aboard this sinking ship
And have a party – that's my tip.

CHAPTER 2

Other Business

GIVING JUNK A BAD NAME

'It's a special sort of pastry-cutter . . . for croissants and, er, stuff like that,' the man in the grey anorak said tentatively, indicating a latticed metal cylinder with wooden handles at each end. 'Over £4 in the best kitchen shops, but I'm offering it for only £1.50.'

It could have been anything, but if he had said it was a satellite television aerial, or an implement used in martial arts, he might have had a better chance. On Sedgefield racecourse on a windswept, drizzle-sodden Sunday morning, fancy patisserie equipment is probably not high on shopping lists. This is the north-east's biggest car boot sale – every Sunday from February to December.

Check your local newspaper, drive around this weekend at random: you will find car boot sales everywhere. Having become popular in the boom years of the 1980s, they mushroomed during the recession into an essential mechanism of the borderline economy, a way of life for regular stallholders and shoppers with nothing better to do. On a good day the Sedgefield event attracts 300–400 stallholders, each turning over, according to the organisers, an average of £80–£100. Multiplied at least 200 times across the country, that indicates an untaxed, unregulated industry with an annual turnover of £400 million, more than that of many famous companies.

By reputation, car boot sales are crawling with dodgy dealers; every Transit van laden with ripped-out car radios and the pick of last night's burglaries. Certainly the police like to keep an eye on them, and promoters claim to be keen to help victims who spot their own toasters and videos for sale on the stalls. 'Strictly No Photography' signs may suggest complicity between villains and the organisers, but, in fact, are often there to shield a less detectable, even more widespread form of dishonesty: semi-professional stallholders who are not declaring their profits to the taxman, while claiming unemployment benefit or avoiding the Child Support Agency.

But what is extraordinary about most car boot sales is not the bent electronic gear at bargain prices, or the occasional discovery of a missing Gainsborough: it is the absence of virtually anything of any recognisable value. Most car boot sales are a sea of non-biodegradable trash, picked over, discarded, occasionally shifted from one field to another.

As a newcomer I was amazed – at Sedgefield, Stokesley Sports Club and Pickering Showfield, to name but three north-eastern sites – to find hundreds, perhaps thousands of people absorbed in desultory trade reminiscent of the flea markets of Warsaw and Kathmandu, or even the garbage-dump dwellers of Manila.

Sedgefield, of course, does not otherwise resemble any of those places. It is the constituency of Tony Blair, who has yet to be spotted buying or selling on Sunday mornings. But as a self-proclaimed expert on free enterprise economics, he should; these events offer a glimpse of market behaviour at its most elementary.

Some stalls (one of them the contents of the boot of a white Rolls Royce) consist of heaps of old clothes and worn shoes tipped on to the ground. Others run makeshift counters and display stands. Some have a speciality, like the video man whose demeanour suggests something really nasty in the back of his van. Others offer a random selection: at the top of the range, the sort of glass decanters which, when he still had shops to sell them in, Gerald Ratner unwisely described as 'crap'; hideous souvenir crockery; rusted tools, taps and washing-machine parts; cracked light switches hacked from walls of repossessed houses; hubcaps of joy-ridden Astras; Buckingham Palace jigsaws in boxes held together by Sellotape, sure to be missing the last three pieces; back numbers of *Viz, Fiesta* and the *Journal of the Alpine Garden Society*; bottles, jars, buckets, broken hairdriers, useless bits of wood.

If you ever wondered what happened to Ray Conniff, James Last or Bert Kaempfert, rest assured that LPs scratched but intact, change hands all over the country, along with *The Stars On Sunday Album* and *The Mighty Hammond Organ*.

Somewhere out there *Kylie: The Video* and *Swamp Killer* jostle for space with paperbacks of Dennis Wheatley and J. T. Edson, Mills & Boon, thrillers with swastikas on the covers, third-rate erotica like *Naked Came the Stranger* by 'Penelope Ashe' (haven't seen that one since I was a schoolboy) and the odd forlorn copy of *Against Goliath*, the autobiography of Sir David Steel.

The VAT-man is not missing much in this bonanza of bottom-grade bric-a-brac, because there is rarely any value added. In car boot sales, as in large parts of the legitimate British economy these days, people do not seem to make things to sell; they simply clear out cupboards. I found it impossible to imagine that buyers actually want this dismal merchandise, other than as a special form of currency; there is a kind of after-the-bomb quality about it, as though the monetary system has broken down and the survivors have devised their own surreal rates of exchange: two left boots are worth a 1977 *Jackie* annual, a box of assorted coat hangers and a chipped beer mug equal a Jane Fonda fitness video.

Here and there are signs of more creative activity. The truly ubiquitous car boot sale item is the *Haynes Owners' Workshop Manual*, the hardback bible of DIY car repair. There is one for every model, and in many cases the books have long outlived the vehicles they describe. Is there, anywhere in Britain, a working example of a 1976 Datsun Cherry, or a Hillman Avenger, or a Talbot Horizon? Probably not, but there is a Haynes Manual being lovingly pored over by a car-boot-sale punter, perhaps to add to his collection, perhaps to hoard in the hope, one day, of finding an uncorroded Datsun locked away in some forgotten garage.

Along with the car buffs and the obsessional bargain-hunters are the lightly battered husbands, a breed of subdued middle-aged men happiest in garden sheds, fiddling with obsolete bits of machinery and polishing their wood-carving tools. There are young mothers with pushchairs and black bin-liners, buying broken toys and toddlers' clothing; and young grandmothers with short, metallic hair and big loop earrings, browsing and gossiping like dowagers in Harrods.

When the grandmothers were toddlers, most of the families would have been in church or chapel on Sunday morning. But in the modern material world, the substitute for religion and the hub of community life is often, it seems, not much more than relentless shopping – even for rubbish, in the rain, in the middle of a field.

Daily Telegraph, May 1995

— ✳ —

SEX AND STUPIDITY

Lunching with a beautiful girl at Mon Plaisir in Monmouth Street, I let slip that *The Spectator* would be grabbing headlines this week with a special issue on the theme of sex and society. As the business columnist, I explained, my assignment was to analyse how consumer trends reflect current sexual attitudes, and to highlight sectors that investors should keep an eye on accordingly. 'Oh-ho,' she said – rather huskily, I thought – 'We'd better pop into Coco de Mer after lunch. It's just next door.' I looked blank. 'Come on, you must have heard of Coco de Mer, the hot new thing in lingerie and erotic accessories? It's run by Anita Roddick's daughter Sam, and it's incredibly chic and sophisticated. I buy lots of her feathery ticklers for my girlfriends' hen parties.'

I started to perspire, but luckily my research gave me plenty to talk about. 'You've hit the nail on the head,' I said. 'Women are more and more self-confident and self-sufficient, sexually and economically. They spend oodles of money on treats that make them feel good about themselves – and they seem to enjoy, ahem, sharing these experiences with other women.' She looked a bit cross about that last bit, but agreed that the designer lingerie market is growing at a phenomenal rate, from Marks & Spencer upwards, and that vibrators shaped like pebbles and seashells are the new iPods. She said I should check out Myla, 'the world's first luxury sex brand for women', with its flagship store off Bond Street and outlets from Marbella to Moscow; or talk to Julia Gash, Sheffield's award-winning knickers-and-toys entrepreneur who says her philosophy is all about 'empowering women'.

Quite so, I responded, but where does that leave us men? The 'male grooming' market has flourished in recent years, and I once overheard two middle-aged men on a train discussing which moisturisers they preferred. Male cosmetic surgery is also, apparently, enjoying a mini-boom. But does this reflect growing self-confidence, or the opposite – a desperate feeling of stress-induced premature ageing and sexual uselessness? What's a bloke to do when the internet sends him twenty unsolicited reminders a day about erectile dysfunction and the girls are all giggling over feathery ticklers?

Well, one thing blokes do these days – I referred to my notes – is spend £80 million a year on magazines based on a formula of 'sex, sport and stupidity'. *Loaded* pioneered the genre in the mid 1990s, but the soaraway success of two rival weekly titles launched in January 2004, *Zoo* from the Emap stable and *Nuts* from IPC, has contributed to sales growth in the 'men's lifestyle' segment of the magazine trade of 150 per cent in the past two years. And what a lifestyle they offer: *Maxim*'s '35 grubbiest places to get laid' in Nottingham and Nuneaton; *Zoo*'s 'five-minute facial' for dealing with blackheads; *FHM*'s guide to getting 'as pissed as possible in 60 seconds flat'; plus acres of untouchable flesh and adverts for 'hot'n'horny' chat lines – giving you the chance to talk dirty, for £1.50 a minute, to what a publisher of one of the titles tells me is usually a middle-aged housewife in a shed.

So that's the picture, I concluded. If I was a Branson or a Sugar I would back business ideas that play to modern woman's self-image as a pampered sexual princess, and modern man's oafish sexual inadequacy.

My lunch date reached for the restaurant bill and paid it with a flourish of her executive gold card while I fumbled for my wallet. 'Come on,' she said urgently, 'Coco de Mer.' I followed her into the dark-red cave next door, where we browsed suspender belts, spanking paddles and aphrodisiac massage oils. I mopped my brow as we re-emerged into the daylight. Huskier still, she grasped my arm: 'And it's terribly handy for the Covent Garden Hotel opposite . . .'

But me, I'm a bloke: I made an excuse and left, in search of some wrinkle cream and a copy of *Nuts*.

March 2006

— ✳ —

THE TORCH'S TRUE MEANING

The symbolism of the Olympic flame, last seen meandering through Kent towards the M25, has been much misunderstood. Forget the propaganda about '8,000 truly inspirational torchbearers . . . shining a light on local communities'. When Toby Young took his children to watch the relay pass through Dartmouth, he found it 'not merely tarnished, but ruined by the heavy-handedness of the sponsors' – Lloyds TSB, Samsung and Coca-Cola – whose convoy preceded the torch itself. The following week, I wrote in defence of the idea that companies cannot be expected to put up seven-figure sums for 'feel-good causes' without high-profile publicity in return.

But both of us missed the point. A pageant made up of a bailed-out bank, a cut-price Korean consumer electronics giant and a nutritionally worthless fizzy drink that reaps $50 billion a year from the world's poor is a perfect representation of the man-made monster that is twenty-first-century capitalism. And it's been on the run all summer, pursued by a mob with flaming torches.

If the tracksuited heavies who surround the torchbearer had been issued with official pitchforks, the metaphor would have been even more vivid. With a week to go, the beast is cornered and whimpering: Coca-Cola general manager Daryl Jelinek pleads that his product should be seen as part of a 'holistic lifestyle', while McDonald's and Cadbury, sole purveyors of food to the Olympic masses, tie themselves in knots to avoid suggesting that the best way to watch world-class athletics is with a cheeseburger in one hand and a Crunchie in the other. As for G4S, the contractor that failed to supply the requisite number of security guards and became this week's political show-trial defendant, many of its recruits were so frightened of public hostility that they opted not to show up at all.

I tell you, there's an ugly mood out there, and before the final celebrity torchbearer touches the flame to the cauldron at the climactic moment of next Friday's ceremony, business owners everywhere should check their fire insurance policies.*

July 2012

— ✳ —

KNOCK DOWN BATTERSEA POWER STATION

About ten years ago I had a friendly debate with the late Giles Worsley about Battersea power station. The distinguished architectural writer said Battersea was an industrial icon that should certainly be conserved and – like its sister station-turned-gallery at Bankside – found a new purpose. I countered that if an industrial icon has ceased to serve the purpose for which it was built, there was no need to strive at great cost to save its hulk, especially if we've kept another just like it a mile downriver. Assuming it's physically possible to knock the brute

---

* The Olympics were, in fact, a huge success: it was a year earlier, in August 2011, that a wave of riot, arson and looting had broken out in London and elsewhere.

down, I argued, why not create a fit-for-twenty-first-century-purpose landmark in place of the old one?

I'm not sure who's winning this argument so far, but the news is that London's great pink elephant has just seen off the latest in a line of developers and is for sale again. Having switched off its turbines in 1975, Battersea was sold in 1987 to a developer who was going to turn it into an industrial-history theme park. Laden with debt, the project fell into the hands of Bank of America and was sold on to a Hong Kong company called Parkview, which for thirteen years tried without visible success to advance a controversial shopping mall scheme.

Parkview, in turn, sold in 2006 to an Irish crew, Real Estate Opportunities, who trumpeted a new £4 billion plan but have gone the way of all boom-time Irish property punters, leaving debts of £324 million to Lloyds and Ireland's National Asset Management Agency. The next queue of possible buyers is rumoured to include Russian-owned Chelsea Football Club. In effect, while Battersea's fabric has been slowly decaying, its post-industrial fate has offered a virtual theme park of financial fantasy. Whoever the next owners are, my advice – if they're not allowed to demolish – is to get with the *zeitgeist* and start digging: who knows what mineral deposits lie beneath.

December 2011

———— ✳ ————

THE LUCK OF THE IRISH

The screen at Manchester airport tells me I'm about to board Aer Lingus to Dublin, but there's a Lufthansa plane at the gate. 'This bail-out's moving fast,' I mutter. I'm at the wrong gate, however, and it's an Aer Lingus stewardess who becomes the first of many people during my short visit to wish me 'the best of luck'. Luck looms large in the Irish psyche and it's what they need right now – an oil find, perhaps – plus a bit less attention from world markets and media. For a country whose economy is little bigger than Manchester's, the glare of global attention is traumatic. The last thing they want, I guess, is another doorstepping foreign columnist.

So thank goodness for talkative taxi drivers. The first offers a rant about the cronyism of the Irish political class. 'Here's where one of the big fellahs drinks,' he says, as we pass Fagan's Bar in Drumcondra, where Bertie Ahern, who presided as Taoiseach during the decade-long boom while fending off multiple allegations about his personal finances, can be found supping Bass and contemplating his country's ruin.

The next driver tells me he's behind on his mortgage and business is thin, 'but all I need's a couple of good months and a bit of luck, an' I'll be fine'. A third points out a sign of destitution I haven't seen since Eastern Europe before the fall: entire blocks of flats, in mid-evening, with not a single light on. But he roars with laughter as he tells me about a man from his own flats who was a sandblaster by trade but claimed to be a builder when the boom came, won contracts, bought a string of racehorses and lived the Irish dream. How's he doing now? 'The banks have him by the bollocks, he's completely fucked.'

Later, a racing man tells me the other side of the same story. In some trainers' yards, every horse was owned by new-rich builders. But just as there were no bidders last week (even at a slashed reserve of €300,000) for an apartment complex in Donegal once valued at €9.5 million, so there are no buyers for the builders' nags at bloodstock sales – and owners often don't bother to collect them if they're unsold.

I was wrong to think no one would want to talk to me: everyone does. But it seems to me that Dubliners, as people in shock often do, are obsessing about the wrong things – the shocking €85-billion size of the bail-out and the €20,000 debt per citizen it implies. But those are just numbers, I tell them: what matter more are market mood-swings. To stabilise investor sentiment you need leaders who declare robustly that Ireland has taken every painful step demanded by the IMF to shrink the fiscal deficit; that there is a way to keep Irish banks alive without imposing a haircut on bondholders which might cause Europe-wide panic; and that Ireland's inward-investment success story, bolstered by its ultra-low corporate tax rate, still offers real hope for the future. I'm hearing all that from businesspeople, but not from rabbit-in-the-headlights politicians.

Halfway through dinner, there's a hand on my shoulder. It belongs to Vincent Browne, a cult figure in the Irish media who's riding high after telling the current Taoiseach, Brian Cowen, at a press conference that he should apologise for 'screwing up' the country and resign as a matter of patriotic duty. Vincent wants me on his late-night TV3 chat show to give a British view of Ireland. I assure viewers that we Brits still have far more affection for our Irish cousins than we do for the EU powers and their doomed currency. But Vincent, too, is obsessing about numbers: what's a fair rate for Ireland to pay on the bail-out? The answer when it came won't have pleased him: 5.8 per cent is more than Greece had to pay, and could mean €5 billion a year in interest costs. Again I argue, the numbers won't matter if markets believe Ireland has a viable recovery path – because much of the bail-out will never have to be drawn down.

Dublin airport's Terminal 2 opened, a year late and massively over budget, on the day the IMF men flew in. Ryanair boss Michael O'Leary (who had argued to be allowed to build and run his own low-cost terminal) damned the new showpiece as 'a statement of modern Ireland, a big, bankrupt property development'. But at 7.30 on a Friday morning, Terminal 1 is heaving: everyone has a cheap ticket to leave the country. Ryanair planes buzz in and out of the departure stands, intent on their twenty-five-minute turnaround target and offering a demonstration of what the Irish can do when they get their act together. 'That's the fellah should run the country, that Michael O'Leary,' said my last taxi driver. 'An' the best of luck to you, sir.'

December 2010

—— ✳ ——

KERRY GOLD

This column comes from County Kerry, where I'm staying in a lovely Georgian house in the middle of a golf course that offers a view of MacGillycuddy's Reeks and a parable of boom and bust. The verdant eighteen-hole course used to be the home farm in the days when landowners in these parts prospered by supplying creameries that made Kerrygold butter. By the mid 1990s, golf looked a better bet, and then came Ireland's real-estate bonanza. My host was approached by a new-rich builder: 'He offered x for the golf course with planning permission for a hotel. It was a lot of money, but we didn't want to sell. Then he offered one-and-a-half x, and finally in September 2007, $2x$. We really couldn't say no.' The hotel scheme sprang out of the ground behind the old farmyard, but the builder – who had borrowed 100 per cent of his funding from Irish banks, putting not a penny of equity into the project – swiftly went bust.

Now it's all about to be offered for sale again by the National Asset Management Agency, Ireland's 'bad bank' repository of foreclosed real estate assets. At what sort of price? 'Maybe a quarter of x,' says my friend. 'There's not much demand for golf courses these days.' But there's plenty of demand for agricultural land, which according to Savills fetches almost £19,000 per Irish hectare compared to £15,415 in the UK, having soared in the boom and stayed high. So cattle might once more graze this rich pasture, ivy will slowly clad the hotel's half-built shell like an abandoned Ascendancy mansion, and what happened to Ireland these past few years will be remembered as a kind of dream.

April 2014

— ✳ —

FRAGRANT VISIONS

I always thought a 'hammam treatment' was what happened to that American youth in a Turkish prison in a film called *Midnight Express*. But I experienced one in the spa of a West End hotel the other day, and came out feeling thoroughly enlivened. The fizz with which I went through the rest of the day had less to do with the application to my skin of a combination of fragrant oils and what felt like an industrial pan-scrubber, and more to do with the information that the basement treatment room had previously been the vault of the London branch of the Bank of Nigeria. I had been lying on a stone slab where there once might have been a stack of gold bars labelled 'Personal property of President Sani Abacha'.

It's good to think that much of the late dictator's loot has been recovered; more philosophically, it's good to discover examples of how buildings find new uses as economies are transformed. The rest of the hotel, the Sofitel St James in Waterloo Place, used to be Lloyds Bank's Cox and Kings branch, descendant of the eighteenth-century agency that administered the payroll of British regiments at home and abroad. In more recent times, it was no doubt busy shovelling money to West End property developers and hedge funds. As the fall-out from the financial treatment continues, and as the HSBC-led exodus gathers momentum, many other former banks will find more 'socially useful' purposes – though I'm not sure what Lord Turner's position is on hammam treatments.

Allowing this train of thought to roam free – as one does on the massage table – I imagined how invigorating it will be if future Chancellor George Osborne's application of an industrial scrubber to departmental budgets caused great swaths of the public estate to find new life in the private sector. The picture that came to me, I know not why, was of Quarry House in Leeds, the vast, fortress-like headquarters of the Benefits Agency. I imagined it emptied of civil-service jobsworths and refilled with bioscientists, software designers, web entrepreneurs, green-tech exporters, venture capitalists, chocolatiers, video artists and tapas bars. And in the vault where they used to keep the abandoned plans for welfare reform, a fragrant, steamy, vision-inducing spa.

September 2009

——※——

LUSH PLACES

In the spirit of William Boot, the 'Lush Places' nature columnist of *The Beast* who was accidentally despatched to cover an African war in Evelyn Waugh's *Scoop*, I can announce that coots have nested atop the concrete pipe that runs just below the surface of the lake in St James's Park. This is such a charming sight that I now regularly enjoy a lakeside breakfast picnic on my way to Old Queen Street. It's all thanks to work carried out during the winter, when the previously murky lake was completely drained and scraped – making it rather less of a plashy fen for Boot's feather-footed questing vole and rather more of a fragrant habitat for water-birds. I rang the Royal Parks department to congratulate them, but with an ulterior motive: I wanted to know how much the clean-up cost and whether it came in on budget, since it offers a perfect example of the kind of public spending that brings quality-of-life benefits but which in the current climate we can scarce afford. Disappointingly, their spokesman refused to reveal the figure, but I'm guessing several hundred thousand pounds. Even so, there's an opportunity for positive headlines on this one. 'Malodorous slime banished', Boot might have reported, 'New freshness pervades Westminster air' – and we thought that wasn't due to happen until next week, when parliament rises for the summer.

July 2009

——※——

CHRISTMAS MESSAGE

My vicar David Wilbourne asked his flock to come up with favourite biblical texts for the Christmas issue of the parish magazine. Most people went for familiar snippets from the Nativity story. But with both the self-destructive behaviour of the financial community and Charles Moore's crusade against BBC smut in mind, I opted for James 1:21: 'Wherefore lay apart all filthiness and superfluity of naughtiness and receive with meekness the engrafted word which is able to save your souls.' Alleluia to that, I say – but we can also still learn from the parables of popular culture.

How should we respond to financial storms? Follow the phlegmatic example of Nessa, the amusement-arcade cashier in the award-winning comedy *Gavin and Stacey*, who we saw last week, rather improbably, on the phone to her broker. 'Shall I sell now?' she asked, 'Or wait for Tokyo to open?' Sensibly, she decided to wait: in volatile markets, never trade in haste.

How should we behave more generally in these harsh times? My new role model is Roy Cropper, *Coronation Street*'s well-meaning but far-from-streetwise café proprietor. When a drug dealer was peculiarly nasty to him in the café but left a mobile phone behind, Roy set off to return the phone – and found himself arrested as the dealer's suspected supplier. Why had he bothered to try to help someone so vile? asked Ken Barlow in the Rover's Return when it was all over. In a wicked world, said Roy, 'we should never forget the power of random acts of kindness'. That's my final message this Christmas.

December 2008

—＊—

NEGATIVE STEREOTYPING

I t's only fair to warn you – especially if you're Greek, Irish or Chinese – that this column contains negative stereotyping and I'm bracing for the Twitter storm.

My propensity to commit this category of thought crime was first pointed out to me by Giorgos Papakonstantinou, the socialist former finance minister of Greece. A graduate of the LSE, George to his friends, he was his country's most fluent spokesman during the earlier stages of its financial crisis – and last May I came up against him in a debate about the pros and cons of 'austerity'. I argued that the word itself was merely a synonym for the frugal, uncorrupt government supported by willing taxpayers which was largely absent in southern Europe, but that it was being larded with an excess of emotion about the temporary suffering it might cause. 'That hits a nerve,' retorted George: there were 'too many stereotypes flying around' when what was needed was empathy with his country's plight and 'a more relaxed fiscal path'.

That last phrase came to mind when I read that George now faces criminal investigation. He is accused of removing the names of three of his relatives from the 'Lagarde list' of 2,000 Greek citizens who held accounts at HSBC's Geneva branch and may have been evading domestic taxes. This was sent to George as finance minister by his French opposite number Christine Lagarde (now head of the IMF) in 2010, but no investigation in Athens ensued. After he left office, the Lagarde spreadsheet was thought to have been lost – but has now turned up again on a memory stick, the French having provided a copy of the original for comparison.

Meanwhile, a journalist who published a version of the list was briefly arrested for breach of privacy. And the Lagarde list is not to be confused with others said to be in the hands of the authorities – of Greek holders of accounts in Luxembourg and Lichtenstein, Greek owners of super-yachts registered in the Netherlands, and (this one getting longer by the day) Greek buyers of luxury properties in London, not to mention a master-list of 54,000 Greeks believed to have taken

€22 billion out of the country between 2009 and 2012. Is there a pattern here, or would that be stereotyping?

I wouldn't like to say ... but news that Tesco Everyday Value beef-burgers supplied by an Irish company, Silvercrest, have been found to contain 29 per cent horsemeat reminded me of a snippet I picked up in Dublin when I reported two years ago on the spectacular bursting of the Irish real-estate bubble: 'In some trainers' yards, every horse was owned by new-rich builders,' I wrote. 'But ... there are no buyers for the builders' nags at bloodstock sales – and owners often don't bother to collect them if they're unsold.' I'm grateful to the *Irish Times* for the statistic that the number of horses slaughtered in licensed Irish abattoirs rose from 7,000 in 2010 to 12,575 in 2011. That represents colossal quantities of prime horseflesh for export to Italy, France and Germany, while an unknown number of horses was also being shipped live to meat plants in Poland, France and Spain. Larry Goodman, the Irish tycoon behind Silvercrest, has queried the validity of DNA tests on his products while fingering a Dutch supplier of 'burger filler' as a possible source of horsemeat originating from South America. Meanwhile, cookery writers reassure us that horse steak makes healthy eating.

But what with all that exporting and importing in a trade described by welfare groups as inhumane, poorly tracked and prone to 'identity swapping', I can't help wondering whether some of those unsold non-runners have been finding their way back to processing plants in their home country.

Or am I being unfair to Irish horse dealers? Meanwhile, one story with a happy ending this week was the private sale, for more than £20 million, of an eighteenth-century Qianlong vase which had previously attracted a winning auction bid of £43 million from a 'Chinese billionaire', who then refused to pay up. The sellers, retired solicitor Tony Johnson and his mother, now have ample cash in the bank, and both the original auctioneer in Ruislip and Bonhams, who negotiated the private sale, have been remunerated, so all's well.

But – amid a booming multibillion market in Oriental artworks and antiques – non-payment by Chinese bidders has become a plague on international auction houses as well as suburban ones. Sotheby's in particular has pursued a string of lawsuits against defaulters in its Hong Kong sales, and at one stage introduced a requirement that potential bidders on premium lots should pay a HK$1 million (£80,000) deposit to establish their bona fides.

The problem is delicately described as 'cultural'. All handbooks on doing business in China warn that contracts there are merely frameworks for negotiation; auction bids are apparently seen the same way, as the starting point from which to chisel prices down again in private. Likewise 'face' is all-important: bidders lose it if they stop bidding, even if they have gone beyond their means, but take offence when asked to pay a deposit – so may not bid at all, resulting in lower hammer prices all round. Some winning bidders also resort to claiming that the dignity of China itself will be affronted if they pay top dollar for artworks which they belatedly realise were looted by foreigners in the first place.

And some just see the Western auction mechanism as an opportunity to outwit the *gweilo*. I gather it's not unknown for the winner and the under-bidder to be representing the same dealer, who has already agreed an onward sale at an even higher price and wants to reassure his customer of a lively, rising market – but if the customer pulls out, so does the dealer. Alongside *caveat emptor*, the slogan of today's auction world must be beware the wily Chinaman. Oh dear, I think that's a hat-trick.

January 2013

— ✳ —

UNSINKABLE

Other contributors have already saluted the centenary of the loss of the *Titanic*, but this column will continue to celebrate the doomed ship's timeless legacy to financial journalism, the *Titanic* metaphor. Impossible to count the number of icebergs that have loomed in the night and bands that have played on as the decks splintered in coverage of the banking and economic crises of recent years. But the prize for the most extended and imaginative use of the genre must go to Estonian historian Anti Poolamets, whose 'Welcome to the *Titanic!*' campaign in 2010 failed to persuade his countrymen not to abandon their own currency, the *kroon*, for the euro – making Estonia 'the passenger that got the last ticket'.

In the spirit of Poolamets, rest assured that the great wreck will never rest quiet on the ocean floor as far as Any Other Business is concerned, even after next month's anniversary has passed. Meanwhile I am discovering more food for thought on every page of Richard Davenport-Hines's brilliant social history *Titanic Lives*, including this observation as to why the British are more hostile to wealth than the Americans, even though the gap between the first-class super-rich and the poor down in steerage was and still is so much wider over there: 'The hungry beggar who glimpses a sumptuous feast feels more marvel than hatred. Envy occurs when people become capable of mutual, and invidious, comparison.'

March 2012

———✳———

TRIPLE PLAY

In our next Investment Special we will look at the pros and cons of putting money into India, bloodstock, forestry and spread-betting. By way of an appetiser, let me introduce three other things – all in different ways related to fashionable concerns about climate change and environmental health – that I would be tempted to invest in, having recently encountered them for the first time.

The first is the tricycle rickshaw. Tottering out of the Garrick Club, I hailed one of these contraptions to take me to Bond Street: despite a chilly evening it was a surprisingly enjoyable ride. A fleet of rickshaws transports tipsy tourists in the West End at night – but why not all day and in much greater numbers, instead of some of the black cabs which are among the capital's worst polluters? The constraint is cost: a state-of-the-art Pedicab Rickshaw from Cycles Maximus of Bath will set you back £3,145. But there must be Chinese factories that could knock them out in kit form for a quarter of that. It's a market open for the taking.

My second hot tip is snuff. Tottering into the Savile Club (I hope I'm not starting to sound like a clubland bore), I found myself urged to snort this aromatic substance off the back of my hand. It didn't do much for me except tickle, but when the smoking ban takes effect in July it will be the only tobacco product that can legally be consumed (apart from chewing plug, which is too disgusting) in any public building or work-place. In Sweden, there are now a million users of 'snus', or moist snuff, the majority of them ex-smokers. Expect a huge boom in demand for the products of historic British snuff-grinders such as Samuel Gawith of Kendal – which offers a snuff for every taste, including scented ones called Lavender and Otterhound.

Thirdly, black truffles – which I have just been hunting with a neighbour in the Dordogne and his labrador Orchys. If our climate is really becoming more prone to droughts and storms we might one day have the right conditions for these fungi, which have been selling at up to €900 a kilo this winter; we already have plenty of chalky soil and oak trees. I admit it's a very long-term punt, and yields are uncertain – but what a lovely way to spend Sunday morning.

February 2007

———✴———

THE TRUFFLE INDEX

Have Anglo-Saxon habits infected the truffles of Périgord – or is another rogue trader at work? Sunday morning found me at the annual *fête de la truffe* in the medieval town of Sarlat, hoping to bring home some vox pops about Standard & Poor's downgrading of French government debt from triple-A to double-A-plus. But the crowd was too absorbed in the serious business of gastronomy: sampling *amuse-bouches* offered by local chefs, all based on the pungent *tuber melanosporum* and ranging from truffled cappuccino of ceps (delicious) to truffled macaroons (yuk).

But what really caught my attention was the behaviour of wholesale truffle prices. In the big freeze of 2009–10, these passed €1,000 per kilo, but after the recent mild autumn they opened in late November at €400, doubling to €800 by mid December when the volume traded also doubled. Post-Christmas they dropped to €500, but have perked up to €600 again. That's what I call volatility. There's something sinister about these '*diamants noirs*', and someone's making a killing in them.

I tried to spot the villain amid the gourmet throng. Maybe it's not a human being, I fantasised, but a laptop lurking behind one of Sarlat's shuttered facades – a bit like the super-computer in Robert Harris's *The Fear Index*, which I happened to have been reading all weekend. 'One could no more pass moral judgement on it than one could on a shark,' writes Harris at a climactic point in his gripping narrative. 'It was behaving like a hedge fund.'

January 2012

———✳———

OUR MAN IN THE CAR PARK

An hour imprisoned in a gridlocked multi-storey car park close to Old Trafford on a home-game evening gave me an opportunity to ponder what was once called the beautiful game. I was a Chelsea fan in my youth – the heroic era of Cooke, Wilkins and Droy – but I'm irritated by the modern fashion for corporate chiefs to declare their club allegiances in the interest of looking blokeish. I'm prepared to accept that the governor of the Bank of England has a lifelong passion for Aston Villa, on the basis that no one would make that claim to impress, but – to take two examples I stumbled across this week – who really cares that the chief executives of Standard Chartered, Peter Sands, and the advertising agency M&C Saatchi, David Kershaw, are devotees of what Kershaw refers to in his official bio as 'the mighty Arsenal'?

So I'm not a natural supporter of the Red Knights, the consortium led by Jim O'Neill of Goldman Sachs, financier Keith Harris and hedge-fund player Paul Marshall, who are trying to wrest control of Manchester United from the Glazer family. That's not to say I'm in sympathy with the rebarbative Florida resident Malcolm Glazer and his sons: among the few facts known about Glazer *père* when he first expressed interest in the club in 2003 were that he had never set foot in Manchester and didn't like sports, and that a US judge had once described him as 'a snake in sheep's clothing'. He has loaded the club with debt and alienated its loyal fans, but it has picked up plenty of trophies under his ownership and there's no obvious reason why a coterie of super-rich City types should be more in tune with the diehards in the stands. Frankly, the whole game – motley owners, overpaid and oversexed players, dodgy agents, financial shenanigans – has become a grotesque circus of greed. I'd rather be stuck in a darkened car park than have anything to do with it.

March 2010

— ✳ —

A VOTE FOR RYANAIR

I'm composing this paragraph in my head on a crowded Ryanair flight from Bergerac to Stansted. It would be physically impossible to type it, because the rigid plastic seat-back in front of me is too close for me to open my laptop – and anyway the flight attendants (Irish and Polish) keep interrupting, trying to sell me snacks, scratchcards, phonecards, perfumes, train tickets to London and 'smokeless cigarettes'. I hope their rock-bottom wages, and the costs of buying their own uniforms, are offset by commission on in-flight sales. The ruthless Ryanair business model has become almost a caricature of itself – a flight quoted at £22.99 costs you more than £90 by the time you've ticked all the boxes in the online booking system, rising to £125 at the gate if you try to board with a second item of hand luggage, even if it's only your duty-free shopping. But that's still a cheap flight, with a better than 90 per cent chance (so the PA system declares, with a comic fanfare, as we land) of arriving on time. As a result, the airline that systematically rejects conventional notions of respect for the customer now has a market capitalisation almost twice that of beleaguered British Airways and expects to report profits for the year to March of £275 million, while BA clocks up giant losses.

No wonder Ryanair's Michael O'Leary was willing to drop his customary in-your-face animosity and express sympathy for fellow countryman Willie Walsh of BA during the recent strike. I'll vote for any politician who can work out how to apply Ryanair principles to the running of public services.

April 2010

———— ✳ ————

RICHER LIST

I have a suggestion for Philip Beresford and his *Sunday Times* 'Rich List' team to refresh their annual research exercise now that it has passed its twenty-fifth birthday. They already include a subsidiary 'Giving List' of philanthropists ranked by 'proportion of total wealth donated or pledged to charity'. But how about re-ordering the entire parade of our 1,000 wealthiest residents (who needed £75 million to qualify this year) according to their 'total contribution to the British economy'? Readers are welcome to submit their own formulae for this, but mine would be calculated by adding up how much each Rich-Lister paid during the year in all forms of UK tax and charitable gifts, plus the salaries attaching to UK jobs he or she has created, plus or minus the gains or losses of fellow UK investors in the ventures concerned.

Non-doms clearly start at a disadvantage in this reckoning, but redeem themselves by creating wealth for others – which is the supposed justification for their favoured status anyway. Even if we add 'fees paid to UK lawyers, accountants, estate agents, decorators, PR spivs and security firms' to the formula as a further element of trickledown, it's a safe guess that the top five would no longer sound as exotic as Usmanov, Blavatnik, Hinduja, Mittal and Abramovich.

Meanwhile, I'm compiling the more exclusive Any Other Business Rich List, and you'll swiftly spot how it works. I've excluded Richard 'Richie' Rich Jr, the richest kid in the world, on the basis that he's a comic-book character, and the Californian rapper Richie Rich on the basis that he has done jail time and writes appalling lyrics. But I'm including Marc Rich, the Swiss-domiciled commodities trader and former US tax fugitive (until Bill Clinton pardoned him) who is said to be worth $2.5 billion, and, of course, Rich Ricci, the racehorse-owning former sidekick of Bob Diamond who has just left Barclays having cashed in an £18 million share bonus to add to the fortune the bank had already awarded him.

Again, readers may like to submit other names that fit, but the only admirable one I can find is Yorkshire-based retail entrepreneur Julian

Richer, who has amassed £115 million, gives 15 per cent of his profits to charity, is described as having 'perfected the art of staff motivation', and plays in his own jazz band. Surely that's what being rich is all about.

April 2013

———✳———

INTERNSHIPS MADE ME

My thanks to 'AndyB', the only reader who posted an online comment on my column last week. It was 'Don't you ever go on holiday?' and the answer is yes I do, and here I am deep in the Dordogne, lunch on the terrace in prospect, scanning cyberspace for fizzing ingredients to make an Any Other Business cocktail. Upbeat economic news from home, led by 'CBI lifts growth forecast amid optimism', merely adds to the mellowness of mood. As for local issues to raise the pulse, there isn't even a decent ruckus to be had over shale gas, since François Hollande has barred exploration of it beneath French soil. '*Non au Gaz de Schiste*' declare some rather redundant banners, on which I'm tempted to spray '*Vas te faire fracker, Monsieur le President*' in the hope of getting myself arrested so I could write about French police brutality.

But instead let me turn to the topic that has had *Spectator* readers in a froth this week: unpaid internships. Brendan O'Neill's essay describing interns who agitate to be paid as 'nauseating' in their sense of entitlement attracted no less than 114 online comments, many of them very cross indeed. That certainly puts my single message from AndyB in the shade, and tells me I'd better jump on this bandwagon before our younger readership assumes I'm permanently out to lunch on the terrace. So, kids, here's a horror story to cap any of yours: unpaid internships turned me into a banker.

It's true. When I went from school in 1972 for an interview to get into Oxford and was asked my ambition, I answered 'to write for *The Spectator*'. But my banker father thought I'd better brace up, and fixed me an unwaged gap-year internship in a Barclays branch at Biarritz, the grand resort on the French Atlantic coast. It was a stylish induction – on the Avenue Edouard VII behind the Casino Municipal – but it was also a lesson in the greed and fear that rule the money world. My duties included arranging remittances from home for British customers who blew all their holiday money at roulette, sometimes returning repeatedly after being drawn back to the tables. I also helped count, and exchange for gold bars, bundles of Spanish pesetas brought over the border illicitly in shopping bags by wealthy Spaniards who were petrified that a socialist revolution would follow the death of the ailing General Franco.

All very interesting for an eighteen-year-old, but still I thought I wanted to be a journalist – and my father clearly thought I needed a second dose of sense. So two summers later I found myself in a posh City merchant bank called J. Henry Schroder Wagg. The work consisted of handling bills of exchange issued by companies to finance trade, 'accepted' by the bank and sold to discount houses in a daily routine unaltered since the nineteenth century. It was duller than Biarritz, but boredom was relieved by a clerk called Piers Pottinger – later a successful PR man, now based in Singapore – who spent his afternoons constructing elaborate practical jokes and making prank phone calls, on one occasion to the office of Mrs Betty Ford at the White House. Was this really the life for me? I wasn't sure – until my last day when I was summoned to see the chairman, the urbane Earl of Airlie, who said, 'Do come back and see us next time you're in the City', as though I had popped in for a post-lunch snifter.

An offer of a graduate traineeship followed, and that's how I was trapped for fifteen years in the great fortress of finance before I tunnelled out and turned into a writer. But here's the moral of my story, kids. Life is not a straight line. For you, as I wrote recently, life is about chances and choices, not entitlements – about snakes and ladders and unmarked doors through which a path will eventually emerge. So grab every experience you can, paid or unpaid, home or abroad. Accept the tedium, discomfort and shortage of pocket money. Yes, you were unlucky if you left school or graduated in the midst of a financial disaster wrought by your parents, but your choices will fructify as recovery advances. So get on with making your own luck.

August 2013

— ✳ —

POSTCARDS FROM KILLARNEY

The Beaufort Bar

The pub looks closed, its windows dark
Inside a dozen men clustered at the bar
Some silent as if deep in prayer, others
Discussing sport or war in voices softer
Than the creamy head on the black stout
They sip between murmured profanities
That serve as noun or verb or salutation
No one seems to glance in my direction
As I order Guinness, wine, lager shandy
My accent slicing through the heavy air
As if I'd challenged them to fight anew
And yet their banter ripples on unbroken
The failings of their Gaelic football team
Outweighing those of Anglo-Irish history
'That feckin' fellah, he's no feckin' use'
And me, I'm just a ghost they cannot see

56

The Meeting of the Waters

Fifty-somethings, fat, unfit
On unfamiliar hired bikes
With unforgiving saddles
Whizzing along wooded paths
Like Enid Blyton's Famous Five
Pause for breath on a little bridge
Beauty spot between the lakes
'Poohsticks,' says William
'Pick your branch or log or twig'

And so we did, and let them drop
On count of three, and ran across
To see them ride the gentle current
Nudge each other, change direction
The vigorous become becalmed
Unlikeliest emerge the winner
The child in all of us released
In re-enacting adult lives

CHAPTER 3

Heroes and Villains

RICHARDSON DESERVES A STATUE

When I first met the former Bank of England governor Gordon Richardson, at a bankers' jamboree in Japan in 1987, I remember thinking that he was smaller than I had imagined.* So I was not surprised to read Sir Win Bischoff – long ago Richardson's junior at Schroders and now chairman of Lloyds Banking Group – making a similar observation in David Kynaston's history of the City: 'I think his personality was such that he seemed to be quite tall but he wasn't. Very elegant; very imposing. A God.'

Lord Richardson died last week, aged ninety-four, and Bischoff must be one of the few bankers working today who observed him at the height of his powers. His leadership of the City through the 1973–4 banking crisis, and his marshalling (with his able deputy Sir Jasper Hollom, who is still with us at ninety-two) of high-street banks to fund the 'lifeboat' scheme for smaller banks in danger of collapse, was the Bank's finest hour in modern times.

---

* Lord (Gordon) Richardson of Duntisbourne, a former chairman of Schroders, was governor from 1973 to 1983; Lord Kingsdown (Robin Leigh-Pemberton) from 1983 to 1993; Lord (Eddie) George of St Tudy from 1993 to 2003; and Professor Lord (Mervyn) King of Lothbury from 2003 to 2013.

And although Richardson's self-taught patrician manner (he came from a middle-class home in Nottingham, where, like Ken Clarke, he was educated at the high school) could be intimidating, it certainly stiffened City sinews at a difficult time. My father, a lifeboat crewman on behalf of Barclays, secretly admired the governor's way of commanding meetings across a vast desk empty of papers, with a silent male secretary sitting in a corner taking notes. And it must have been another Barclays man who – in the hearing of the Treasury minister and sometime *Spectator* columnist Jock Bruce-Gardyne – was brave enough to remark jocularly to Richardson that 'of course, the Bank hasn't always been right', citing Montagu Norman's hostility in the 1920s to the creation of Barclays' overseas arm, which, Richardson's interlocutor declared, had turned out a great success. 'That,' replied the governor icily, 'remains to be seen.' But he was not always icy. When I once described him as 'austere' to a grand dame who had recently sat next to him at dinner, she suffered what looked like a hot flush: 'Oh no, he's . . . he's dazzling, utterly charming . . . the handsomest man in London.'

Financial storms have a way of overturning central-banking reputations. Just look at the fallen star of former US Fed chairman Alan Greenspan, also once widely believed to have divine powers, and the comeback of his predecessor, Paul Volcker, who after two decades in Greenspan's shadow has popped up at Barack Obama's shoulder as the architect of his controversial bank reforms. But Richardson's standing is untouched by time; the City should commission a statue, perhaps in robes of the Roman senator he might have been in another life.

January 2010

———✳———

WHY GORDON WAS RUDE TO EDDIE

I n Tokyo in the mid eighties, I bumped into a very senior Japanese investment banker who had just been to London to negotiate an operating licence. 'We met …' he paused for effect, bowing slightly at the neck and adopting what I can only describe as an obsequious grimace, '… Eddie-George-*san!*' The other Japanese present sucked their teeth in accord. Lord George, who died last Saturday aged seventy, was a big name long before he became governor of the Bank of England in 1993. He was also a model public servant: modest, calm, courteous, firm-principled and a master of market technicalities.

It was perhaps because he was so universally respected that he was treated so brusquely by Gordon Brown, whose 'tripartite' regulatory structure – which removed the banking supervision role from the Bank and handed it to the FSA – was imposed without consultation within a couple of weeks of the 1997 election. Only George's loyalty to the Bank stopped him resigning in fury. Brown's reform was spun at the time as a response to the Bank's weak handling of BCCI and Barings; but with hindsight, we can see it as a characteristic paranoid manoeuvre to weaken the governor's power-base, lest it should threaten Brown's own. And we have seen the consequences, in the abject failure of regulatory oversight at Northern Rock, HBOS and Royal Bank of Scotland.

My predecessor Christopher Fildes warmly recalls Eddie George's last Mansion House dinner as governor in June 2003 – alongside Brown, who, as ever in those days, refused to obey the dress code but was received with formal politeness. The retiring governor ended his gracious speech with a joke about making the transition from *Who's Who* to 'Who's he?' – and the assembled City rose to its feet and cheered him for a full five minutes.

To me, George was friendlier than I probably deserved, having written (on editor's orders, but that's no excuse) a rather savage piece about him in the *Daily Telegraph* during the difficult early days of his governorship. We were last in contact a few months ago, when I tried to persuade him to be interviewed in these pages on the subject of bankers behaving badly. He rang from his splendid Cornish garden, no doubt with a cigarette in his hand, to say 'Yes, but not yet.' I'm sad we shall never hear what he might have said.

April 2009

—— ✳ ——

THE GOVERNOR'S SOUP

I'm no WikiLeaker, but I am prepared to reveal that I have, on two occasions, lunched *à deux* with Professor Mervyn King in his private dining room at the Bank of England. Not a single word of what he said will appear in this column or anywhere else. But I think it's probably OK to tell you about the soup.

At our first encounter, as soon as this smoothly indeterminate vegetable broth was served, the governor filled his spoon, raised it halfway to his mouth, and embarked on a *tour d'horizon* to which, having been a notably poor student of economics long ago, I felt able only to reply 'Mmm.' Two minutes in, my own plate was empty; twenty-five minutes in, the governor's was still full, his spoon immobile, his butler darting in and out and dancing from foot to foot in frustration at being unable to clear for the main course, which was going cold outside.

But the second time, I went better prepared. I read and reread the *Financial Times* from cover to cover. I blew the dust off textbooks untouched for decades. And when the soup arrived, I launched into my own extended take on the global monetary situation. The governor gradually emptied his bowl – mission accomplished, I felt – while regarding me through his spectacles with the same mildly puzzled look that my Oxford tutor used to assume, as if to say 'Why on earth did we let this boy into the college?' A third invitation has not been forthcoming.

I tell this tale to explain that the governor is an economics teacher at heart. That's what he did for a living before he moved to Threadneedle Street, it's why he still calls himself 'Professor', and it's why he cannot hide his exasperation at politicians who put electoral gamesmanship ahead of serious economic policy formation. He barely concealed, in Mansion House speeches or Select Committee hearings, his suspicion that Gordon Brown's blueprint for 'financial stability' was more about maintaining political control than it was about smart regulation. And it comes as no surprise to learn via WikiLeaks that King told the American ambassador before the election he was worried about the inexperience of David Cameron and George Osborne and their tendency to see every issue in political terms.

That's what everyone was worried about at the time. So it's absurd to suggest that the independence of the Bank was compromised when the governor urged the Conservative team to draw up detailed plans for deficit reduction – and even sillier to call it an 'unforgivable sin' that requires the governor's resignation, as the motor-mouthed former Monetary Policy Committee member David Blanchflower has done. Rather, it was an example of the governor in economics-tutor mode, soup spoon in mid-air, explaining a basic point to a couple of undergraduates who clearly had not spent sufficient hours in the library.

---❈---

MERVYN MARCHES OFF WITH HONOUR

Mervyn King was his own man to the end: professorial, downbeat, against the tide. At last week's Mansion House dinner – as in his final vote in favour of more QE, on which his Monetary Policy Committee colleagues bid him farewell by defeating him six to three – he was still worrying about a potential reversal of the fragile recovery. Even as he packs his collection of Aston Villa programmes and

MPC minutes into plastic crates, the prospect of collateral damage from another euro-storm must be furrowing his brow.

So his last speech as governor was short on jokes and long on warnings: about 'unfinished business', lessons unlearned, and 'the audacity of pessimism' as an antidote to complacency. The ovation that followed (to answer my own question as to how fulsome it would be) was no more than polite: as he ended with the traditional toast to the Lord Mayor, the assembly shuffled to its feet – but sat again, a little awkwardly, within half a minute.

Neither the City nor the media nor the politicos at what he called 'the other end of town' ever loved Mervyn. He steeled himself to the loneliness of that position – and it liberated him to stick to his principles, right or wrong. All he can do now, as he heads for the House of Lords, is ignore valedictory swipes and await the judgement of history. He will have in mind the example of Alan Greenspan of the US Federal Reserve, saluted as a monetary genius on his retirement in 2006, damned last month (by *Time*) as one of '25 People to Blame for the Financial Crisis'.

How judgement gels in King's case depends on whether the economy hits another shock while a portion of blame can still be heaped back on him; but it must also take account of what-ifs. Would the Bank have had more clout, or better relations with Downing Street, or taken different decisions, if Gordon Brown had appointed the europhile Andrew Crockett or the media-friendly Howard Davies back in 2003, instead of King? What if King had won more arguments, and we'd had less moral hazard, more QE and less 'funding for lending'? In truth, it's awfully difficult to say whether King's personal part in the drama of recent years actually made matters better or worse.

What can be said is that, under the new structure which includes the Prudential Regulation Authority chaired by the governor, he leaves the Bank in a much stronger position than he found it, a decade ago, shorn of responsibility for banking supervision and adrift in Brown's 'tripartite' stand-off with the Treasury and the FSA. And in relation to King's attributes of intellectual obstinacy, righteous indignation at bankers' misbehaviour and disdain for shallow politics, let me echo Churchill's tribute to Neville Chamberlain: as 'history with its flickering lamp stumbles along the trail of the past . . . the only guide to a man is his conscience; the only shield to his memory is the rectitude and sincerity of his actions . . . with this shield, however the fates may play, we march always in the ranks of honour.'

June 2013

——✳——

THATCHER AND THE CITY

'Margaret had no love for the banks,' Nigel Lawson wrote in *The View from No. 11*. The idea that the amoral greed of the City and the banking crisis it fuelled should be blamed on Margaret Thatcher has been much bandied about this week. Let me try to put it in perspective.

In her early years in power, Thatcher thought of the City as another enclave of the 'Wet' public-school types who so annoyed her in the Conservative Party. The high-street banks were, in her view, a complacent cartel that reported embarrassingly large profits during the 1981 recession (hence the windfall tax), refused to contribute to Tory coffers, and did nothing to promote recovery. Dining at Barclays in February 1982, she harangued directors on the need for bolder lending – my father found it 'sexy'. When a Barclays branch later leaked details of one of Denis's companies to a Sunday paper, her hostility increased.

Meanwhile, she saw the stock exchange as another smug closed shop – when what she wanted was a dynamic market that would sell huge privatisation issues, raise capital for conquering British businesses and give Wall Street a bloody nose. If she instinctively disliked pin-striped idlers and Bank of England Keynesians, she was attracted to raffish deal-makers who flattered her: Sir Michael Richardson of Rothschilds, Lord King of British Airways, the transatlantic takeover player Lord Hanson. But she also wanted to make examples of those who transgressed, hence her urge to see criminal convictions in the aftermath of the 1986 Guinness scandal.

In many respects, she got what she wished for. Heightened high-street competition made a mortgage market fit for a home-owning democracy. London-based investment banks led the triumph of privatisation at home and abroad. The City's renewed status as pre-eminent global financial centre owed much to foreigners' admiration for the Thatcher spirit.

And yes, it's true: the bonus-hunting, the ill-considered risk-taking with other people's money, the lust for financial sophistication, all were by-products of the reforms she instigated. But all could have been shaken out by wiser managers, and by politicians less dazzled by City riches, in the decades that followed. In finance, as in many other fields, Margaret Thatcher was a positive force for change; it was human nature that led those changes astray.

April 2013

———❋———

ARE YOU THERE, BRUCE?

As a professional obituarist, I observe that 2009 has been a mercifully lean year for the business world. We said farewell to hard-partying Ernie Harrison of Racal in February, and chain-smoking Eddie George of the Bank of England in April. But perhaps the most potent name to be inscribed in the great book was that of Bruce Wasserstein, the Wall Street deal-maker who died in October, aged only sixty-one. 'Bid-'em-up' Bruce, latterly chairman of Lazard Frères, had a hand in more than 1,000 takeovers during a thirty-five-year career, all of them highly remunerative to himself and fellow investment bankers, rather fewer of them generating decent returns for shareholders of the companies involved. Famously, he brokered the dotcom marriage of Time Warner and AOL that came to be regarded as one of the worst deals of all time, then set out to make another bundle out of breaking it up again. Asked why he maintained such a relentlessly aggressive pace when he had already made himself a couple of billion, he answered: 'Frankly, I never considered the alternative.'

So it must irk him, from the place he now occupies – I'm picturing somewhere rather like a crowded Dubai nightclub with locked doors, no air-conditioning and no BlackBerry signal – that there are so many fat fees he can no longer collect. Deconstructing financial giants and reassembling them in different shapes will generate billions for the next generation of Bid-'em-ups, and meanwhile Kraft-versus-Cadbury (in which he was an early adviser to Kraft boss Irene Rosenfeld) rumbles on and on. This has the feel of a bid battle from a distant era – like switching on the telly to find yourself watching Noel Edmonds's *Deal or No Deal* – and in the absence of Wasserstein, today's financiers must find themselves having to phone long retired former colleagues for tactical advice. Now that Nestlé and Hershey may be teaming up to outbid Kraft, the entire global confectionery-to-convenience-foods industry seems to be engaged, and any chocolate-related news item, even the Fairtrade KitKat, takes on sinister new meaning. As for the announcement – on the *Daily Telegraph* obituaries page, of all places – of a recall of Kellogg's Choctastic Pop Tarts, what's the secret signal in that? A spoiler bid by Cadbury for the great American cornflake maker? Set up the Ouija board and call for Bruce.

December 2009

— ❋ —

THE DIAMOND LEGACY

'**M**y dad once said that the only time he'd ever heard me say "never" was when I was asked if I'd had enough,' Bob Diamond told me in 2009. You might guess, given the nine-digit fortune he scooped from Barclays during a sixteen-year tenure – latterly as chief executive – which ended this week, that what he could never get enough of was cash in his own deposit account. But actually he was talking about the pressure of steering Barclays through market storms in the face of relentless personalised hostility: 'I love the challenge, Martin, I love the business.'

I believed him and, as I've written before, I admired him for it. Diamond was the most formidable trading-floor chief of his generation in London. From unpromising beginnings he built a hugely successful investment bank in Barclays Capital and never let it run out of control. He pulled off the deal of the decade in the middle of the banking crisis by picking up the best bits of Lehman Brothers for next to nothing. He was a charismatic leader who always stood up for his boys.

But now he's gone, it's time to examine what Bob did to the culture of Barclays – which is, as regular readers may know, my *Mastermind* special subject: I wrote a book about it called *Falling Eagle*. My father worked at Barclays for forty-seven years and as its senior general manager, the 1970s equivalent of chief executive, he was a direct predecessor of Diamond. I worked there myself for a decade, made lifelong friends, and hope one day (if they haven't damaged the fund as badly as they have damaged the bank's reputation) to collect a Barclays pension. So I have never pretended to be objective, but I have always tried to be even-handed. And unlike many reporters on the Barclays story, I actually know what I'm talking about.

What was the culture like in better days? It was not the sleepy sort of bank that employed Mr Mainwaring of *Dad's Army* as branch manager at Walmington-on-Sea. It was surprisingly feisty. Senior managers wanted to give the competition a kicking. Lending bankers liked to take big but calculated risks, and went in hard to get the money back when they had to. There were stand-up rows and turf wars, between head office and the provinces, between domestic and international, between old-timers and smartarse youngsters like me. And until twenty-five years ago there was another source of friction: a class structure providing accelerated promotion for sons of the founding families, which my father, a gifted grammar-school boy, fought but never defeated.

Even so, it set a tone which allowed Barclays people of all ranks to look down on their rivals at classless NatWest as oiks. Stronger than the internal tensions were the collective loyalty and the shared norms: every department and territory had its own design of tie, but all included the Barclays eagle and everyone wore them. If there was a 'code of conduct' I never saw it, but I know what it would have said: work hard, do everything by the book, never let the side down, and we'll look after you for life. 'It was a funny old place,' one of my former bosses said recently, 'but it was a bloody good bank.'

And then along came Bob – or rather, to be fair to him, along came the intake of less able financiers who tried to build an investment bank before he got there. The old Barclays solidarity had already struggled for a decade against the new tide of bonus-hunters and job-hoppers that arrived with the Big Bang market reforms of 1986. 'We want a share of the goodies,' one of them told me, and no strategic decision could henceforth be taken without reference to the individual pay-outs it might generate. Colleagues no longer trusted each other, because they barely knew each other: by the time Bob got down to some serious hiring and firing in 1996, the average length of service in the investment bank was less than two years.

What did Bob himself bring to the party? It was being so darned competent that made his influence so pervasive – and ultimately corrosive – across the whole banking sector. His confrontational style made him so hard to manage that the board largely let him get on with it, surrounded by his tight-knit crew. When he presented his annual bonus list, topped by his own, the directors acquiesced, muttering to each other that it was only what Wall Street would pay to poach him, after all, and that investors weren't complaining. If he was unloved by many of his underlings (one in my hearing compared him to Tony Soprano) he was still their role model, the apotheosis of how powerful, rich and cool it was possible for a trader to be. It was the psychotherapist Lucy Beresford, once a Barclays executive, who told me that when Bob first arrived, 'everyone wanted to touch his golden sleeve'.

And so in the end the bank was remade in Bob's image, and the rest of the City tried to follow: it was all about the hard sell, the big bucks, the traders' testosterone – and it bred the Libor-fixing scandal, whether or not Bob's own fingerprints were all over it. His gentlemanly chief-executive predecessor John Varley, for many years the bank's last cultural counterweight, retired at 55 to make a new career in the charity sector. The chairman Marcus Agius never gained much sway over Bob, but fell on his sword in a last effort to save him – and nimbly fell off it again when the Bank of England and the FSA whispered in Bob's ear that enough was enough.

In *Falling Eagle* I argued that companies like Barclays are not 'machines for making money' but more complex, idiosyncratic human organisations, not unlike historic regiments. That parallel came to mind again this week. It was all there: hierarchy, ritual, discipline, *esprit de corps*, campaign honours, past heroes, everything but the marching band. It bonded people together, taught them how to behave, brought the best out of them. Then mercenaries like Bob arrived and were allowed to take command. Their day must surely now be over, but I'm watching the shaming of Barclays with sadness.

July 2012

——— ✳ ———

BRANSON GOES TO BOLLYWOOD

So here I am on a flight from Delhi to Mumbai, sitting next to an Englishman in his early sixties with bright blonde hair and a heavy cold. He has his feet up on the bulkhead and I'm distracted by his sensible black lace-ups: his wife packs for him, an aide whispers later. He's Sir Richard Branson, the billionaire entrepreneur about whom I've written so much over the years, often sceptical and unflattering, but never previously met. Between visits to Warsaw and Cairo he's in India for forty-eight hours to re-launch Virgin Atlantic's Mumbai route, which closed four years ago when too many carriers got in on the act and passenger demand dropped after the financial crisis.

I'm a guest for the jamboree and this is my one-to-one slot. Other hacks have put him through his paces on the West Coast rail franchise (his bad-loser stance so far triumphantly vindicated) and the award of a London–Moscow route to EasyJet rather than Virgin (he'll take his bad-loser beef on that one all the way to the Kremlin). So I've asked him about philanthropy instead. These days, I gather, he'll pop up as the face of the airline, the train company, the bank or the broadband-to-mobile business when need or opportunity arises, but spends the bulk of his time on projects close to his heart, such as the Ocean Elders, a pressure group that campaigns against marine abuses such as the harvesting of fins from live sharks for Chinese soup: 'We've persuaded them to stop serving it at state banquets.'

Then there's the other Elders, who he's about to meet up with in Egypt: 'the twelve people in the world with the highest moral authority', as he puts it, adding swiftly in response to my raised eyebrow, 'No, I'm not one of them.' They are the likes of Desmond Tutu, Jimmy Carter, Kofi Annan and Mary Robinson. His role, along with the rock star Peter Gabriel and others, is to fund and facilitate their conflict resolution missions around the world.

There's a touch of Tony Blair about Branson in all this: the perpetual youth, the messianic gleam, the access to presidents. But our stilted chat also reminds me of the elderly Yehudi Menuhin, who held forth between catnaps about the intelligence of insect communities in the African desert. Branson still has an appetite for hard deals and dangerous fun (kite-surfing with a naked blonde on his back, for example), but in other ways he has clearly moved on in search of something more meaningful. He has seen off most of his business detractors, but it irks him that the British media responds so cynically 'when you're a celebrity trying to do something positive'. On this occasion, then, and not just because I enjoyed the curry buffets, let me not slip into that habitual mode. I'd certainly rather be on a desert island with Branson than Blair – and since he already owns one in the Caribbean, I'm sure he'd be a handy companion. Perhaps he'll teach me to kite-surf.

One reason the British establishment has never liked Branson is his irritating, in-your-face informality, not so much a conscious protest against convention as a deafness to social nuance. At a lunch party hosted by our acting High Commissioner in Delhi, everyone obeys the 'lounge suit' rubric except the tie-less star guest in jeans, who makes a stumbling, jokeless speech in which he thanks 'the ambassador'. On the tarmac at Mumbai, his encounter with an official welcome party looks excruciatingly awkward, because he won't shake hands – not wishing to pass on his cold, he says – and doesn't seem to want the proffered bouquet.

But everyone, high and low, wants to touch his sleeve. His megawatt grin and entourage of Virgin beauties (real flight crew, who love these assignments) make him a media magnet. On the Mumbai seafront a comic cavalcade assembles: the great man, in Indian bridegroom robes, clambers on the roof of a battered taxi which is escorted by Bollywood dancers and flag-waving flight crew towards a mass of cameras. As he passes me at the front of the crowd, he shrugs and says sheepishly, 'The things we do . . .' It's the most human moment of our encounter.

The pictures, lit up by Virgin red and Indian gold, are fantastic. They're all over the local media, and it's mission accomplished. Only one negative: Britishness is represented by Indian male models in ill-fitting guardsmen's uniforms topped by limp bearskins worn at the wrong angle. There's my *Spectator* strapline, I whisper to a nervous Virgin press officer: 'Branson insults historic regiments.'

November 2012

— ✳ —

A GIFT FROM ASIL

Asil Nadir, the Cypriot tycoon who fled Britain in 1993 to avoid trial for £34 million worth of fraud charges following the collapse of his Polly Peck empire, has instructed lawyers to see whether he might be granted bail if he came back to face justice. His return would certainly add colour to what promises to be a drab autumn. Polly Peck was a modest textile business until it was bought by Nadir, merged with his fruit-packing businesses in Cyprus, and turned into one of the hottest stocks of the 1980s boom. It came to own an exciting portfolio of brands from Russell Hobbs appliances to Del Monte canned fruit – but everything went pear-shaped in 1990 and the fraud squad came to call. When the assets of the group's Berkeley Square head office were catalogued in the bankruptcy they included a fleet of BMWs for the use of what Christopher Fildes called 'fourteen ladies who seem to have been consultants'.

That chimed with my own knowledge of Nadir's modus operandi. When I worked in Hong Kong in the late 1980s, Nadir dropped in by private jet and hosted a lavish party. His PR man, an acquaintance of mine, fixed me an invitation, while confiding that he had been surprised to find his duties at stops en route from London included popping into town to find ladies – who, as it were, seem to have been consultants – to keep the tycoon amused. Each guest at the party was given a flashy gold pen, but I always felt embarrassed about having received a gift from the hand of Nadir. Some months later, I found myself spending an evening, as you do, in the station bar at Erlianhot on the Chinese–Mongolian border, where I had a long conversation with a barman called Liu who had been learning English via the BBC World Service. As a token of friendship before my train left for Ulan Bator, I gave him the gold pen. I hope it has outlasted Nadir's exile.*

June 2010

---

* Nadir was found guilty in 2012 of ten counts of theft totalling £29 million, and was sentenced to ten years in prison.

FRED'S CURSED LEAF

My invitation to the World Economic Forum in Davos got lost in the post yet again. But who wants to dine on Alpine ragout – or even pizza with Dave* – when you could be at home remembering Robert Burns with haggis and a dram? I enjoyed double measures this year, two nights running of the irrepressible *joie de vivre* of Scotland's national poet triumphing over Yorkshire blizzard and storm. Burns's financial affairs, like his love life, rarely ran straight, but in a week when RBS shareholders launched a £4 billion lawsuit against their collapsed bank and its former directors, I wondered what he would have thought of the demise of Scotland's reputation for prudence – or perhaps he knew it was never really so.

His tenant-farming father William felt the impact of the collapse of the Ayr Bank in 1772, which destroyed the wealth of local landowners, and the poet was later chased for his own debts by the Bank of Scotland. He heaped praise on James Gracie, the Dumfries branch manager who seems to have bailed him out, but Gracie himself went on to found a bank that failed, and died a bankrupt. So Burns might not have been as shocked as modern Scots by the disgrace of HBOS and RBS, and his 'Lines Written on a Banknote' in 1786 would make a nice tattoo on the buttocks of Fred Goodwin, who allegedly insisted that only notes bearing his own printed signature should be issued by ATMs at RBS headquarters, and who will now be obliged to emerge from exile or seclusion for the court case:

> *. . . thou cursed leaf!*
> *Fell source o' a' my woe and grief! . . .*
> *For lack o' thee, I leave this much-lov'd shore,*
> *Never, perhaps, to greet old Scotland more!*

January 2013

---

* The prime minister and his entourage had made a point of being seen dining in a pizzeria in the ski resort.

RISK AND REWARD

Let me stretch the boundaries of Any Other Business to pay tribute to two ambassadors of our native genius who have died. The Hull-born actor Ian Carmichael was a North Yorkshire neighbour – across the moors, that is – and a supportive patron of the project, which I led, to create an arts centre in Helmsley. Lunches at his home in the Esk valley were long afternoons of fine wine, theatrical gossip and worldly, well-informed conversation that belied the silly-ass image he so elegantly perfected on screen: curiously, the first question he ever asked me was 'What d'you think of that Lonrho chap, Tiny Rowland?'

It's many years since I was in touch with the jockey turned author Dick Francis, but he was one of the first people to encourage me to try my hand as a writer, after we had spent a week together on a yacht in the Mediterranean – he and his wife Mary as guests of honour, me as the deckhand. I can scotch the rumour that it was Mary who really wrote his thrillers, though she certainly did much of the research; what struck me about Dick was his down-to-earth attitude to his work. He produced a cracking bestseller every year in those days, on a contract timetable by which, so long as he delivered a new manuscript in time for the pre-Christmas hardback market, all his previous titles stayed in print. And he earned a commendation from John Blundell of the pro-free-market Institute of Economic Affairs for creating 'self-employed small business characters who are heroic yet humble; problem-solving and law-abiding; self-reliant and self-interested but not selfish'.

It was a tough slog for Dick, and he was always worried (as Ian Carmichael was too, and as creative people so often are) about staying ahead of the taxman. The yacht, incidentally, was the one he used as a setting in *Risk*, though I can also scotch the rumour that I was the model for its intrepid, lady-pleasing hero.

February 2010

— ✳ —

75

WRITING ABOUT MONSTERS

It was Tom Bower, doyen of British investigative authors, who first told me how good *The Last Tycoons* is – and other experts clearly agree. William D. Cohan's 'secret history' of the banking house of Lazard won last year's *Financial Times*/Goldman Sachs Business Book of the Year award. It is, without doubt, a masterly example of the specialist genre of investment-banking-laid-bare. So meticulous is its layering of anecdotal detail, its verbatim capture of authentic Wall Street voices, its unravelling of complex deal-making and corporate politics, that you know without reading the bio-blurb where Cohan spent his first career. He's an insider, an ex-banker with six years at Lazard itself on his CV.

In fact – I realised as soon as I met him – Bill Cohan is remarkably like me. He's American and I'm British, but that apart we've led parallel lives. His true ambition, like mine, was to be a journalist, but the financial world offered better pay and a certain spice, so for some years (seventeen in his case, fifteen in mine) we pursued that path instead. He moved on from Lazard to JP Morgan Chase; I moved on from Schroders to what became BZW. We both achieved the title 'managing director' – handed out liberally in such firms, but rarely involving management or direction. Then we both had the experience of being, in his words, 'summarily zotzed', which is Wall-Street for being handed the bin-bag and the P45. And we both went on to write books about the foibles and follies of our former employers – mine, *Falling Eagle*, being about BZW and its parent, Barclays.

Both of us have, therefore, had to wrestle in our second careers with the dilemma of just how savagely to bite the hand that so handsomely fed us during our first. 'I admit that when I was working on Wall Street I was as overpaid as anyone else,' Cohan begins. 'I have respect for the practitioners in the financial world; many of them are hardworking, honest and incredibly bright and skilled.'

But he's in no doubt that being as overpaid as the entire investment banking industry has arguably been for the past two decades is bad for not only for the moral fibre of the recipients, but also for the fortunes of their clients – and ultimately for the stability of the global economy. 'I believe the levels of compensation [in investment banking] now are leading to one boom-bust cycle after another, each cycle more disastrous than the one before, faster and more furious.'

He worries, too, that the values of Wall Street have pervaded far beyond the world's major financial centres, corroding standards everywhere as small-town businessfolk seek to ape the swagger and cynicism of the bankers and traders they see on cinema screens – or read about in books written by the likes of Cohan and me. So, I unleash my killer question: 'Why don't we just stop writing about these monsters? Aren't we just playing to their over-inflated self-image and encouraging them to behave even worse?'

He looks genuinely startled at the suggestion that, for the greater good, we should voluntarily give up doing what we know best. But it was a rhetorical question, after all: I'm not really about to stop writing about City big-hitters, and Cohan has already embarked on a new book on the downfall of Bear Stearns. The raw truth is that there's just so much to be written about these people – unlovable they may be, but some of them are truly extraordinary. And in that respect, I have to admit that Bill Cohan has the advantage. The characters I write about are, for the most part, uptight Brits imitating the kind of high-stakes players they've met in New York or Aspen or Gstaad. Bill's, on the other hand, are the real thing: true cosmopolitans whose wealth, arrogance and stamina are matched by their huge appetites for everything from real estate and fine art to mistresses and big-game hunting.

At Lazard they even think of themselves as 'Great Men', a concept which helped create the mystique of a firm whose success has derived far more from its wits and connections, in New York, London and Paris, than from its capital. No British firm would ever talk about Great Men, you might think: Warburgs in its heyday had leaders who were similarly revered, known more modestly as 'uncles'. But at Lazard only the office furnishings were modest: the egos were imperial – and the all-controlling monarch of modern times was Michel David-Weill, billionaire scion of the firm's French founding dynasty.

One of the best passages in *The Last Tycoons* details David-Weill's cigar habit: he loves big $20 Cuban stogies, and unlike lesser men who merely puff on them, he not only inhales them deeply but even recommends them as a cold cure. It was his invariable habit, having lit one and drawn on it three or four times, to leave it in the ashtray and light another: one of his junior partners would wait until the chairman left the room, then clip both ends of the abandoned smokes and slip them into his pocket, 'so every Monday I had two $15 cigars, and no one ever knew'.

Then there was Felix Rohatyn, a Viennese-born émigré from Nazi-occupied Paris who became Lazards' most potent deal-maker, earning the appropriately immodest label of 'the greatest investment banker that ever lived'. Credited with saving New York from bankruptcy in the 1970s, he also served as US ambassador to France in the last years of the Clinton administration. Hell to work for, he was a habitual destroyer of the careers of younger partners who crossed him, failed to deliver, or tried to steal the limelight; relishing his legendary status, he was 'like a larger-than-life Mickey Mouse' in the Disney World of Lazard.

In confirmation of their status as Renaissance as well as 'Great' men, Cohan records that David-Weill gave Rohatyn a Monet as a wedding present, and followed it with a Bonnard. But Cohan also recalls the icy, unrecognising stare with which Rohatyn used to pass him in the corridor – and the charm which was switched on when Cohan made it known he was writing a book in which Rohatyn would feature. Do such people have any redeeming features? I wondered.

Cohan thinks they do. 'To be a success in that world you have to be in some way a flawed person, with very sharp elbows,' he concedes. 'The objective is to make as much money as possible and garner as much power as possible. There was really no limit to how nasty you could be to your own colleagues.' But still the older generation deserved respect because they lived their business and risked their own fortunes in it: 'Once upon a time wisdom was venerated. It was a time when giants roamed the earth. But theirs were the days of private partnerships with unlimited liability.' The difference in today's shareholder-owned firms is that the big-hitters are in it merely for the short-term bonuses: 'There's no collective responsibility.' The new generation of investment bankers are disconnected from the risks they take with other people's money, which means they're prepared to run closer to 'the moral edge'.

I guess he's right: it is possible to admire old-style banking grandees without actually having to like them. And let's face it, Rohatyn and his ilk are sweeties by comparison with another big character in *The Last Tycoons*, David-Weill's son-in-law and one-time heir apparent, Edouard Stern, once described by the *Spectator* columnist Taki as being 'as close to a monster as anyone can be and still be free to walk around in society'. Cohan has a story about Stern at a business dinner in Paris cutting his own finger with a knife and allowing a drop of blood to fall into the soup tureen, as a test of the loyalty of those who were about to drink the soup. And the whole world knows the story of Stern's death, in Geneva in 2005, clad in a flesh-coloured full-body latex suit without even holes for the face, shot by his mistress in the midst of sadomasochistic frenzy.

Stern was a one-off perhaps, a man whose true purpose in life was to end up as a cautionary tale of the rewards of unlimited greed and arrogance. Of course, there are some wholly decent people in the investment banking world: it's just that they're the ones who don't bully, stab and claw their way to the top, and they don't have books written about them. The consolation, Bill Cohan and I agree, is that sometimes they're the ones who get out and have the fun of writing the books.

June 2008

—✳—

HEAVENLY BREAKFAST

It was Sir John Harvey-Jones, the former ICI chairman and television 'Troubleshooter', who handed me the only award I have ever received for journalism, but that yellowing certificate is a source of far less pride than the accolade of a mention in the final chapter of the late Hugh Massingberd's *Daydream Believer*, where I am listed with a dozen other 'young writers' whose careers Hugh encouraged. So let me add an anecdote to the eulogies that have appeared elsewhere – and one which gives credence to the famous story of the Connaught breakfast.* When Hugh and I once boarded an early-morning train from York to London, he was horrified by an apologetic announcement that the restaurant car was out of action. 'I'll get the bacon sandwiches,' he muttered disconsolately, heading for the buffet queue – to return moments later beaming with the news that the announcer was wrong and a table awaited us. Porridge, kippers, the full InterCity sizzler and second helpings of black pudding followed; the chef shook our hands; the astonished waiter received a tenner tip; and at King's Cross the great man strode off Lord's-wards, replete, rubicund, radiating bonhomie. I hope the heavenly dining car is as satisfying; at least, as far as we know, it's not at the mercy of Network Rail.

January 2008

———✳———

---

* Hugh Massingberd (1946–2007), the *Daily Telegraph*'s obituaries editor from 1986 to 1994, was said to have eaten, in 1972, the largest breakfast ever served at the Connaught Hotel, beating a record set by King Farouk of Egypt.

THE CITY'S PEERLESS JOKESMITH

Christopher Fildes's 'City and Suburban' column first appeared in June 1984 and notched up over a thousand appearances; before that, he served as business editor under Nigel Lawson in the late 1960s. As a chronicle of modern City life, the Fildes oeuvre has only one equal and that comes in the weighty form of *A Club No More*, the last volume of David Kynaston's magisterial history of the Square Mile. In the lighter field of daily and weekly journalism, Christopher has been peerless in his combination of wit, learning, firmness of judgement, appetite for gossip and enthusiasm for lunch – preferably at the Savoy Grill before its tragic refurbishment.

As the governor of the Bank of England, Mervyn King, wrote in his introduction to *A City Spectator*, the selection from City and Suburban which I assembled in 2004, Christopher has combined 'a real affection for the City – both old and new – with a readiness to be trenchantly critical when the occasion demands, criticism which is all the more effective when it comes from a knowledgeable friend'. He has also been very kind to me personally, so I hope he won't mind me telling some old stories about him in lieu of the speech I might have given if *Spectator* largesse had stretched to hiring a sufficiently capacious venue (Epsom racecourse would have been ideal) to invite all his loyal readers to a farewell party.

One afternoon, back in my banking days in 1989, I was staring idly across Hong Kong harbour from my office window when a colleague rang from London to ask whether I knew who Christopher was. Of course, I said. Not only was I a long-time *Spectator* fan, but his bowler hat, buttonhole flower and general bonhomie had made a big impression on me when he lectured to my graduate training course in 1976, and had made me wonder even then why on earth I was trying to be a banker when being a journalist was clearly so much more fun.

His name had been familiar at home before that, I recalled. My father, as general manager of Barclays Bank during the City crisis of 1974, had been introduced by Christopher, then at the *Daily Mail*, to the idea that when the going gets tough in the markets, lunch at the Ritz is the best possible investment. Despite or because of this evident *joie de vivre*, my father's chairman, the redoubtable Wykehamist Sir Anthony Tuke, had declared Christopher the only City journalist who was to be allowed to set foot in his office.

Well, said my colleague – who had probably not expected such a comprehensive answer – he needs someone sensible in Hong Kong to advise his goddaughter, and you're the man for the job. I feared this might concern tangled affairs of the heart, but Christopher himself rang to explain: Charlotte Ashby was a student film-maker who had been living in Beijing, where she had become involved with a radical cinema co-operative – a high-risk venture in more ways than one in the aftermath of the Tiananmen massacre. She was proposing to invest a slice of her inheritance in it, and Christopher thought this might not be a terrific idea. Could I talk her round?

Charlotte duly came to see me. Before her money reached the cinema, she told me, her Chinese friends proposed to multiply it by investing it in a sure-fire import-export deal, possibly involving the same consignment of metals being exported and then re-imported, or vice versa. My view of emergent Chinese capitalism has always been cautious, but back in 1989 such fast-buck dealings were even more dangerous. 'I really wouldn't do that if I were you,' I told Charlotte, as kindly as I could. Luckily she didn't, but she did go on to make a fine career in the film industry, starting with an award-winning documentary series, *China: Beyond the Clouds*.

A couple of years later, when I was back in London and out of work, Christopher repaid the Hong Kong favour by sending me a picture postcard of 'London County Council Tramways No. 1763 Class E/1 Built 1920/11'. On it he wrote that a mutual friend 'tells me you're thinking of leaving the fat cattle country of banking for the badlands of journalism. If that's so, I've come across something which may be of interest. Ring me and let's meet with glasses in our hands.' What was remarkable about this gesture was that it came very soon after the terrible car accident in Morocco in which his second wife Frederica was killed and Christopher was badly injured: his scalp still bore a livid scar when I went to see him at the *Telegraph*'s City office.

The something he had in mind for me turned out to be the role of business obituarist at the *Daily Telegraph* – a niche I have occupied with great enjoyment from that day to this. I think Christopher must have put in a good word for me in Doughty Street as well. He was certainly an encouraging tutor. 'An absolute corker!' he declared when one of my early efforts passed muster, but when I took to interviewing silver-tongued City dealmakers he warned me sternly against 'letting old villains off too lightly'. Later – another lapse into naivety on my part – I remarked to him that Gordon Brown's 1997 *Spectator* lecture expressing his eagerness to help British enterprise flourish 'sounded rather reasonable'. 'But not to old-fashioned libertarians like you and me,' Christopher retorted, even more sternly. That exchange came back to me as I listened to last month's dismal Budget.

But what I will treasure most from Christopher's work, and enjoy in the rereading, is the quality of his jokes, the best of which have long outlived their victims. Few of us, for example, recall anything about the tenure as first president of the European Bank for Reconstruction and Development in London of the ludicrous Mitterand-crony Jacques Attali, except for the fact that he clad it in three-quarters of a million pounds worth of marble. But I bet many of you remember City and Suburban's headline from April 1991, and you may want to take this opportunity to recite it in unison: 'Knock, knock! Who's there? Attali. Attali who? Attali and completely over the top.'

And having done that, reader, please join me in a rousing toast to Christopher Fildes.

April 2006

———✳———

Wagner on the A1

Between Stamford and Grantham
between boredom and blankness
I retuned the radio
to the irritating station
whose name I won't mention
but you'll know the one I mean

With its syrupy presenters
introducing 'Smooth Classics'
to match the evening calm
with mispronounced composers
and disconnected movements
between ads for mobile phones

But suddenly the mood gives way
to love and death, Isolde's theme
the tension mounts in rolling chords
unbearable, unstoppable, a moment
of epiphany, transporting me
towards the flaming setting sun

If I'd been driving a Ferrari
I'd have overtaken Schumacher
If I'd been driving a Polaris
I'd have torpedoed the *Belgrano*
If Maria Sharapova had hitched a lift at Stamford
I'd have gone to jail at Grantham

The force of Wagner holds me
in a transcendental stasis
till the rapture of release
of unconsciousness and bliss

and a Vodafone jingle
and a trifling little madrigal

But in that passing moment
Left arm out, conducting
Right foot accelerating
Eyes obscured by tears,
I drive a burning chariot
through a forest of dark dreams

And unlike Tristan or Isolde
I live to tell the story
no infernal conflagration
at Little Chef or service station
no juggernaut collision
at the Melton Mowbray junction

Just a flash of inspiration
a blinding revelation
an unfathomable whiteness
eclipsing mighty Wagner: a
Lincolnshire speed camera
and three points on my licence

CHAPTER 4

West to East

MISSION TO ISTANBUL

I'm on a mission, in the steps of Pope Benedict,* to salute expatriate *Spectator* readers in Istanbul. And what a life this city offers. 'Very cosmopolitic!' exclaimed Mustafa the driver, forcing his way through impossible jams. Force your own way through the evening throng in Istiklal Caddesi, Istanbul's Oxford Street, and you might be in Milan or Barcelona; watch Bosphorus ferries at night from a penthouse restaurant, and you might be in Hong Kong; talk to businessmen about the booming real estate market, and you could be in any new-rich city on the planet. But stare up at the dome of the Blue Mosque, as His Holiness and I have just done, and you gain a stronger sense of where you are: Istanbul is neither west nor east but both – and that, of course, is the problem about Turkey's aspiration to join the EU.

'Welcome in Europe!' Mustafa shouted as we crossed the Sultan Mehmet Bridge from the Asian side of the Bosphorus. But the Germans, Austrians and French have made pretty clear that he and his countrymen are not welcome, offending Turkish honour so deeply that poll support for joining has fallen from 75 per cent to half that

---

* Pope Benedict XVI had been in Istanbul a few days before me, visiting the Ecumenical Patriarch.

level, and many public figures are now unwilling to declare themselves in favour. But one politician I met, a member of the liberal Anavatan party, was more frank: 'Of course we should join. It's not just about jobs for migrants. The rules and disciplines would be good for us too. And it would help keep Turkey a secular state. That's the most important thing.' And that's why Britain should continue to support Turkish entry, even taking account of Charles Moore's point that EU membership is an odd thing to wish on your friends.

One former *Spectator* subscriber not represented at my get-together with readers was the British consulate-general. The weekly copy which used to adorn the consular coffee table had allegedly been cancelled by consul-general Barbara Hay to cut costs. Miss Hay operates from Pera House, an imposing palazzo commissioned by Stratford Canning, the great Victorian ambassador to the Sublime Porte; it is one of Britain's finest pieces of diplomatic real estate, and very much the right sort of venue for a *Spectator* party. But rules governing hospitality there nowadays require completion of a questionnaire on the commercial benefits to Britain of the proposed event; my hosts reckoned our assembly would score so few points on this test that they booked a room in a hotel instead.

Half-hidden behind high granite walls, Pera House is impenetrable to most visitors these days – for grim reasons. In 2003, al-Qaeda bomb attacks on the consulate and the offices of HSBC killed thirty-two people, including Miss Hay's predecessor Roger Short and two British colleagues. The damage has been repaired, but one consequence of the blast still causes tension in the British community. The tale of St Helena's chapel is a curious parable of penny-pinching official insensitivity.

There has been an Anglican church on the site of Pera House since permission was first given by a seventeenth-century sultan – indeed, since before there was an embassy there. But the present chapel has been the subject of argument as to who should be responsible for it since a spat in 1928 between the ambassador and the Bishop of Gibraltar in Europe, to whose see it belongs. The chapel was in disrepair until the chaplain, Ian Sherwood, raised money to restore it in 2003 – but a week after the reopening came the bomb, which almost destroyed it. To the distress of Sherwood's congregation, the Foreign Office and the bishop then came up with a wheeze to defray rebuilding costs: the chapel was to be leased to a new hotel next door which would use it for entertainment, allowing worshippers access once a month. FO experts were not put off by warnings that in Turkey's arcane legal system, change of use can cause property to be forfeited. But Sherwood – victor of an earlier campaign to save the nearby Crimea Memorial Church – was not put off. A petition was raised, and questions asked in both houses of parliament, co-ordinated by the unlikely combo of Lord Strathclyde and Glenda Jackson MP. Eventually the FO and the bishop agreed to keep and restore the chapel, but the arguments rumble on: construction of the hotel continues alongside and beneath, and a garden that was to be replanted as a memorial to the bomb victims by Roger Short's widow Victoria (who bravely chose to make Istanbul her permanent home) has suddenly been covered by a thick concrete slab.

Mrs Short was, incidentally, full of praise for Jack Straw, who as foreign secretary flew straight to Istanbul after the bombing, spent time with her and her daughter, and kept in close touch afterwards. Perhaps it's unfair to be surprised that a political animal is also a warm human being, but I was. Even more surprising was the discovery, at the *Spectator* party, of two ardent female admirers of Tony Blair. They were Americans, and they took exception to what I had to say about the Blair-Bush relationship. 'We love him,' said one, a consultant in the stock exchange development. 'He's the best ally we ever had. His speech to Congress [in 2003] is just the best I ever heard. I make my staff listen to it every morning.' She even emailed me the text. So take comfort, prime minister; your ratings may be rock-bottom at home but somewhere in Istanbul, office workers are chanting in unison: 'Free not to bend your knee to any man in fear . . . That's what we're fighting for. And it's a battle worth fighting . . .'

I was unsure what to offer by way of seasonal greetings, our ambassador to Ankara having just set an example of the new correctness by issuing invitations to a 'Winter' reception. Around Istanbul there were plenty of fairy lights and images of Father Christmas – and I'm told some Turkish Muslims enjoy attending Christmas Eve services – but still it seemed diplomatic not to mention the birth of Christ. At last, however, outside a subway station, I found a billboard which gave me what I needed: a message that was universal, yet uniquely British: 'Marks & Spencer – Happy New Year!'

December 2006

— ✳ —

STEPPES AND STRINGS

In January 2003 I was invited to Kazakhstan to cover the first Uralsk International Violin Competition for the Daily Telegraph.

Thursday

It's six in the morning and we've been travelling all night on a cramped charter plane full of oilfield workers. Snow gusts around us as we totter across the icy tarmac towards Uralsk's old Soviet airport terminal. Blocking the doorway is a Kazakh folk group in bright robes and pointy hats, bravely trying to sing a welcome to the accompaniment of a two-stringed dombra, the Kazakh mandolin. We are offered doughnuts, and soured milk to dip them in.

Indoors a crowd of officials, some of them no doubt secret police-men, gathers to watch us. Foreigners other than oil men are a rarity here, but the hand the locals really want to shake is that of their own country-man, the violinist Marat Bisengaliyev, who is the prime mover of the competition and the leader of our crew of musicians, jurors, journalists and children. With his Beatles haircut and his love of cars and gadgets, Marat is a huge celebrity here, a macho Central Asian Elton John.

Strictly speaking, Uralsk is still in Europe. An old Cossack strong-hold, it sits on the west bank of the Ural River, the true boundary of

Asia. In the Soviet era it was a closed city, devoted to missile manufacture. Now the factories are derelict but the oil is flowing: the $4 billion Karachaganak project – a joint venture by British Gas with Italian, US and Russian partners – is bringing prosperity and cultural renaissance. Our first glimpse of this is the restored, red-plush Philharmonia Hall, where the first round of the contest will take place.

The gala opening is presided over by the Akim, or regional governor, Krymbek Kusherbayev. An appointee of Kazakhstan's all-powerful President Nazarbayev, he is a princely autocrat in a Central Asian tradition that owes more to Ghengis Khan than it does to Tony Blair. But the Akim is also a former education minister, and his plan is to use oil money to put Uralsk on the map as a cultural centre. His ally in this is a young British Gas engineer, John Morrow, chief executive of Karachaganak, who is ushered on stage by a sonorous fanfare. But the biggest star is Marat, who is hailed as 'Honoured Art Worker of Kazakhstan'.

The audience is fascinating. Kazakhstan has a hundred tribes whose physiognomies range from Slav to Mongol to almost-Polynesian. The women have small-featured, almond faces, framed by winter furs; some have the exotic beauty of Balinese temple dancers. The children are button-eyed in wonderment, and remarkably well behaved. The men, by contrast, fidget constantly with mobile phones: many are heavy-jowled from good eating, and I amuse myself trying to guess which ones are secret policemen. The first one I pick turns out to be the minister of culture.

Friday–Saturday

The first round of the contest. Each of fourteen competitors will play a Bach sonata, a Paganini caprice, and a virtuoso piece of their choice. First up is the French-born Israeli Naaman Sluchin, a student at the Juliard School in New York and an exponent of the authentic baroque approach to Bach. At twenty-four he is the oldest participant, and a mature creative artist. That cannot be said of the five Kazakh players we hear on the first day. Only one, the elegant Arzhan Khozbanova, excites the judges with moments of dancing musicianship – but her eyes are downcast, avoiding audience contact. The best moment is provided by Jia Zhang, from Szechwan province in China, with a sinuous account of Ysaÿe's Sonata No. 3.

We begin to worry that the locals will be offended if foreigners take all the prizes. A pianist who has rehearsed with all the contestants whispers that there are better Kazakh players to come. 'But watch out for the mother.'

The other journalist in our party has been drafted on to the jury, leaving me the sole representative of the international media. I have been allocated my own interpreter, Nadezdha, daughter of a Russian naval officer at Sevastopol, and a minder, Malik. I ask Nadezdha if Malik is a secret policeman. No, she says, he's the deputy head of the Uralsk education department. 'He thinks you're a secret policeman,' she tells him. He smiles enigmatically.

The pianist is right: the best Kazakh players have all drawn places on the second day. Botakoz Mukasheva and Almaz Kurmangaliyev (seventeen-year-old girl and boy respectively) are outstanding. Almaz's performance of Sarasate's Carmen Fantasy is a high point, and we hear that the local betting has him hot favourite for first prize. The audience also warms to Welsh-born Rakhvinder Singh – daughter of a Sikh father and an English mother, and a former BBC Young Musician finalist – and enjoys the Russian Dmitri Torchinsky's playing of Ravel's Tzigane. But the drama of the day is provided by the two youngest Kazakh contenders.

A sixteen-year-old Uralsk girl, Maria Hokhryakova – a Slav with the long-legged look of a potential supermodel – plays with coltish abandon until she breaks a string on her cheap violin. The string is quickly replaced, but the instrument is so awful that the judges have to rule her out of the final. She becomes an instant local celebrity instead. Meanwhile, the youngest player, fourteen-year-old Ahan Meyrbekov from Almaty, turns out to be the one with the mother. He is a child star of Kazakh television and a favourite of President Nazarbayev, so when the jury fails to name him as a finalist, his mother goes ballistic. The jury has picked all four foreign contestants plus three Kazakhs from Astana, the national capital. Having sat in on the jury discussion, I can attest to its absolute fairness. But Ahan's mother thinks she smells a plot against Almaty. For Marat, trying to create a first-rank international competition while pleasing the Kazakh powers-that-be, the politics have just begun.

Sunday

The Akim has invited the men of the party (this is a very male chauvinist society) to lunch at his dacha, 30 miles out in the steppes. The landscape is a vast, flat snowfield, with birch scrub and a few huddled villages. But the dacha, in a private nature reserve, is charming, and the lunch is sumptuous. It is served by two pretty waitresses from our hotel, who I am convinced are secret policemen. Between courses, the Akim plays his dombra and sings. He finishes each song, endearingly, by shouting 'Bravo!'

He also tells a joke about violin competitions. To get it, you have to know that Felix Derzhinsky was the founder of the KGB, and that when Russian virtuosi travelled abroad in the old days, KGB men always went with them. At one prestigious competition, a Russian prodigy is the winner; two other Russian entrants, the KGB men, come equal last. The first prize is a Stradivarius, and the winner weeps as it is handed to him. 'Why's he crying over that old bit of wood?' says one KGB man to the other. 'Imagine if the prize was Derzhinsky's own pistol. That would really be worth competing for.'

Monday–Tuesday

The final round. The competition has moved to the brand new Drama Theatre, also funded by oil money. The external design (it was the Akim's idea) resembles a yurt, the traditional round tent of Kazakh nomads. But its steps and floors are of shiny marble inside and out, lethal in icy conditions. We stagger arm-in-arm for stability, hoping our dignity will be saved by the tall fur hats we have bought in the bazaar.

The remaining competitors will now play Bach and Mozart

concertos. The problem is the orchestra, which has been bussed in from Samara in Russia, 200 miles away. Whether because they are worn out, or cowed by their fearsome Australian conductor, Andrew Wheeler, or just because they are very Russian, they seem listless and gloomy, offering little help to the soloists. The acoustics do not help, making performances seem smaller than they might have done elsewhere. But there is one shining highlight of the first day: Rakhvinder Singh's expressive playing of the slow movement of the Bach A minor. She is lovely to watch, though afterwards I offer to buy her a more glamorous pair of shoes.

The second day is harder to judge. The Chinese girl Jia Zhang has a heavy cold, but still gives an impressive account of the Mozart D major. Mukasheva and Kurmangaliyev are hugely popular with the audience – though the latter has the edge because, an audience member explains to me, 'as a man he is expected to lead'. Last to play is Sluchin, who again displays exceptional artistry – particularly in the opening passages of the Mozart G major – but is surprisingly out of tune with the orchestra. As a travelling companion he has been intensely self-contained; that is also the nature of his playing, but we all agree he is a major talent.

In the jury room – the Akim's marble and leather hospitality suite – there are strong opinions on the musicianship of Sluchin and Singh, but swift agreement that they should be named equal winners. Zhang is placed third, and there are runner-up prizes for Mukasheva and Kurmangaliyev. Marat, to his credit, allows a consensus to form without any hint that political sensitivities have to be accommodated. This is not going to be like the old days, he says, when competitions were always fixed to satisfy the powerful interests. He braces himself for the flak to come.

When the announcement is made, there is a favourable response to Sluchin and Singh, but scattered booing for Zhang. The angriest person in the hall is no longer Ahan's mother – who seems to like the result – but a lady professor from Astana whose three pupils were the Kazakh finalists. She is convinced the foreign jurors have favoured the foreign competitors, with whom they have been closeted (as, indeed, has she) in same hotel for the week. It is made plain to us that the $8,000 prize money shared by the three winners is a fortune in Kazakhstan, where average wages are $50 a month. The Kazakh runners-up share only $1,000, and the professor's resentment is not to be assuaged.

Wednesday

The professor was right to observe that the foreign party has formed a close bond, though wrong to suggest that it affected the judging. At the comfortable, British-owned Chagala Hotel, we have become a castaway family, with the American juror Mark Malkovich, veteran director of the Newport Festival, as honorary grandfather, and the young violinists as teenage children. Now the mood is subdued and conspiratorial, as the lady professor holds court in one corner of the dining room and the jurors conduct their post-mortem in another.

The final gala and banquet are still to come. Marat has to construct a programme which pleases the crowd and reinforces the verdict: he does so in spades. Kurmangaliyev reprises his Carmen, but not so convincingly. By contrast, Zhang – now really quite ill – plays her Ysaye piece with a passionate strength that stuns any remaining doubters. Touchingly, Sluchin and Singh play a movement of the Bach double concerto together. And one of the British jurors, Malcolm Layfield from the Royal Northern College of Music in Manchester, announces that he is going to give the English violin on which he learned to play as a boy to unlucky Maria.

After that, there's hardly a dry eye in the house. The Akim and Marat are full of plans for next year's competition. Even the secret police chief (I am convinced I have spotted him) is beaming from ear to ear. Ahan's mother is our new best friend, and the lady professor is nowhere to be seen. At dinner, everyone makes speeches. On behalf of the world's press, I construct an elaborate toast to competition, whether in violin playing, in transcontinental oil and gas projects or in the price of fur hats. 'Competition leads to excellence,' I declare. 'Competition leads to friendship. I wish you joy for future years.' And I truly mean it.

Daily Telegraph, *January 2003*

BEWARE OF KAZAKH TAXIS

I have been following with special interest – not to say unrestrained glee – the spat between the government of Kazakhstan and 'Borat Sagdiyev', the latest alter ego of the comedian Sacha Baron Cohen. Kazakhstan's autocratic President Nursultan Nazarbayev has evidently failed to see the funny side of Borat's characterisation of Kazakh men as brutal racists and Kazakh women as mulish peasants who are treated as chattels by their menfolk. London ambassador Erlan Idrissov called Borat 'stupid, belligerent and charmless', while other spokesmen have suggested that Baron Cohen is cowardly and politically motivated as well as plain wrong. What particularly got up Idrissov's nose were Borat's claims that a Kazakh wife can be bought from her father for '15 gallons of insecticide' and that 'Throw the Jew Down the Well' is a popular local folk song.

Happily I can adjudicate in this dispute, having once spent a week in the old Cossack stronghold of Uralsk in north-west Kazakhstan. Indeed, I count as an acquaintance – I hesitate to say friend – one of Nazarbayev's most trusted henchmen, Krymbek Kusherbayev, who was until recently ambassador to Moscow but at the time of my visit was Akim, or governor, of the oil-rich West Kazakhstan *oblast* of which Uralsk is the capital.* Sunday lunch at the Akim's dacha in the frozen steppes – preceded by a rifle shooting contest, washed down with fine claret, watched over by a thick-necked secret policeman who hissed 'Akim will read what you write in your newspaper' as I left – was a memorable occasion, though not one for asking awkward questions. This is not a regime which embraces inquisitive journalists, let alone cutting-edge satirists.

But I can report that Borat really has got much of his portrayal wrong. Kazakhstan is a society where men are men, but women are elegant and self-confident. Uralsk, an attractive town astride the Ural River which marks the boundary of Europe and Asia, is a multi-ethnic

---

* After Moscow, Kusherbayev went on, briefly, to become deputy prime minister.

96

meeting-point where Orthodox Christianity and Islam, having both survived Soviet oppression, seemed to co-exist without friction. I was told that when snow made travel difficult it was not unusual for Muslims to pray in Orthodox churches, and Christians in mosques.

Borat is right, however, to imply that Kazakhstan has a darker side. It is certainly not a country where I would rush to do business, despite a rising tide of oil-fuelled wealth. Foreign contract workers whispered lurid tales of corruption and intimidation, and I met one British entrepreneur who on a previous visit had been kidnapped as soon as he arrived at Almaty airport. The kidnapper – apparently tipped off by a passport officer – greeted him warmly by name, chattered about the many folkloric attractions of Kazakhstan, ushered him into a cab and set off at speed into unknown territory. Luckily for the visitor, a powerful connection, a steady nerve and a mobile phone enabled him to escape. The moral of the story is beware of Kazakh drivers who sound like Borat. Unfortunately, they all do.

November 2006

—— ❋ ——

TREKKING TO KATHMANDU

The first business article I ever wrote, in 1987, was a colourful (I'd have to say now, wildly overwritten) profile of the Nepal stock exchange, which in those days consisted of a polite man in Kathmandu who facilitated sales of shares in the handful of local companies that had achieved a basic public listing. 'See Nepal and buy?' was the jaunty headline . . .

'Forget bulls and bears. Yaks and yetis are being traded beyond the horizon of even the most adventurous emerging-market investors . . . In the bustling Dillibazar district, behind a throng of black scooter-cabs, ancient Datsuns, hawkers of roasted maize, hill-people walking to market, wandering cattle and sundry livestock, stands a neat white villa announcing itself to be the Securities Exchange Centre . . . an illustration of how capital markets can evolve and function even in the most adverse of circumstances. Nepal is officially classified, together with regional neighbours such as Laos and Bhutan, as one of the world's least developed countries . . .'

The article was commissioned by Robert Cottrell, a correspondent for various British papers who doubled as editor of an investment magazine published in Hong Kong by the bank where I happened to be one of the bosses at the time. So Robert didn't really have the option of spiking my copy, or even knocking out my superfluous adjectives, and, indeed, he politely encouraged me to write more. The rest, in my case, is history – and it's always fun to catch up with someone who once shone a light on your path. I was startled to discover that Robert now runs a second-hand English bookshop in, of all places, the Latvian capital of Riga. He also runs an elegant website called The Browser, which recommends a selection of the best in daily journalism from around the world; the least I can do to thank him for my debut is to draw The Browser to your attention.

You're probably also curious to know what's happened to the Kathmandu stock exchange. Well, like me, it has come a long way since 1987. It has 168 listed companies, an index (the Nepse), and a busy volume of trade. But the Nepse peaked in August 2008 at 1175 and is currently languishing at 475, having shown no sign of following the recovery path of neighbouring exchanges such as Mumbai's. One broker blames the Nepse slump on a 'titanic' rush of new listings, swamping the market with more shares than local investors can absorb. Ah yes, supply and demand: whether for cars, books or shares, it's what makes the world go round. High time I trekked back to Kathmandu for a follow-up piece.

March 2010

— ✳ —

YOU LUCKY BLIGHTERS

'You blighters don't know how lucky you are, Mohammed,'
growled Walter to the syce ... [who] nodded and smiled
politely, holding out the umbrella for Walter to step under
and ignoring the rain that hammered on his own unprotected
shoulders.

This snippet from J. G. Farrell's exquisitely crafted novel *The Singapore Grip* captures the entire psychology of Anglo-Malaysian relations. In doing so, it lights the background to the strange burst of petulance from Prime Minister Datuk Seri Dr Mahathir bin Mohamad which threatens to cost Britain billions of pounds in lost trade.

To extract full value from Farrell's forty words, we have to deconstruct them: we need to know that the author is writing in 1978, from a perspective of post-imperial guilt, about the events of 1940–42. He disapproves of Walter Blackett, chairman of Blackett & Webb, whose fortune comes from Malayan plantations and who is about to behave rather badly when the Japanese advance on Singapore. Farrell's sympathies, expressed through the thoughts of the novel's hero, Matthew Webb, lie strongly with the locals, both Chinese and Malay.

In the scene quoted – in which Walter has been musing about what would happen to the 'strong-flowing river of wealth' which Malaya represents to him if the British civil and military elite there were to be removed by 'some higher force' – are glimpses of several factors in the Anglo-Malaysian equation: the Malay habit of subservience to hierarchy, and of concealing true feelings, often bitter ones, under a nodding and smiling exterior; the British sense of superiority, even now not completely subdued; a relationship of mutual economic advantage, rather than kinship; a certain eccentricity on both sides; and the effect of the weather.

I was myself, in a small way, a propitiatory offering to Malaysia during the era of Mahathir's 'Buy British Last' campaign. At no profit to my London employers I was despatched to Kuala Lumpur to advise on privatisation, that potent export of Thatcherism which the wily doctor was the first Asian leader to adopt.

For ten months I sweated in badly air-conditioned rooms over the prospectus for the sale of shares in the national airline – the country's corporate flagship, run by a multiracial management, some of whom had been to Harvard. The government took crisp decisions; the shares were sold to 40,000 citizens; the whole exercise was evidence of the efficient, new, industrious nation which Mahathir likes to advertise. Outside the office, Malaysia was as verdant and superficially smiling as its tourist brochures.

But all the time, just below the surface, was a kind of unpleasantness which I rarely encountered anywhere else during seven years in Asia. Sometimes sinister, sometimes comic, well described in the Malayan novels of Anthony Burgess and Paul Theroux, these dark undercurrents gradually wore me down.

An insignificant incident serves to set the tone. One weekend, a retired Malay general-turned-arms-dealer (a common career change) took me to see his fish farm in the mountains. The sky was leaden, the humidity overpowering. The general ordered all his staff, including his driver, into the chest-deep, mud-churned, leech-infested ponds, where they spent their afternoon stumbling in line abreast from end to end, driving glittering sultan fish, much prized in expensive Chinese restaurants, towards landing nets.

As we watched them struggle, the general chatted amiably about, among other things, Tottenham Hotspur, and how he came to own the fish-farm land. It was, he hinted, a bit of a scam: an influential syndicate had bought a huge area of unreclaimed secondary jungle for a song, in the expectation that the government would declare it 'federal territory' and acquire it from them at a much higher price to build a satellite township.

It was unusual to hear such things at first hand. Tales of dubious speculations and of more blatant forms of corruption were common currency, but foreigners rarely felt they understood what was really going on. I have no idea whether any of the hundreds of stories I heard about dodgy land deals, arms procurement scandals, 'commission' payments and conflicts of ministerial interest were true or false; all I can say is that they were consistent. The only bribe I ever actually saw was one that passed from me to an airport policeman to allow me to park at the Arrivals door; all the rest is hearsay, circulated avidly, indeed viciously, by the Malaysians themselves behind each other's backs.

Within the organisation to which I was attached, a manager known to be the chairman's personal spy would take me for fish-head curry lunches, and fill my ear with poison about malfeasance by our colleagues. Introducing me to a well-known Chinese tycoon, someone would whisper, 'He has all the ministers in his pocket, you know.' One local dignitary told me it was well known that only three men in public life were incorruptible. Mahathir was not one of the three names mentioned: everyone had heard the gossip about him, usually connected with Japanese contractors, but few were brave enough to voice it above a whisper.

Ill-tempered, vindictive, uncharismatic, Mahathir has never been loved by his citizens even if he is respected by them for the success of his economic policies. The only national politician ever held in real popular affection was his genial Cambridge-educated predecessor, Tunku Abdul Rahman – the epitome of everything Mahathir hated about the British colonial legacy, and in old age, the only Malaysian newspaper columnist who could say what he thought about the doctor, even allude to his financial affairs, without fear of persecution.

I saw Mahathir only once, in curious circumstances. On another torpid Sunday afternoon between downpours, I came across him having a riding lesson in the stable yard of the Selangor Polo Club. Then aged about sixty, he looked woefully uncomfortable. So far as I know, he progressed neither to chukkas with the local princelings nor to mounted inspections of his personal bodyguard, but the equestrian cameo certainly accords with the awkward delusions of grandeur that colour his appearances on the world stage.

I might perhaps have seen more of the elusive premier if I had taken the flat which was offered to me in a castellated Hollywood-style mansion called Camelot, home of an ageing Chinese *chanteuse*, wife of another general, who was rumoured to have been on terms of intimate friendship with both the prime minister and the then king, the dangerously excitable Sultan of Johor. She had a white grand piano, erotic murals in the bathroom and a Jacuzzi on the roof. 'I usually keep my jockeys in here,' she said of the vacant apartment. I made an excuse and left.

Life was like that every day: slightly discordant, full of secret suspicions. The strange Malaysian attitude towards Britain was, it seemed to me, partly a reflection of Malaysians' strange attitude to each other, the prickliness and distrust between religious and political factions, between races, between colleagues, between a vulgar elite and a diffident populace.

A debate on whether the British legacy to Malaysia – courts, parliament, civil service, plantations, mines, railways, hill-stations, Chinese and Indian immigrants, wartime Japanese occupation, defeated communist terrorists – was on balance good or bad would be fascinating to hear, but it could not be conducted rationally in Kuala Lumpur. The subject is charged with emotion. Senior Malaysians with flats in Bayswater, accounts at Harrods and tables for the Boat Race Ball at the KL Hilton would instantly take umbrage at the suggestions that Britain has contributed to Malaysia's success or might still have something to offer. Any plain-speaking British comment on Malaysian affairs is instantly interpreted as racial and ex-colonial prejudice.

If the relationship is one of love-hate, Dr Mahathir has called the tune for the hate side ever since he came to power in 1981, when he launched 'Buy British Last' because Margaret Thatcher decided to stop subsidising overseas students at British universities. Our high commissioner at the time, William Bentley, made the mistake of reminding local journalists (off the record) that British blood had been spilled during the 1948–60 Emergency to keep Malaysia from communism. For this he was publicly vilified by the new premier, and cold-shouldered for the rest of his term.

The ordinary cut-and-thrust of commerce became fertile ground for anti-British fire-stoking. When a Malaysian institution bought the plantation company Guthrie in a dawn raid on the London stock exchange, the subsequent rule-change to prevent such sudden-death takeovers was interpreted as an insult to Malaysia. The denial of additional landing slots at Heathrow for the Malaysian airline was treated, repeatedly, as a major diplomatic slight – on which we eventually gave way every time, and will probably do so again to defuse the current row. In my own modest assignment, exposition of the subtleties of privatisation had to be presented with extreme caution at all times, lest I should suggest in the tiniest degree that what we did in London was ethically or intellectually superior to the practices of the rackety local capital markets.

Towards the end of my time in Kuala Lumpur I found I was counting the remaining days in my diary. Some locals had been kind and helpful, many had not. Some displayed, in irrational patterns, both polarities of the love-hate problem. I remember particularly the brilliant, volatile Malay surgeon-turned-banker (once a colleague of Mahathir, the doctor-turned-statesman) who was capable of fierce bursts of anti-British resentment, but treated me personally like a son.

These unprompted flashes of hostility were rooted, it seemed to me, not only in the history of British involvement there, but in the suppressed tensions of the society the Malaysians have created for themselves – and, trivial though it may seem, in the effect on the temperament (theirs and sometimes mine) of an unbearably sultry climate.

Like many other expatriate Englishmen before and since, I did my best for them and I was glad to be getting out. In letters to friends I used sometimes to recite another quotation from the ample literature of the South China Sea, this one from Joseph Conrad's *Youth*:

> *I have seen the mysterious shores, the still water, the lands of brown nations, where a stealthy Nemesis lies in wait, pursues, overtakes so many of the conquering race, who are proud of their wisdom, of their knowledge, of their strength.*

March 1994

A CULTURE OF WHISPERS

Malaysian Airlines, whose flight MH370 has strangely disappeared, is a national flag-carrier in the broadest sense – a symbol, along with the Petronas Towers in Kuala Lumpur and the Proton car, of its home nation's aspirations as an Asian Tiger. Hived off from the former Malaysia-Singapore Airlines, it became, in 1985, one of the first state-owned Asian enterprises to be privatised – and the young banker from London who sweated for ten months to write its prospectus for flotation was none other than your columnist.

The airline had every appearance of a modern international business, including a Harvard-educated chief executive. But my assignment was made challenging by a culture of fear and whispering which seemed to pervade the whole country under the rule of its then prime minister, the notably anti-British Dr Mahathir Mohamad. Speaking the plain truth was not encouraged – especially for a British expatriate – and I recall an uncomfortable afternoon in an airless boardroom when almost every interesting fact I had inserted in the draft prospectus was struck out again by my own local colleagues.

It's possible that I even tried to include an account of the crash of flight MH684 from Singapore to Kuala Lumpur in December 1983 – an incident which (though it involved no fatalities) caused national embarrassment when it was revealed that the pilot had taken over the controls in a heavy rainstorm on the final approach, ignoring instrument warnings, and slammed the plane down in a swamp a mile short of the runway, to the surprise of nearby villagers. The story of MH370 looks far more sinister. But whatever its secrets, don't expect the Malaysian authorities to offer them readily to the world's media.

March 2014

———✳———

LEARNING TO LOVE JAPAN

It was midway through Earl Mountbatten's funeral when I realised how much I liked the Japanese.

The former Supreme Commander South-East Asia, it will be remembered, left instructions that no representative of Japan was to be invited to his elaborately planned obsequies. He could never forgive the Japanese for their treatment of British prisoners of war: when he took the surrender in Singapore on 12 September 1945 he recorded in a diary his impression of the officers facing him: 'I have never seen six more villainous, depraved or brutal faces in my life. I shudder to think what it would have been like to be in their power. When they got off their chairs and shambled out, they looked like a bunch of gorillas, with great baggy breeches and knuckles almost trailing the ground.'

The Admiral of the Fleet's view of Japan is still shared by many Britons, including, perhaps, those who (until sensitivity prevailed) were planning to re-enact the Hiroshima bombing, complete with mushroom cloud, at this week's Elvington air show. But, though I have studied them closely to see what traces of their wartime viciousness persist, it is far from my impression of the modern Japanese.

I was not invited to Mountbatten's funeral either. On that day, in 1979, I was in Tokyo, having been sent for training with a Japanese bank. It was my introduction to a metropolis which felt at first like the capital of another planet. I was in jet-lagged shock at so much concrete and neon, so much ambient noise, so many thousands of identical people crossing the streets when the lights turned to green. Since I was junior, ignorant and spoke no Japanese, my hosts were distant, not really knowing what to do with me. But one of them, Kunio Osugi, invited me out for a night on the town.

At the hour of Mountbatten's final procession, I was ensconced with Osugi and his cronies in a tiny bar near Shimbashi station, under the care of a kimono-clad hostess called Setsuko. We were drinking whisky and discussing the world. It was one of those rare moments when a window unexpectedly opens on to a whole new horizon of life. Osugi (born during the war, the son of a professional soldier) became a kind of Japanese elder brother to me: I taught his children English, attended his silver wedding party, and discussed the world with him in all kinds of bars over the years, from Nagoya to Yorkshire and back again.

On that first encounter, we delved straight into the sensitive subject of Mountbatten's last wish (a master of fractured but discursive English, Osugi kept referring to 'Lord Mountain-Baron'). I revealed that my own father had fought the Japanese in Burma.* Far from causing uncomfortable silence, these topics led to vigorous discussions among my drinking companions about the affinities between Britain and Japan as naval powers innately superior to their continental neighbours. Much was made of the fact that Britain had assisted Japan in its war against Russia in 1905, and parallels were drawn between Mountbatten (who must have been spinning in his coffin) and Admiral Yamamoto, the veteran commander who had argued against war with the USA until the eve of Pearl Harbor. It was only by some perversion of the natural course of history, my new friends argued, that we had ever become enemies.

All of this was sincerely expressed. Similar arguments were put to me many times when I returned to live in Japan in the mid 1980s. No mention was made of prison camps or atrocities, the history of which was largely not told to the post-war generation. Instead, we turned in due course to the topic which the Japanese male invariably discusses when drinking: sex. We debated, inconclusively, whether the average Japanese was more of a 'horny guy' than his British counterpart. Osugi – a big fan of 1950s 'sweater girls' – held forth eloquently on the charm of European breasts. By the end of a digestive marathon of raw fish, iced whisky and karaoke, the Japanese no longer seemed hostile or inscrutable; very

---

* Like many of his generation, my father Deryk Vander Weyer rarely spoke of his wartime experience: commissioned in a Yorkshire regiment, the Green Howards, he was posted to India where he served with the Maratta Light Infantry, commanded a signals school at Poona, and rose (at twenty-one) to become one of the youngest majors in the Indian army. He saw action in Burma, but never told me anything about it.

different, certainly, but hospitable and open people. And they seemed to like me. Genuine cultural exchange had been achieved.

In many subsequent visits to Japan, and a period of residence there, I came to love the food, the art, the rock-gardens, the gracious service, the perfectly groomed girls with squeaky voices, the system of getting everyday things done which worked so well if you found out what the system was and rigidly conformed to it. I came to regard Tokyo, in all aspects except its relentless traffic, as more civilised than London. I became the only foreign regular in the little Shimbashi bar and (it was my job, you understand) I discussed the world with amiable half-pickled bankers in Sapporo and Fukuoka, Kanazawa and Aomori. In the office, I found the Japanese diligent and committed; after a while I learned to read the tensions below the courteous surface of their working relationships.

All the time, I tried to observe the side to the Japanese nature which had driven them to do such evil things in the war. It must still be here, I thought, in their motionless, helmeted riot police standing guard over government buildings, and their crazed rightist and leftist cliques, shouting slogans through loudspeakers from armoured trucks; at a different level, in their appetites for sexual violence in films and comic-books and their humour of physical cruelty.

But, for the most part, the dark side of Japan was either oddly institutionalised or heavily disguised. Yakuza gangsters with extreme right-wing connections were instantly recognisable by their dress and demeanour, and apparently operated in cheerful coalition with big business, stock-market manipulators and elected politicians – but there was no burglary, vandalism or casual violence, and women walked the streets in safety. The then prime minister, Yasuhiro Nakasone – on 'Yasu' and 'Ron' terms with President Reagan – had been a wartime naval officer and protégé of Yoshio Kodama, an ultra-nationalist yakuza godfather. When the Royal Opera came to Tokyo, one of their smiling sponsors was billionaire 'philanthropist' Ryoichi Sasakawa; he had run his own black-shirted militia in the 1930s, and was a Grade A war criminal.

As to old soldiers, none boasted of glorious deeds. Two of my colleagues had fought in the war, but their stories could only provoke sympathy. Mr Eguchi, our driver, had been a trainee pilot, living on starvation rations and cowering under his bed as the Allies bombed his airfield to rubble. A charming, dignified man, he was always eager to learn new English idioms; searching for him one day, I found a note in his handwriting saying 'For all I know he's gone to the airport', and so he had. Mr Hirayama, with whom I shared an office, had been a teenage conscript in Manchuria, and described how officers had driven raw recruits into battle at the point of a gun. He was hard-edged and chauvinistic but loyal and humorous; I liked him immensely.

It was with Hirayama that I had my closest encounter with the modern storm troopers of Japanese nationalism, the bureaucrats of the Ministry of Finance. We needed an operating licence, and more than twenty times in two years we were summoned to the Ministry's dim corridors to jump through Kafkaesque hoops of regulation, the interpretation of which was altered at will to slow our progress to the Ministry's pace. Our pallid, unsmiling interlocutor, Mr Fujitsuka, was never rude to foreigners, but one sensed the fanatic underneath. On the sole occasion when we tried to circumvent him, through the Bank of England and the Japanese embassy in London, Fujitsuka telephoned Hirayama and blasted him savagely for disloyalty to Japan.

There were other such flashes. When we wanted urgently to move into new premises, we were told that we could only use the building's official contractor for fitting them out, and that we would have to wait to do so at the back of a queue of obscure government departments which were moving in on other floors. Acting like one of his wartime officers, I sent Hirayama in to battle on our behalf. He returned from the first meeting of interested parties looking as white as boiled rice. The building's supervisor, he said, had ignored all Japanese conventions of oblique, consensus-forming discussion; he had simply harangued the meeting, expressing special contempt for foreign intruders. We decided to wait our turn.

But, this being Japan, the problem was solved in the end. We were given a date when the offices would be ready, and they were, in every perfect detail. In a pragmatic society, there always was a solution in the end: to me, the challenge was to decipher the subtleties of the Japanese mind, and to try to break down the barriers of deep xenophobia.

They were, of course, practically impossible to do business with, but it was a pleasure not doing business with them. I was often told that I would never really get to know the Japanese, but in some cases I did, and the more I knew the better I liked them. I also met many older Japanese who were stone-faced in their unfriendliness, because they thought of foreigners as commercial enemies or coarse-mannered aliens – like my Japanese girlfriend's uncle's golfing partner, who on first seeing me exclaimed loudly in Japanese (I had learned some by then), 'Look at the size of this *gaijin*, I bet he drinks like a fish.'

But among the Japanese brought up after the war I did not meet any of Mountbatten's 'villainous, depraved or brutal faces'. One weekend I travelled by myself to the pleasant port of Nagasaki, with its reconstructed Dutch settlement and its 'Madame Butterfly' villa – and its Mitsubishi shipyards, which made it the late second-choice target for 'Fat Man', the atomic device dropped on 9 August 1945, three days after the smaller but more devastating bomb on Hiroshima. I visited the black marble obelisk which marks the epicentre of the explosion, and I saw the plain domestic wall-clock retrieved intact from the rubble with its bent hands recording the precise time of day when the city was obliterated: 11.02 am.

I was glad to be alone, because I could not have spoken. Perhaps I am naive, but I believe that at that moment, in that place, the dark side of the Japanese nature must have been buried deep in the ashes and transmuted into something better.

August 1995

———❋———

SMOKE IN MANILA

Whenever I let rip in print about bankers' morals, I come clean by slipping in a mention that I used to be a banker who occasionally received bonuses. I was quite excited about them at the time – the late eighties – but to illustrate the difference of scale, the biggest annual pay-out ever tossed my way was roughly equivalent to a single working day's remuneration for Royal Bank of Scotland employee Jay Levine, who collected £40 million between 2005 and 2007. With hindsight, the real reward of my banking career was not the cash but the opportunity for exotic travel and human observation – and I'm slowly reliving it all by using up the vast collection of matches I amassed on my tours. This week, it's a box from the dining room of the historic Manila Hotel, once General MacArthur's headquarters, where I stayed during a banking conference in 1988. Dinner was made memorable by a beautiful Filipina, clad in a white toga, whose job was to sell cigars from a trolley. For each customer, she went through an elaborate routine of cutting, rubbing and warming the cigar, dipping it in brandy and eventually lighting it: the performance was so erotic that every fat-cat banker in the room had to have one, the bigger the better, until the smoke was so dense we could barely see each other. Reader, I had one too: let me take this opportunity to say 'Sorry.'

February 2009

---❋---

AFTER THE TYPHOON

The Philippines government has been widely criticised for the inadequacy of its relief efforts in the aftermath of Typhoon Haiyan, amid allegations that political bickering and rampant corruption have impeded emergency services and the delivery of international aid. It might be worth pausing to ask how our own county councils would cope with the passage of the strongest tropical cyclone ever to make landfall – but I'm also reminded of the impressions I formed for myself when I was a regular visitor to Manila in earlier days.

That was during the presidency of Corazon Aquino, mother of the present incumbent Benigno Aquino III and heroine of the 'People Power' revolution of 1986 that put an end to the brutal US-backed regime of Ferdinand Marcos and his ridiculous wife Imelda. Mrs Aquino's husband, Benigno II, had been shot dead at Manila airport by soldiers loyal to Marcos as he tried to return from exile to lead opposition in 1983; I once spent an unhappy afternoon stuck at that very boarding gate, contemplating the failures of democracy in Asia.

Buffeted by big-money and military interests, the Aquinos (a rich landowning clan themselves) have periodically tried to take a stand against corruption, but the country remains an example of what Professors Daron Acemoglu and James Robinson, in *Why Nations Fail*, labelled an 'extractive' regime – one that is ruled in the interest of an elite that controls vital economic resources and has scant interest in sharing wealth or promoting progress. Far more admirable than the people who run the place are the millions of hard-working and often exploited Filipino expatriates – maids, waiters, seamen, nurses, construction workers – whose remittances feed families at home.

I have even more uncomfortable memories of stepping over the bodies of sleeping families on the pavements of Manila's nightlife district, and of attending a bankers' party in the grotesque Coconut Palace built by Imelda for the visit in 1981 of Pope John Paul II, who according to legend refused to set foot in it. Progress has now been knocked back again by the forces of nature, and you will perhaps sense a note of atonement when I say that we should not let tales of misappropriation or incompetence deter us from sending donations.

November 2013

— ✳ —

BLUE LAGOON*

In the modern world your chances of being shipwrecked in the South Seas are increasingly remote, but should it happen and you have any choice at all in the matter of direction, head for Bora Bora in the Society Islands, 240 kilometres north-west of Tahiti and an enormously long way from anywhere else.

If you have dreamed of a verdant tropical isle in a limpid blue lagoon, this is absolutely it. As your ship goes down, however, you would be well advised to fight your way into the purser's office and grab all the travellers' cheques you can find, since, like all great rarities, Bora Bora is extremely expensive.

You don't have to arrive on a raft. A catamaran skipper told me with shining eyes and perhaps only a little hyperbole that he had just made the crossing from Tahiti in a single eight-hour tack on nothing but a double-reefed mainsail, his boat skiing from one Pacific roller to the next.

The sedentary traveller can come as I did, by the fifty-minute Air Polynesia flight from Tahiti and, as I did, he will probably make the mistake of asking one of Bora Bora airport's two or three employees where the taxi queue is. The airport (built by the US Navy when the island was an important wartime staging post) is on a small outer island, part of the reef. A leisurely ferry takes you across the lagoon to the main village of Vaitape, and a rattling school bus takes you to your hotel.

It's best to arrive at night, to savour the mysterious dark shape of the island and its scattered lights against the huge night sky, and to awake to the full beauty of the place in the clean light of early morning. The only appropriate time to leave is, of course, at sunset.

The main island is an irregular crescent formed from the rim of an ancient volcano and rising to two sinister vertical crags, Mount Pahia

---

* This was my first piece of paid journalism. The editor who commissioned it, in Tokyo, was Claudia Cragg – whose home is now in Evergreen, Colorado, where she kindly retrieved a copy of the article from an archive box in her barn.

and Mount Otemanu. It has a circumference of 32 kilometres, three or four beguiling but uncomfortable hours on a bicycle, of which more later.

All around the island is the lagoon, its surface the veritable Impressionist's palette of cliché – electric turquoise in the sandy shallows to blackish purple over the coral and sea-green in the deep. Beyond the lagoon a permanent white wall of surf breaks thunderously against the reef, a constant, distant rumble which, as you listen from the beach, you may well imagine to contain all the traffic roar and city vibrations you left so far behind.

Below the lagoon's surface is another world, a quiet coral landscape teeming with fish in extraordinary profusion of shape and colour-scheme, some barely distinct from their habitat, others no more camouflaged than a peacock or a London bus: the spectacled parrotfish, the moorish idol, the milletseed butterflyfish and its cousin the raccoon butterflyfish, the reef triggerfish, the forceps fish, baby barracudas like silver propelling pencils, clams with ridiculous bright blue lips – all of this available within a few feet of the beach to the idlest snorkeller armed only with a morsel of bread from the breakfast table, a great deal more available to the serious diver who ventures out to the reef.

Apart from its natural blessings, the pleasure of Bora Bora is the amiability and style of its people. The Polynesians are a distinctive race: great warriors, fishermen, musicians and dancers, their native dignity and independence of mind largely undiluted by the encroachments of tourism and modernity.

Both men and women tend to the strongly built, heavy-limbed, going to fat in middle age; the men huge in the neck and chest like great rugby players, the women languorous in their simple cotton pareus, exactly as Gauguin painted them, reminding us how scrawny is the late twentieth-century Western female ideal.

The islanders are not effusive in their welcome but they are civil and humorous and they don't mind you being there. The tourist industry has changed things, but a cycling tour of the island reveals that, for the most part, life is much as it must have been for a century or so: an old man sits in his vegetable patch patting a black pig, a boy stalks an unseen prey with a home-made bow and arrow; plump women stoop in muddy shallows gathering fish, mongrels lie on the road, land-crabs scuttle for cover, white churches stand in the sunlight.

The Polynesian nature is most evocatively caught in music and dancing. Every hotel and restaurant has its group of musicians, big men with guitars and ukuleles, tiny in such huge hands, sometimes a one-stringed broom handle for a bass. Throughout the evening they keep up a flow of close-harmony folk songs, breaking off now and then to swig beer from the bottle.

The village dance troupes who tour the hotels are family affairs, parents and grandparents singing, small boys drumming like demons, teenagers dancing. The girls in their grass skirts and coconut shells and flower garlands generate a cheerful natural eroticism whose wholesomeness is only slightly debased by the inevitable call for audience participation, ungainly pink tourists making lewd fools of themselves for their wives to photograph.

Small and far away it may be, but Bora Bora offers a very sophisticated selection of places to stay, all of them in bungalow style. Aficionados of that highly successful institution will opt for the Club Med. French existentialists may enjoy the Yacht Club, which has basic facilities and a transvestite barman, while Foreign Legionnaires will feel more at home among the strangely military clientele of the Revatua Club. There is an ambitious but unfinished Hyatt development at the northern tip nearest the airport, and going up the scale of luxury to the south is the Hotel Marara, built by Dino De Laurentiis to house the crew for two now-forgotten films, *Hurricane* and *Shark Boy*. But top of the list in every respect (including the price) is the Hotel Bora Bora, truly the Cipriani of the South Pacific.

The best hotels are nearly always privately owned by wealthy enthusiasts: the Bora Bora has been owned since 1963 by a Californian drug-store millionaire, who has ploughed back profit to improve facilities and maintain its exceptional ambience. The thatched-hut rooms are dotted around a manicured garden, some built out over the water, and designed with an attention to detail which extends to Gauguin's *Et l'or de leur corps* reproduced on the book matches.

The discreet professionalism of the management does not overwhelm the slightly lackadaisical charm and unpredictable gaiety of its local staff. As well as large numbers of nubile Polynesian beauties, these include the bulkiest and beeriest of the island's guitar groups, lapsing suddenly from folk songs to jazz blues, and a pair of jovial boatmen who, if the breeze is stiff, will take you for a terrifying sail in an outrigger canoe, crashing across shallow clumps of coral with great guffaws of laughter.

The Bora Bora's cuisine is not particularly Polynesian: the best option for lunch is a hamburger at the beach bar, served, if you're lucky, by the most Gauguinesque of all, the mischievous cocktail waitress Sylvana. Dinner can be quite grand, with the alternative just down the road of a restaurant called Bloody Mary's, a kind of Californian-Polynesian-Bohemian joint venture where you can eat plain grilled local fish and hear yet another splendid folk group.

The clientele of the Bora Bora is largely American, many of them honeymoon couples, some of the latter all-male. The remainder are a mixture of European jet-setters working on their tans, and a handful of Japanese. Such is the cost of getting there and staying there that one suspects it is a once-in-a-lifetime experience for most visitors.

But the island's lesser hotels are not substantially cheaper, and frankly, if you're going that far, go for the best.

If, indeed, you do go, spend what's left of your pocket money before you come back on cassette tapes of the local musicians. Play one to yourself in the car in a traffic jam on a wet Monday. Then you'll know with absolute certainty that the venture was money well spent.

The Magazine (Tokyo), *November 1986*

——✳——

Sunday lunch in Tahiti

Tahiti should be glamorous,
Gauguinesque,
Voluptuous,
But it shuts for lunch on Sundays
Except one bistro by the port
With a shifty little waiter
Perhaps a convict on the run
Who'd murdered his French mother
Back in Clermont-Ferrand.

He came to take our order
With a cockroach
On his shoulder
Bigger than a crayfish,
Waving its antenna.
If it had been a crayfish
It wouldn't have been offensive
But a cockroach, for Christ's sake . . .

'Monsieur,'
I said with dignity,
'Vous avez un grand insecte
Assis sur votre epaule.'
He flicked,
And shrugged,
As though it happened all the time.
It darted for safety
Amid the comforts
Of the sweet trolley.

We ordered wine;
A sad-eyed waitress brought it

With an extra encrustation
On the bottom of the carafe.
'*C'est un escargot?*' I asked.
'*Non, monsieur,*'
She countered,
Offended by my sarcasm,
'*C'est du chewing gum.*'

CHAPTER 5

Chinese Takeaways

MONGOLIAN STROGANOFF

When the weekly Beijing–Ulan Bator–Moscow train leaves China, it departs from a station called Erlian in the timetable, Erlianhot or Erenhot on maps. An otherwise undistinguished place on the southern edge of the Gobi Desert, it is known to railway buffs as the halt where the Chinese carriages have their wheel-bogies adjusted to fit the wider gauge of the Russian and Mongolian tracks. But it also deserves to be known for the attractions of the station house to which passengers are herded during a lengthy pit-stop.

Surely unique in the whole of China's dilapidated public-transport system, its waiting rooms include not only a television lounge, bank and post office but a fairy-lit bar-cum-discotheque boasting a revolving mirrored ceiling-globe of the kind once favoured by *palais de danse* ballrooms. All is presided over by Mr Liu, a part-time signalman whose engaging English is acquired from the BBC *Follow Me* series and polished on British travellers.

This interlude on the Trans-Siberian Railway is the second major surprise of an extraordinary five-and-a-half-day journey. The first surprise is the charm and comfort of the train itself – if you are fortunate enough to have secured a deluxe-class sleeping car. Spacious, wood-panelled, brass-fitted, accoutred with cut-glass water decanters and chintz-shaded table-lamps – the compartments are every romantic's image of the grand transcontinental travel of a bygone era. With or without waxed moustaches and murder weapons, this is the real thing, of which modern replicas are usually but a poor and expensive shadow.

It would not have been difficult to assemble the cast of an appropriately ripping yarn among the multifarious groups of passengers and attendants. There was a convivial English peer with his wife and beautiful, enigmatic daughter; a banker, a clarinettist and identical twins; a vivacious Cambridge undergraduate surrounded by eager German boys; a party of lugubrious Finns; and innumerable candidates for the role of bearded anarchist among the student population of the train's 'hard' class.

And of the self-contained group of Chinese officials in soft class there must have been at least one secret agent. There was the solicitous cabin attendant, Chang, who makes the journey twice a month in each direction, and the official interpreter Zhang, a gentleman-scholar in the old Chinese traditions, patrolling the carriages with his dictionary and phrase-book, occasionally arbitrating tense Scrabble games among the passengers.

Had Agatha Christie's Hercule Poirot been aboard to complete the ensemble, he would have found plenty to occupy his talents. He might have been intrigued by the whiff of corruption in the Mongolian dining car, where a sinister attendant pocketed all US dollars proffered and was spotted unloading food supplies to an accomplice at one of the smaller stations. He might have enquired into the scandal at the Russian bureau de change at Naushki, the only place on the route where roubles are officially sold. A group of Polish travellers had blocked the front of the queue so effectively that almost no one else had time to be served. Once the train was moving again, word passed along that the Poles were offering roubles at exorbitant rates.

Another mystery was the curious mechanism whereby tickets for the train can be bought quite legitimately at a fraction of their normal cost in, of all places, Budapest, allowing enterprising Germans and Austrians to fund their journeys by arbitrage. Poirot might also have investigated the disappearance of one of the German back-packers at Darhan in northern Mongolia, perhaps wandering too far for a fifteen-minute stop. Or he might simply have practised his forensic skills in identifying the footprints in the black Siberian dust on the rim of the substantial deluxe-class lavatory.

But perhaps, like most of us, he would have found himself in a pleasant state of lethargy induced by the passing hours, 130 of them, the kilometre-posts (7,621, no less – 4,735 miles) and the ceaseless rattle and shake of the train. Part of the trick is to keep timetable and guidebook (Robert Strauss's *Trans-Siberian Rail Guide*, for instance) constantly to hand, so as not to miss the intermittent points of interest amid the steppes and birch woods. The obelisk which marks the boundary of Asia 1,777 kilometres from Moscow flashes by in two seconds, the splendid gilded monastery of Zagorsk in ten or fifteen.

There are many strange and atmospheric incidental sights to be collected along the way: a barren Mongolian valley full of military hardware or a vast petrochemical complex smoking and flaring in the autumnal forests; two of the ugliest, grimmest towns on the planet – Zima (the name means 'winter') in Siberia and Datong in northern China. The latter, thickly located in the brown dust of the arid Shanxi plain, is another holy place for railway enthusiasts as it was the home of the world's last operational steam-locomotive factory until it closed last year. In the same region the rivers are polluted to an opaque grey soup, foaming at the banks.

There are also, of course, stations: every three or four hours, an opportunity to jog or stride the length of the train, to buy bread and doughnuts and to take photographs, if the Soviet police don't intervene, which they did with increasing frequency and gruffness as we came nearer to Moscow. The stations themselves are remarkable for the range of their architecture. The remote Mongolian township of Choyr consists chiefly of circular felt tents, but its station is colonnaded and pastel pink. Sukhe Bator has one in ornate Islamic style, Ulan Bator's is elegantly grey and white, Slyudyanka station on Lake Baikal has a kind of rustic Bavarian folly and Yaroslavsky station is tall, with rounded windows and classical stonework.

The social life of the train is another distraction – and attraction. It develops rather as it might on an ocean liner. Chinese passengers, reclusive to begin with, became livelier and more sociable as time went by; Europeans in hard class, perhaps understandably, did exactly the reverse. Up in deluxe we held court, offered each other whisky, coffee and Chinese white wine, swapped gossip and unreliable information, even on occasions exchanged business cards. Once a day we made the long trek to the dining car, which changed at each border. In China the food and service were good, the ambience warm. In Mongolia there was only thin soup, beef stroganoff rumoured to be goat, and sporadic, intimidating service; in the Soviet Union, fresh caviar and a mildly comic head waiter in a greasy bow-tie who responded well to large tips.

This waiter was almost the only Russian with whom any of us made contact, even though a whole carriage of them was added at Irkutsk. No expressions of glasnost were exchanged in the corridors or on the platforms. The archetypal soldiers in greatcoats and 'brick-built' railway workers watched us without curiosity. Passengers on local trains just stared back – those in the guarded carriages with barred windows, at a chilly night stop at Balezino in the Urals, perhaps preoccupied with other thoughts. The Dostoyevskian gloom of the platform scenes was increased by a powerful smell of coal smoke, an aroma almost forgotten in the centrally heated West. Only two things seemed to evince warmer human reactions: the antics of small children and the effects of vodka no longer sold anywhere on the Soviet railway system but evidently an important part of many travellers' luggage.

The train reached Moscow almost exactly on time, in beautiful autumn sunshine. Until then the absence of liquor sales had been the only sign of Gorbachev's reforms. Out in the sticks life just goes remorselessly on, as Siberian citizens had not been slow to tell the General Secretary on his tour of the region. A farewell dinner in Moscow's Taganka Bar, however, afforded us a vivid glimpse of perestroika in action. The Taganka is the most fashionable of the private-enterprise co-operative restaurants now springing up in the capital. It has a floorshow which includes jazz musicians, opera singers, a contortionist and a belly dancer; the atmosphere is bohemian.

At one table a sophisticated elder son was entertaining his family, including hugely fat and stolid parents. The father, perhaps a suburban party official, scowled at the entertainers and drained his vodka glass repeatedly. Finally a violinist in gypsy style provoked him to comment. 'What sort of rubbish d'you call that?' he asked. 'Thank you, comrade,' the fiddler replied. 'The next one is just for you,' and carried on playing right into his ear.

The Peak (Hong Kong), *March 1990*

— ✳ —

EASTERN MENACE

I remember a warm Sunday afternoon at the Singapore Polo Club in the late 1980s. I was drinking beer with the Hon. Mark Baring, ninth generation of the Ashburton branch of Britain's grandest merchant banking dynasty. I never thought of him again until this Sunday, when the telephone lines started to buzz among old Far East hands. In tones of stunned amazement, we exchanged what little information was available about the sudden death of Barings at the hands of a maverick Singapore futures trader.

None of us could understand how rumours of Barings' potential losses could have been current for a fortnight (some say a month) with no apparent reaction from its management, who somehow failed to stop their man in Singapore, twenty-eight-year-old Nick Leeson, from executing the catastrophic double-or-quits manoeuvre which broke the 233-year-old bank. We were all wise after the event about the inherent dangers of the 'derivatives' market: statistically, as Prince Andrew famously informed the grief-stricken citizens of Lockerbie after the Pan Am air crash, this was always going to happen somewhere. But mostly there was sadness, for a stylish competitor brought to a humiliating end; and, among those of us who had managed businesses in Asia's no-holds-barred securities markets, a sense of there but for the grace of God, if perhaps not quite on this spectacular scale, go we all.

On that halcyon day when we met watching polo, Mark Baring – one of four family members still working in what now remains of the bank – was managing its corporate finance business in that part of the world. Though it seems odd now to recall from the comfort of my typewriter, I was then in regional charge of a rival investment bank, Barclays de Zoete Wedd, with stockbroking offices in Hong Kong and Singapore, outposts on the even wilder shores of Bangkok, Manila and Seoul, and connections in Tokyo. Representatives of various other British and American houses were also there; we were all, like the fugitive Leeson, relatively young for our responsibilities; all confident and optimistic about our businesses; all at the mercy of market forces which we could not ultimately hope to understand or control.

As the polo ponies thundered back and forth, we discussed, among other things, the merits of dealing on Simex, the Singapore exchange which (along with a parallel bourse in Osaka) offered Barings the fatal possibility of staking much more than its entire capital on Japanese Nikkei stock index futures. The techniques of derivatives trading – complex ways of betting on future levels of share prices, currencies and interest rates, and of hedging risks taken in other markets – were already well established, but these exotic instruments were only just beginning to emerge as front-line sources of profit, in which every ambitious investment house was eager to stake a claim.

Japanese equity warrants, for example, had provided a sudden bonanza for several firms, Barings among them, which were otherwise struggling for income to cover the costs of hugely extravagant Tokyo offices. These miraculous certificates (representing rights to new shares, to be issues at fixed prices sometime in the future) could be traded to great effect by raw Essex and Watford boys who knew and cared nothing about the fundamentals of the Japanese economy. The warrants just roared up and down in an exaggerated echo of underlying stock price movements, and so long as someone told the traders which way the market was going and stopped them busting their daily limits, fortunes were there to be made. Nikkei futures offered a similar proposition.

But where fortunes are made, they can also be lost. The wise were wary of too much promise, and of the simplistic view that all markets basically behave in the same way, wherever they happen to be on the globe. Hong Kong also had a futures exchange, and when I arrived as managing director in September 1987 I was told by head office to look at it and decide whether to participate. Among the big players I was advised to meet were a Mr Lai, a successful broker, and a Mr Ng, a cheerful Singaporean property speculator. It all looked wonderfully exciting. The cost of access was relatively small. In the first strategic decision of my new appointment, I reported to London that I was keen to buy a seat on the exchange. A few days later, while the powers that be were still considering my proposal, it was Black Monday.

World stock markets plunged. The Hong Kong stock exchange closed for a week, and when it reopened share prices went into free fall. There were fisticuffs on the trading floor as brokers wrangled over failed settlements. The futures exchange had effectively collapsed; the same Mr Ng, it transpired, had bought enormous numbers of contracts in anticipation of a market rise, was now unable to meet his obligations, and was to be investigated by the anti-corruption commission. As a result of the crash Mr Lai's business was in terminal difficulties, and had to be rescued by the Standard Chartered Bank.

Many expatriates reacted to the dangers of Asian markets by excluding locals, whether Japanese or Chinese, from their innermost councils. I tended to take the opposite view. As in any financial community, some locals were totally reliable, some were absolute rogues. I recall a terrifying evening in a nightclub called the Lido with the putative Mr Big of the Singapore market, surrounded by Taiwanese showgirls; and a bizarre 'tea-dance' rendezvous in Hong Kong with a gang of high-rollers who included the money-man for a top jeweller (the gem trade in Asia, I learned later, is often associated with money-laundering), a high official of the Sumitomo Bank of Japan, and another mysterious figure who offered two-way prices in New Territories taxi licences.

I dread to think what deals they were cooking up between bouts of karaoke, but whether good, bad or ugly, these people were the market, of which we, the *gweilo* or *gaijin*, were merely interpreters to the wider world. My job, I decided, was to pick the right locals, persuade them to tell me what the market was doing, and apply a combination of their judgement and mine as to how we should respond to it.

The people I really distrusted, on the other hand, were the white men who thought they knew better. Some were fast-talking salesmen, with only the haziest idea of risk, ethics or inter-racial business diplomacy. But the worst were the aggressive trading types, reporting only to swaggering bosses in London or New York and obsessed with the machismo of 'global' dealing, in which vast sums of money pursue each other across the time zones like space-fighters in a computer game. Dismissive of Asian sensibilities, they operated in blinkered ignorance of everything except the patterns of numbers on the screens in front of them. They were also hugely overpaid, with expatriate benefits and tax breaks allowing them money to burn. It was an unreal life, which brought out the worst in people. It is in this category, by all accounts, that Nick Leeson of Barings fits.

Every day for three years, in Tokyo, Hong Kong or Singapore, I would wander around dealing-rooms, watching these people at work, staring at their faces for signs of unease. Sometimes I would wonder whether the Cantonese speaker was involved in some share-ramping concert party, whether the Japanese speaker was busy repaying an expensive obligation for past favours from a crony in a local firm, whether the suave public-school salesman was dealing on his own account ahead of his clients', whether somebody in the room was constructing a massive, impenetrable fraud. Or whether one of the brash young derivatives traders had simply lost control of his position, as Leeson seems to have done, and was multiplying his losses in an effort to conceal the inevitable catastrophe. And I wonder now whether, if it had actually happened, I would ever have been able to spot it.

After our Hong Kong business passed through the 1987 stock market crash unscathed, the Chinese director in charge of trading, whom I trusted completely, told me that we ought to have a proper ceremony to give thanks for safe deliverance. This turned out to involve bringing a whole roast pig into the office, plastic sheeting having been laid on the floor to catch the dripping fat. Each member of staff in turn clapped hands to attract the attention of the spirits, bowed to the shining red face of the pig and planted a burning joss-stick in front of its snout. Then we devoured the greasy pork with our bare hands. Some of the expatriates refused to participate in this pungent ritual, finding it altogether too pagan and sinister.

But I was glad to bow to the inscrutable beast. Like must else about life and business in Asia, the forces at work were a mystery to me, but I knew I needed all the help I could get. It is a region of powerful spirits, and Barings sadly failed to propitiate them.

March 1995

— ✳ —

CHINA WON'T BE A SUPERPOWER*

M r Zhang Yuchen, a Communist Party member and former official of Beijing's municipal construction bureau, has just built himself a new house in the suburbs of the Chinese capital: it is a replica of the seventeenth-century Château de Maisons-Lafitte on the Seine, enhanced with wings copied from Fontainebleau and gardens based on Versailles. It cost him $50 million, and he displaced 800 peasant farmers to clear the site.

---

* This piece, which briefly garnered a lot of attention from the BBC and elsewhere, was an example of Boris Johnson at his mischievous best as an editor: he rang me over Christmas and said, 'Everyone's saying China's going to be a great world power – why don't we just say exactly the opposite?'

Meanwhile, Mr Liu Chuanzhi – a graduate of Xian Military College, a former nominee for *Time* magazine's '25 Most Influential Global Executives', and the founder of Lenovo, China's biggest computer business – has just acquired for $1.25 billion the division of IBM which makes PCs, an iconic product of the technology age. Closer to home, my Christmas shopping this year consisted largely of bargain-priced but beautiful silk scarves from Shanghai; if I had bought anyone a digital camera it would probably have come from there too, and if I had fulfilled my secret urge and bought myself a Hornby 'Hogwarts Express' train set, it would have come from a factory in Guangdong.

The Chinese, their money and their manufactured goods are everywhere, and pundits in search of New Year themes have been full of predictions about China as the coming global power. The great William Rees-Mogg, never one to hold back from a bold forecast, says this 'is beginning to look like the Chinese century'. The former diplomat Sir Jeremy Greenstock, on the *Today* programme, spoke of China as 'an increasingly large presence on our horizon', conjuring the image of those huge alien spaceships that loomed over the world in the film *Independence Day*.

The People's Republic, we are repeatedly reminded, is sustaining growth of 9 per cent a year, on the strength of massive inflows of foreign investment. It is now the second largest national economy after the USA, measured in terms of 'purchasing power parity', and will soon be bigger than the whole of the EU. It has a prosperous middle class of 100 million people, most of them connected to the internet and among them at least 10,000 whiz-kids like Mr Zhang and Mr Liu, with net assets of more than $10 million each. Every factory enterprise that makes another Chinese fortune destroys jobs in the USA and Europe, while a large portion of the dollars China earns is reinvested in US Treasury bills to finance America's notorious deficit – giving China, one way and the other, a hard-to-beat hand of cards in global economic affairs. Hence superpowerdom is Beijing's for the taking, in this decade or the next.

Or is it? The time is surely ripe to rehearse the counter-arguments on this one, and let me start by declaring a bias: the last day I stood in Beijing's Tiananmen Square was 4 May 1989, which was the first day the students marched in with their banners, there to stay until the tanks crushed them a month later. Before and after that traumatic moment, I made many visits to Taiwan, a country which achieved prosperity and democratic progress by refusing to be part of China. In the same era I was often in Tokyo, where hotel bookstalls were full of tomes by American gurus predicting the rise of Japan as the global giant of the twenty-first century, on the strength of its fabulous industrial and financial strength: after the Tokyo stock market collapsed, never to recover, at the end of 1989, the books were pulped and the arguments never heard again.

So it is worth reminding ourselves why China is not necessarily destined for greatness, and certainly does not deserve our unmixed admiration. First, its present growth rate is very far from sustainable, dependent as it is on slave wage rates, corrupt bureaucracy, near-total absence of environmental controls and a financial system which is at best rickety and at worst, by Western standards, insolvent. Secondly, as Bill Emmott wrote in 2003 in *20:21 Vision*, China today is, in fact, only 'a modest country at best', whose gross domestic product per capita, even on a PPP basis, is still only a fraction of that of neighbours such as South Korea, and on a par with Ukraine.

And although China is obviously far from modest in population, at 1.3 billion, it could be overtaken on that front within a couple of decades by India, which also has claims to superpower status in terms of technology, weaponry and what China most glaringly lacks, a democratic government that the world respects.

To enlarge that last point, many observers argue that China cannot continue to advance economically without reforming politically. The new middle class, concentrated in the coastal provinces, is content simply to get rich by paying its dues to the Party elite, but a younger generation more aware of the freedoms enjoyed elsewhere may not be so compliant. Eventually, lack of democracy will itself become a brake on economic progress, holding back reforms and imposing too many costs – all those bribes for local officials, all those well-paid jobs for their cousins. At that same point, foreign investors will become disenchanted by the lack of an untainted judicial system which might help them enforce contract terms and get their money back.

But the Party will not loosen its grip without a fight, and meanwhile there are still a billion Chinese who are not part of the economic miracle – instead they are underemployed peasants like Mr Zhang's displaced and disgruntled ex-neighbours, whose only hope of a better life is to stare through the fence that keep them out and wait for remittances from their offspring, who labour for a pittance in urban sweatshops. One day they may rise up to cut the throats of the rich and powerful, taking China back to the civil wars of its pre-communist past.

And lastly – my guiding text here is Niall Ferguson's *The Cash Nexus* – we should remember that money is not always the answer to everything. Mr Zhang may be able to buy a chateau, but today's Chinese leaders cannot so easily buy themselves a seat at the top table. International reactions to the two relative unknowns now at the top, president Hu Jintao and premier Wen Jiabao, tend to echo General de Gaulle's remark on first seeing a diminutive Japanese prime minister of the 1960s: 'Who is that transistor radio salesman?'

The truth about superpowerdom is that it is partly to do with economic might, but also a matter of culture, education, science, military hardware and statesmanlike posturing. It is about coercing or persuading other parts of the world to want to be like you – which Britain, France, the Soviet Union and the USA have all achieved in their time and in their spheres of influence. How many French millionaires do you know who want to build replica Chinese pavilions in the suburbs of Paris? China produces thousands of gifted musicians who have adapted to the Western tradition – Lang Lang, for example, was the world's best-selling classical pianist last year – and needless to say, proud British piano marques such as Broadwood are now actually manufactured in China. But how many European musicians adapt the other way, and how many *Spectator* readers have ever willingly sat through a Chinese opera? We have always liked Chinese food and we have recently warmed to *Hero* and *Crouching Tiger, Hidden Dragon* in the cinema, but a survey this week said China is one of the five countries where Britons would least like to live. In a broad cultural sense, it is China that wants to imitate the West, and not the other way round.

As for progress for the benefit of mankind, the Chinese may be queuing round the block for MBA courses taught by professors flown over from Harvard, but their tally of Nobel prizes won on home ground is precisely zero (the roll includes two Chinese-born, American-based particle physicists, Chen and Lee in 1957, and one Taiwanese American chemist, another Lee, in 1986). By comparison, the University of California alone has notched up fifteen laureates since 1980. As for literature, the 2000 prize went to Gao Xingjian, born in Jiangxi province, who had to burn a suitcase full of manuscripts during the Cultural Revolution and find exile in France before he could write freely. Ancient China was a great and splendid civilisation; the China built by Mao and Deng is not.

Militarily, on the other hand, China is very big, at least in one sense – and it has unresolved territorial issues over Taiwan (which the USA might feel obliged to defend) and the South China Sea that might one day lead to conflict. According to a helpful public website provided by the American CIA, China has 208,143,352 men between the ages of fifteen and forty-nine who are fit for conscript military service. But only 2.5 million of them are permanently in uniform, many of their senior officers are busy making fortunes in real estate, the defence budget is surprisingly small because Beijing is so bad at collecting taxes, and the national stock of long-range missiles of the sort that really make you a global player numbers only about twenty, according to the International Institute for Strategic Studies. That would make a pretty short fireworks display compared to what America has in its armoury.

Finally, then, to statesmanship. The Chinese government chipped in £31 million for tsunami earthquake relief, half of what the British public has so far donated and a fraction of Japan's offering, but a hundred times more than miserly South Korea. If China was in any useful sense a leader of its region, this would be the moment for Mr Hu or Mr Wen to step into the spotlight, but they have already been upstaged by President Bush. And no one even bothers to ask them what they think of the continuing war in Iraq.

As for all the other fashionable issues on which statesmen like to pontificate, China scores no points at all on human rights and very few on public health: it made a hash of the SARS epidemic, and has only belatedly faced up to HIV/Aids, which, according to the WHO, could afflict 10 million Chinese by the end of the decade. In the battle to eradicate poverty, it can claim about 300 million successes, but a billion failures. On global warming, China signed the Kyoto Protocol while remaining one of the most shameless offenders on the planet, a situation which can only worsen as its manufacturing prowess increases.

It is, in fact, a vast environmental hazard zone, as any recent visitor to its dustbowl provinces and smog-laden industrial towns can confirm. To quote the CIA again: 'air pollution (greenhouse gases, sulfur dioxide particulates) from reliance on coal produces acid rain; water shortages, particularly in the north; water pollution from untreated wastes; defor-estation; estimated loss of one-fifth of agricultural land since 1949 to soil erosion and economic development; desertification; trade in endangered species'.

So there is no sense in which the rest of Asia or the world should, or does, seek to march to China's drum. And there are a great many reasons to bet that China's economic surge will not go onwards and upwards for long. Let us wish Mr Zhang and Mr Liu a prosperous New Year, but let us not confuse a fast buck with a bid for global leadership.

January 2005

— ✳ —

UNASHAMEDLY UPBEAT

Not four hours since the plane touched down at Hong Kong's new airport, Chek Lap Kok, and I'm howling 'My Way' into a Wanchai karaoke machine to the discomfort of my Chinese friends, who all sing like Charles Aznavour. I'll give some of the credit – for my energy level, not my singing – to Virgin Atlantic's Upper Class 'flatbed'. But I'll give most of the credit to Hong Kong itself: brash, noisy, diesel-fumed, neon-lit, money-crazy, always energising. After the pessimism and backbiting of recession-weary England, what a joy to be in a place that is unashamedly upbeat and – at least by comparison with the tensions when I used to live here – at ease with itself.

Back then, particularly after the crushing of the Tiananmen protests, everyone was apprehensive about what life would be like after the handover to China. Now they've had a dozen years to find out – and very evidently it's business as usual, with no suppression of public debate or of the cosmopolitan raffishness that makes the place fun, and many small improvements perhaps most noticeable to someone who has been long absent. There's more civic pride, more evidence of civil society, even a bit more civility: the roughness of Cantonese manners seems to have been mellowed by advancing prosperity, despite half a dozen cyclical downturns since I left.

It's hard to tell whether the global recession now ending has hit Hong Kong harder than, say, the Asian financial crisis of 1997 or the SARS crisis of 2003. The impact was painful this time, but relatively brief. 'When the economy's down, I really miss the sound of the pile-drivers,' one long-time British resident told me; piledrivers and cranes are not yet back in profusion, but with cash pouring in from the mainland, shares and high-end real estate have been moving ahead strongly, and that always makes Hong Kongers feel good.

Hot news is the £34 million price – an all-time record per square foot – allegedly paid by a mainlander for a new-built Mid-Levels duplex. This gilded apartment appears from the lift buttons to be on what locals regard as the lucky 68th floor, but is, in fact, only forty-three storeys from the ground, an arrangement its developer declares to be 'not misleading at all'. My Chinese friends say the more misleading aspect of the story is the headline-making sky-high price: they suspect it might just be someone puffing hot air into a bubble.

It's almost twenty-five years since I first came here for Christmas 1984, in the week of the Joint Declaration by Margaret Thatcher and Zhao Ziyang that sealed the colony's post-1997 destiny as a special administrative region of the People's Republic. One of the touristy things I did was to take a day-trip to Shenzen, the town across the river that separates Hong Kong from the mainland. I took the train to the border post of Lo Wu, walked across the bridge under the hostile gaze of Chinese soldiery, and wandered the rather desolate main street of Shenzen, where sparse shops sold cheap clothes and souvenirs: I still have the butterfly kite that I bought. But beyond the novelty of setting foot on communist concrete, it wasn't much of a day out.

I repeated the trip this week, and landed on a different planet. The border post has the scale and style of an international airport. Where the kite shop stood, or thereabouts, is a Bentley showroom. A metropolis of shiny towers stretches towards distant suburbs, connected by an eight-lane highway lined with manicured shrubbery. I was shown penthouse duplexes with panoramic views at £2 million-plus apiece – still a fraction of Hong Kong prices, but thereby all the more attractive to Hong Kong buyers. Given that local banks are under-capitalised and heavily exposed to property lending, all this has the feel of an even bigger bubble. But a glance at Shenzen on Google Earth reminds me that beyond the unsold apartment towers are thousands upon thousands of factories now responding to an uptick in order enquiries that – if China's official 8.9 per cent third-quarter GDP growth figure is anything like reality – will swiftly turn into full-blown recovery. Real estate markets, everywhere, are full of froth and puff; manufacturing is what really matters.

If I was twenty-five years younger I'd be back out here by Christmas, hunting for a job or a business opportunity or a book or a column to write. If you're one of those 'recession generation' graduates, or a thirty-something whose City career has imploded, take my advice: just get on the plane and go, you'll never regret it.

October 2009

—✳—

Three Memories of Shanghai, 1989

I

Smokey night
in the jazz bar of the Peace Hotel
(where Noël Coward wrote *Private Lives*)
and afterwards a typhoon
of sheeting, bouncing, luminescent rain.
'No taxi, no taxi,'
the doorman shook water from his hat:
no way home across that deluged town.
But out of the torrents came the tiniest car,
at the wheel a tiny girl,
seventeen, she said, but we guessed twelve
and she drove like a demon
fording sudden rivers
between trucks and trams
and out-of-action traffic lights
like a Jack Russell in a buffalo stampede,
like a rubber duck in a whitewater canyon.
'Nice driving,' we said, 'You take care'
as we squeezed out sweating but unscathed.
I often wonder if she's still there.

II

Jinshan,
the guidebook said,

where peasant women paint
their cheerful scenes of rural life:
we pictured a hilltop village,
ancient stone, cooking smells,
chickens running free . . .
Two hours' slow taxi later,
in rusting industrial hinterland
this artists' commune's a concrete block
in the shadow of a petrochemical junkyard,
the artists mostly old, unsmiling
in bare rooms with iron bunks.
Still I bought a picture
(it wouldn't help not to)
and then I met its painter
a younger, handsome, glad-eyed woman
strong in shoulder, jaw and handshake
but the subject that she'd chosen
was chickens trapped in cages.

III

I danced
with a sailor at the Seagull Club . . .
Well, actually, I danced
with an English girl called Claire,
a ring of jigging Filipino seamen just beside us.
Until a huge blubbery fellow,
ship's cook perhaps,
slapped my shoulder;
'Hey, mister'
he bellowed above the racket,
'I like the way you dance,
please dance with me.'
It seemed rude to refuse,
and anyway

he was twice my size
and let's face it,
Claire was no oil painting . . .
so stiffly, briefly,
terribly Britishly,
I danced with a sailor in Shanghai.

CHAPTER 6

Americana

SATISFACTORY BANGING NOISES

Guns are to American country houses what croquet mallets and Scrabble are to the English. Last Sunday morning, in the course of a birthday-party weekend on an estate in Dutchess County, New York, 90 miles north of Manhattan, I took target practice with a cold, fearsome chunk of sculpted metal called a Colt .44 Magnum. This is the calibre of six-shooter (though his was made by Smith & Wesson) favoured by Clint Eastwood as Dirty Harry: '. . . the most powerful handgun in the world,' he famously remarked to a cornered adversary in mid firefight. 'I don't recall whether I got off five shots or six back there. Do you feel lucky, punk?'

The weapon is heavy enough to do serious injury if you drop it on your foot, never mind the savage jolt to your shoulder when you pull the trigger. It would require superhuman strength to shoot straight one-handed, as Clint does, and you would rapidly go deaf unless equipped at all times with industrial ear-defenders. When I suggested that we raise the target on to a convenient tree-stump on the ridge in front of us, it was pointed out that a bullet which passed over the ridge (rather than embedding itself in the ground) would travel for a mile or so down into the township of Smithfield in the valley below, where it would still be capable of blowing a significant hole in a worshipper leaving the colonnade of the charming Greek-revival church or tending the flag-decked graves of veterans of foreign wars. A Colt .44 is an unusual thing to play with at a birthday party.

But it was only one of many guns on display and in use over the weekend. Invited for a pheasant shoot, one American guest arrived in his 5-litre pick-up truck equipped as though for an assault on the Fort Apache police station in the South Bronx. My hosts, an Englishman and his American wife, have highly civilised tastes: they have built a beautiful house on sloping ground landscaped according to eighteenth-century principles. And they have a gun-rack in their elegant drawing-room which would not look out of place in Saddam Hussein's bunker.

In pride of place is a matched pair of Edwardian 12-bores. There are over-and-under shotguns preferred for clay-pigeon shooting: smaller-bore shotguns perfectly adapted for the mass slaughter of Spanish partridge and Mexican dove. Next are rifles with telescopic sights for deer, woodchuck, groundhog and raccoon, not to mention a .38 revolver and a Luger pistol. The only piece not actually in regular use is a Hemingwayesque blunderbuss suitable for those rare moments when you meet a rogue elephant or have yourself helicoptered into the Yukon in search of grizzly bear.

This glimpse of the pervasiveness of gun culture in the politest of American society may help to understand why, thirty years after the assassination of JFK, even the very limited gun-control measures now under Senate debate – the so-called Brady Bill, imposing a brief waiting period on the purchase of a handgun – are so fiercely resisted.

There are 200 million guns in circulation in the USA, compared with 826,000, most of them sporting shotguns, in Britain. The number of handguns in private ownership has more than quadrupled since 1968, to 70 million. The National Rifle Association, which lobbies powerfully for the American citizen's ancient right to be armed, has three million members. Meanwhile, a young American male is twenty times more likely to be shot dead than his English equivalent, and a young black Californian has a greater chance of being shot dead than of attending the University of California.

But guns are by no means the preserve of the hoodlum, the under-class and the homicidal maniac. They are fashion accessories and familiar household objects, instruments of male-bonding and outdoormanship, symbols of the American belief that a man's land is his own kingdom, to be defended come what may. Killer weapons are everywhere, in all shapes and sizes, owned by all manner of decent, home-loving, fun-loving people.

I rarely shoot in England, but in America I seem to do little else. I have never passed a day in Dutchess County without being invited to blaze away with some component of my friends' arsenal, whether at targets, clays or passing wildlife. Ironically, the only days in the year when they themselves prefer to stay indoors are at the beginning of the deer-hunting season, when their land and all the surrounding country-side is menaced by car-loads of beer-swilling, rifle-waving city-dwellers, revelling in one of the great American rituals of machismo.

Our own hunting days (for pheasant) at the nearby Mashomack Preserve Club, one of the smartest shooting venues in the USA, are relatively restrained, formal expressions of this national fascination with firepower – walking, four guns abreast, through melancholy marshland and uncut maize. Here European notions of etiquette are applied, auto-matic weapons disallowed and the story derisively told of a trigger-happy Texan visitor, seeing that the gun-dog had cornered a live cock-bird on the ground, running up yelling, 'Hold that little sucker, boy, I'm gonna nail him right there where he is.'

Some of the club members could pass for dukes, but our companions were perhaps the more archetypal American sportsmen: on one outing the best shot was Skip, an advertising executive in red baseball cap and fluorescent-panelled, ammunition-laden deer-hunting suit; he and others with us were just the kind of middle-class liberal professional who would abhor guns and bloodsports if they were English.

The weekend experience would be incomplete without a visit also to the local gun-store, where the purchaser, whether sporting or psychotic, has only to show a New York driving licence as proof of residence within the state to buy all the munitions his heart desires. On special offer, for example, was a short-barrelled, pistol-grip, pump-action shotgun.

'What game is that for?' I asked innocently. 'Self-defence', was the matter-of-fact reply. The short barrel (as with a sawn-off model) gives a wide scatter of shot which ensures that at short range, even when firing from the hip through a closed bedroom door, you can't miss. The distinctive clunk-click of its automatic cocking action somewhere in a darkened house is enough to deter many an experienced burglar; a tape-recording of it would be almost as effective, and a lot less frightening to handle.

In some states – like Texas, proud of its red-neck, gun-toting frontier traditions, and Kentucky – there are no state laws to be complied with at all before tooling up for a hunting trip, a bank raid or a Waco siege. Florida, conscious of the bad publicity associated with the casual murder of foreign tourists, is slightly stricter: a three-day waiting period for purchases and a ban on ownership by juveniles. But a friend of mine, who has a riverside house there and likes to shoot poisonous water-snakes, found it impossible to register his armoury with the local police.

'We don't even have a form,' the desk officer told him, adding helpfully that it is quite legal for a citizen to keep a loaded handgun in his car so long as it is not concealed, and finishing with some homely advice: 'Any o'them niggers start comin' through the windows, you-all just go ahead and shoot 'em.'

Back in Dutchess County the visceral thrill of our Sunday shooting practice was increased by using targets which exploded dramatically if you hit the little pink bull's-eye. In a curious echo of the adult male psychology involved, we returned to the house for lunch to find two four-year-old boys, made to stay indoors during the shooting, jumping on a sheet of plastic bubble-wrap to achieve their own satisfactory banging noises.

Explosions are fun, guns are exciting. Perhaps, like me, you have always imagined that a Colt .44 Magnum exists only in films. When offered the real thing, you will find it feels good; it fits just right in the masculine hand. So God bless America, but thank Him also for British gun laws.

November 1993

142

AND SO TO LAP-DANCING

O ver the past decade, I have had a go at most forms of journalism except war reporting, but I have avoided this winter's most
overworked assignment: the visit to a lap-dancing club plus interview
with a dancer who's really a drama student and doesn't feel exploited.
There seem to have been dozens of them, and the *Guardian* set a new
record for gratuitous space-filling last week with a double-page feature
devoted to a new branch of the American chain Spearmint Rhino in,
of all places, Harrogate. That's just down the road from Helmsley, but
I'm glad that no editor thought fit to send me for a follow-up. I confess
that I have already experienced this phenomenon – on a stag night for
a British bridegroom at The Gold Club in Atlanta, Georgia, a couple of
years ago. Far from being the chic post-modern art form described by
devotees, lap-dancing turned out to be jaw-clenchingly dull and creepy,
requiring a kind of tantric detachment on the part of both dancer and
customer. Conversation seemed superfluous, and laughing out loud –
the only correct British reaction to a tacky American invention taken
so seriously – would have got us thrown out quicker than grabbing the
nearest G-string. It reminded me of a line by Martin Amis, in *Money*,
about watching pornography: 'Hard to tell who was the biggest loser
in this complex transaction: her, him, them, me.' To which we can add
this season: readers, editors, and journalists desperate for work.

March 2002

———✳———

RAFTING IN THE ROCKIES

I 've been invited to Banff in Alberta to address the annual meeting
of the Canadian Investment Dealers Association on the subject of
'Why China isn't going to be a global superpower' – a theme I explored

recently in *The Spectator*, in contradiction of eminent pundits who had gone large on the coming 'Chinese century'. To be negative about China in any gathering of investors is to invite the response provoked by H. M. Bateman's Man Who Asked for a Double Scotch in the Grand Pump-Room at Bath, and this turned out to be especially the case in Alberta, which has oil reserves second only to Saudi Arabia's and sees the Chinese as huge future customers. So I followed an eminent China-watcher to the platform with some trepidation and started with a low trick to get the audience on my side: a joke about that well-known former-Canadian investor Conrad Black.* I'm sorry to say it went down rather well, and I think I made some unlikely converts to sinoscepticism.

I certainly made more friends than the star lunchtime speaker, James A. Baker, the US elder statesman and Bush loyalist who has recently come out of retirement to negotiate the cancellation of Iraq's debts. He offered a grimly militaristic view of America's role in the world – harder-edged, I suspect, than anything he would have subscribed to when he was Bush Senior's Secretary of State – that did not hide contempt for Canada's refusal to go to war in Iraq. The audience was polite, but a gang of feisty Quebecois told me afterwards they had been relying on me, as a member of the notoriously impolite British media, to have a go at Baker in the Q&A session. I'm afraid I let them down. I lobbed up a G8-related question about debt forgiveness and American hypocrisy, but I'm no Paxman: the leathery old Texan drove my limp googly straight to the boundary and left us none the wiser.

All this took place at the Banff Springs Hotel, a baronial fantasy in granite much visited by British royalty. According to family legend (my family, not hers), the Queen once recommended it to my late father in one of those stilted receiving-line conversations – though my mother, whose memory is sharp, now says she has no recollection of this what-ever. So I passed up the extra point I might have scored if I had slipped the anecdote into my speech after the Conrad Black joke.

---

* Lord Black of Crossharbour was the proprietor of *The Spectator* from 1988 to 2004.

The hotel is so vast that at close quarters it feels as big as the Rocky Mountain behind it, but seen at a distance it is a mere cabin in the woods in such a monumental landscape. It was conceived in 1886 by Cornelius Van Horne of the Canadian Pacific Railway, a man of unstoppable drive who was given ten years to complete the ocean-to-ocean rail link and did it in five – the sort of challenge only the Chinese would attempt today. But his work has stood the test of time better than I suspect much of theirs will, and the hoot of his mile-long freight trains curling through the high passes is still a hauntingly beautiful sound.

I have been involved, secretively, in a significant challenge of my own: to lose a stone and a half in twelve weeks. After a succession of big lunches in the Alps in March, my annual skiing party decided collectively that we had run to flab, and one friend came up with a scheme to raise money for the British Ski Club for the Disabled by each achieving specified weight-loss targets. Remarkably we all did it, and our heaviest contestant, a very big boy indeed, shed an awesome 36lbs on a regime of brown rice, oily fish and industrial muesli. The boring thing about dieting is talking about it – hence the secretiveness – but the pleasing thing is that it makes available eras of wardrobe that you never thought you would visit again. I'm already back in my 1987 cream linen suit, and if I keep going I can see some wicked batik shirts and flared trousers at the end of the rail.

What with all those elk steaks and breakfast muffins in Banff, the last couple of pounds were putting up a valiant rearguard action as the deadline loomed. I baulked at colonic irrigation in the hotel spa but I thought terror might have the same effect, so I booked a day of white-water rafting. What I actually signed up for was the 'family fun' introduction to rafting, but it was cancelled due to heavy rain and I found myself instead on the 'extreme' version, in helmet and wet-suit, hurtling down the Kicking Horse River with a crew of RAF fighter pilots on leave. It was a startling contrast to my last river outing, the *Spectator* staff 'booze cruise' on the Thames at Henley. But I was so busy trying to paddle or hang on as instructed by the supremely macho

Canadian helmsman that I forgot to be frightened. And it worked: I weighed in on the nose.

July 2005

———✳———

BOSTONIAN LADIES

I've been in Boston for the annual conference of the British-American Project, this year discussing education. We heard a lot about a school in Chicago – not the school of economists led by Milton Friedman, but Westside Preparatory School in the impoverished district of Garfield Park, founded by Marva Collins, an Alabama-born black educationist who uses the great texts of English and classical literature to improve children's vocabulary and reasoning. Her speaking style is a bizarre jumble of half-quotations from Shakespeare and Kipling interspersed with pithy aphorisms of her own, but she seems to have produced remarkable results from pupils whose life chances had previously been minimised by exposure to the worst of America's public (that is, state) school system. She has attracted national attention, not least from corporations such as IBM and Anheuser-Busch who have hired her as a motivational speaker. She refuses to accept government funding – telling President Bush that 'none of my pupils could have failed without government help', a remark that might have been scripted for her by Milton Friedman – and unlike most radical British educationists, she encourages positive attitudes to capitalism and entrepreneurship in children of primary-school age. 'I teach them how the stock market works,' she declaimed. 'If they argue over who has the best trainers, I tell them: "Don't fight over the trainers. Own the company that makes the trainers."'

Just how good a piece of advice that is was highlighted by an article about shoes in the business section of the *Boston Sunday Globe*. Retail footwear sales in the USA have risen by 19 per cent in the past five years: for women's fashion shoes, the rise is 17.3 per cent, compared to only 2 per cent growth in clothing sales. American women now buy a staggering 884 million pairs of shoes a year. Why? Because globalisation has made shoes so cheap that fashion-conscious shoppers wear them twice then throw them away; because online shoe shopping is quick, easy and offers a vast array of choice; but most importantly – so I was told by two Bostonian ladies-who-lunch – because of *Sex and the City*. 'Carrie Bradshaw made it OK to have a shoe fetish.'

November 2006

—— ✳ ——

VAUD AND THE VILLAINS

Long before I became a journalist I taught myself to absorb the essence of an unfamiliar city by staying alert in the taxi from the airport: Los Angeles offers a particularly vivid first encounter. As the yellow cab barrels out of the precincts of LAX on to an angry avenue called La Brea, images and warnings crowd in. Neon signs in Korean and Spanish tell me this is one of the planet's most multi-ethnic conurbations. Half-crazed vagrants haunt the sidewalks, their random possessions piled in shopping trolleys. Radio ads offer a catalogue of modern American neuroses. Behind on your mortgage payments, facing foreclosure? Here's the number of a friendly lawyer. Expecting the unexpected? Book yourself a mammogram at Kaiser Permanente. Still believe your luck might change? Win, win, win at Pala Casino Resort. To which a placard on the fence of a derelict site adds 'Divorce – Child Custody – Visitation Rights – Call 0800-123-DADDY'.

But the in-your-face alienation of urban America is so often countered by unexpected charm. 'Sir, are you British?' the world-weary Hispanic driver asks as we pull over for a screaming police car. 'There's a

British TV show on cable I really like, it's called *Keeping Up Appearances*. But I can't say the lady's name right.' 'You mean Mrs Bucket, pronounced "*bouquet*"?' 'Yeah, that's her,' he brightens up and enunciates: 'Hiya-cinth Boo-kay.'

I'm here for the annual British-American Project conference, the veritable Bretton Woods of transatlantic networking. This year we're due to talk about popular culture, but, of course, there are only two topics anyone really wants to discuss: the economic crisis and the triumph of Barack Obama. One modest contributor to his campaign proudly shows me on her BlackBerry the personalised emails his team sent out in the final days, culminating in one which began 'Dear Susan, in ten minutes I'll be leaving for Grant Park … And it's all down to you.' It's clever stuff, but the emotion of the crowd and the near-universal admiration for his coolness, his eloquence, his black-but-not-quite-blackness, his sheer Obama-ness, cannot conceal the blank space where the coherent response to economic crisis ought to be. We know he wants to bail out the auto industry, but does that mean a bail-out for every sector in trouble – and how will he square the cost with his promise of tax cuts for '95 per cent of workers and their families'? Is he going to cane the rich 5 per cent, many of whom, in liberal LA at least, are now so eager to embrace him? If I had a vote here I'd have given it to Barack the beacon of hope rather than McCain the has-been – but by the time Obamamania subsides, I hope the new emperor has found some convincing clothes.

Speaking of clothes, one of our conference sessions is about the tastes and values of the age groups who make up most of today's consumers. We learn about Generation X, born in the sixties and seventies, who have, according to *Time* magazine, 'a monumental preoccupation with all the problems the preceding generation will leave for them to fix': that certainly applies to Obama, born in 1961. Then there's pain-in-the-ass Generation Y, the pampered twentysomething offspring of (usually divorced) baby-boomer parents. And Generation Jones – I doze at this point – which is a post-boomer pre-Gen X slice so thin that quite possibly everyone in it is called Jones.

But I'm awoken by a documentary film by Lauren Greenfield, 'kids + money', depicting an as-yet unlabelled generation of pre-teen girls who are morbidly obsessed with shopping – little princesses of the era of over-consumption, who yearn for the 'four-digit' ($1,000-plus) outfits and accessories that win them admission to the best cliques, pronounced 'clicks', at school. It's horrifying, not so much for the brainwashed state of the children as for the moral vacuity of their parents. But there's a foretaste of a different era to come in a new fashion category, the 'recessionista' – one who makes a virtue of dressing stylishly on a tight budget – with which I strongly identify. Me, I'm a two-digit shopper: my top outfit for the trip is a £69 linen suit from Burton in Leeds. Several American ladies tell me I look sharp, so I tell them that when I went back for a second suit, all that was left in my size was a £75 jacket which I would have dismissed as too expensive, except it came with a free pair of trousers: that's what I call a bail-out.

I think it's ill-mannered of Brits in our party who have succumbed to Obama-mania to keep telling our hosts what a relief it is that 'it's OK to love America again'. We should always love America, not for its leaders – who generally turn out as disappointing as our own – but for its vitality, its collective belief in the possibility of renewal, its vast anthology of personal stories. The perfect metaphor for the America it's impossible to dislike is on stage at the down-at-heel Fais Do-Do nightclub off La Brea Avenue. It's called Vaud and the Villains, it's an eighteen-piece band plus burlesque dancers, and we like them all so much we book them to play in our suffocatingly bland conference hotel, where they blow the roof off with a unique New Orleans-gospel-soul mix officially described as 'what rock'n'roll would sound like if they played it back in the Thirties'. A Democrat lawyer en route to the White House transition team is heard to mutter, while watching the dancers: 'Now I know what Dr King meant when he said he had a dream.' Among the line-up is a gravel-voiced, heavily tattooed chanteuse who's in rehab; a dancer who's a bit-part soap-actress single mother; a tiny, smiling man in a pork-pie hat, Filipino perhaps, with a voice as big as Pavarotti's; and a black lead singer with the loose-limbed elegance and energy of – yes, him again – Barack Obama. I'm not easily swayed by the emotion of the crowd, but I have to tell you, as one New Yorker grabs the mike to declare, 'I feel the lurve.' Vaud and the Villains give me hope for America.

November 2008

——✳——

NO EYE CONTACT WITH ED

I'm intrigued by profiles of Ed Miliband saying what a normal, amiable fellow he really is. That doesn't sound like the Miliband Minor with whom I was stranded in November 2000 in an executive lounge at Newark airport in New Jersey, waiting for a plane to take us home from a conference. It was during those fraught few days when teams of lawyers were arguing over the Florida recounts that eventually enabled George W. Bush to claim presidential victory over Al Gore. Young Ed – then a speechwriter for Gordon Brown and evidently a Gore devotee even before the former vice president became the Messiah of climate change – sat on a bar stool glaring furiously at CNN, occasionally breaking off to berate airline staff for not finding a plane to get him back to his desk at the Treasury. It was understandable that he didn't want to exchange banter, or even eye contact, with me (in those days I was often rude about Gordon in the *Daily Mail*), but the impression he gave generally was of an intense, humourless and unapproachable political obsessive. Still, at least he took a few days off for our conference: I remember being told by a Labour Party insider a few years earlier that Ed's big brother David was just too brilliant, too deep-thinking and too obviously destined for greatness to be asked to mix with ordinary mortals. I'm afraid, despite all the efforts of their spin teams, both brothers look to me like the work of a *Doctor Who* scriptwriter.

September 2010

DEAD NUTS AT THE WHITE DOG

Two years ago on Sunday, I had a long lunch with three friends – English, Irish, Californian – at the Boa Steakhouse on Santa Monica Boulevard and Ocean Avenue, alongside a table of a dozen leggy, honey-tanned models from a 'golf event hostess agency'. This Sunday the four of us got together again in the White Dog Café on Sansom Street in Philadelphia, with rather less to distract us. We drank copious quantities of a zinfandel from Paso Robles in California called (I'd love to know why) Dead Nuts, of 2008 – which means the grapes must have been pressed at the very zenith of Obama-mania. But the wine had not soured, and neither had our spirits. We discussed lessons learned since we last met, and new projects for 2011 and beyond. American optimism, even if temporarily subdued, gets into the blood.

November 2010

———✳———

THE GREATEST NATION?

I love America, and if you look at my rather curious Wikipedia entry – which I have neither the vanity nor the know-how to bother to edit – you might suspect that I've been brainwashed to say so, because I am 'a leading figure within the British-American Project'. I am, indeed, active in that excellent networking organisation, which has never been anything like the sinister Reaganite propaganda vehicle that Pilgerists and Guardianistas imagine it to be. And it has given me valuable insights into the national characters of the up-and-comers from both sides of the pond who form its membership.

The Brits, mostly arts graduates, tend to be argumentative free-thinkers with opinions about everything. The Americans, many of them lawyers, are more courteous, less comfortable in debate, more inward looking, and far more respectful of their own leaders and institutions. At one of our conferences the Americans decided to sing 'The Star Spangled Banner'; when 'God Save the Queen' was called for in response, half the Brits left the room.

But if there is much to admire about Americans in that comparison, they can also be irritating: I winced when I heard Barack Obama tell his fellow countrymen that 'we live in the greatest nation in the history of the world'. They don't, and neither do we, and all of us should leave that judgement to future historians. More to the point, what they live in is probably no longer even the greatest capitalist economy in the world, since it is so damaged by the shenanigans of its own financial sector and is rapidly being overtaken in manufacturing strength by China. Only a handful of innovative US companies with global reach – Google, Apple, Boeing – still stand as beacons.

As for the American way of government, it too often just looks ramshackle, parochial and ill-informed about the wider world. Remember the 'hanging chads', the half-punched ballot cards on the counting of which depended the outcome of the 2000 presidential election? Or the federal government's hopelessly inadequate response to Hurricane Katrina in New Orleans? Or the look on George W. Bush's face in front of an elementary-school class in Florida when they told him a second plane had hit the World Trade Center?

And now this ridiculous debt fiasco. The possibility of a default on US government debt – averted by a compromise on Sunday night that delegated the toughest decisions on deficit reduction to a bipartisan commission which must report by November – was, we're told, 'very remote' and could only ever have been temporary.

But it was close enough to leave Admiral Mike Mullen, chairman of the US joint chiefs of staff, unable to reassure servicemen in Afghanistan they would continue to be paid; close enough to traumatise markets and shake business confidence everywhere, notching upwards the chance of a global double-dip recession; and disturbing enough to leave the Triple-A rating of America's public debt in doubt.

Even if the deal goes through Congress with no further hitches, the episode has been a disaster for America's standing in the financial world – and for Obama himself, knocked off his own policy agenda by Tea Party Republicans, disowned by left-wing Democrats, and revealed as no more than an unusually eloquent version of the lawyerish, inward-looking archetype I know so well. If there's any positive outcome, it is that America has been forced to debate its debt problem. But what an incompetent and unimpressive way to go about it.

August 2011

———✳———

CREATIVE DESTRUCTION

Never say this column doesn't offer global perspectives. OK, it sometimes comes in folksy parables from Yorkshire. But a fortnight ago I was eyeball to eyeball with Richard Branson in Mumbai and this week I'm speaking to you from the Louisiana Superdome. Yes, I'm standing right on the plastic turf of one of America's most hallowed football fields, watching the New Orleans Saints warm up for a crunch game against the Atlanta Falcons and contemplating the Schumpeterian theory of creative destruction. You'll get weightier economics on the op-ed page of the *Financial Time*, but you don't get opening lines like that.

The proper name of this giant concrete bubble, by the way, is a parable of globalisation in itself: the Mercedes-Benz Superdome. But its place in modern American folklore was secured in August 2005 when it served as a refuge for more than 20,000 New Orleanians displaced by the inundation of most of their city in the aftermath of Hurricane Katrina. The suffering of the trapped evacuees – under armed guard, without food, water, sanitation or medical help for several days – was so shaming for America and so traumatic for those close to it that many felt the storm-damaged stadium should be razed to the ground; the Saints, temporarily shifted to San Antonio, Texas, looked set to stay there.

Indeed, many commentators (including me) asked whether it was even worth trying to revive the city at large, given that all but its most historic districts were built on sub-sea-level reclaimed land which the levees were clearly unable to defend. Wouldn't it be better for the displaced masses to make new lives elsewhere, where they might find better schools and job prospects and lower murder rates? Isn't migration a good thing when it leaves insoluble deprivation behind? Go ahead and restore the heritage sites, we suggested unhelpfully from afar, but get real and abandon the ghettos.

Well, that wasn't how the local folk saw it – or most of them. Around 100,000 of the city's 450,000 inhabitants have never come back. But those who did, or never left, have become part of a renaissance which is already wrapped in its own mythology. The trombonist Delfeayo Marsalis (son of pianist Ellis, brother of trumpeter Wynton) talked about Katrina as a 'baptism' and a 'rebirth' – and about the importance of jazz in the refusal to be defeated.

This is now officially 'America's fastest-growing city' of its size; we're told it's a hot new hub for digital entrepreneurs; that tourism is booming like never before; that underperforming schools have been transformed by giving power to better teachers; that corrupt local government is a thing of the past; that the city's university, Tulane, is overwhelmed with undergraduate applications from all over the States; that the Saints, once so hopeless they were known as the Ain'ts, won the 2010 Super Bowl to become the mascot of New Orleans's reborn self-confidence. As for the 2008 financial cataclysm, it was a mere tremor compared to what the hurricane had already wrought: 'We didn't have a subprime crisis because we didn't have any houses left to mortgage,' says one local. 'We're ahead now because we've been recovering since 2005.'

All this – brought about by a mix of massive federal spending, large- and small-scale capitalism, charity, a change of mayoral regime and the spirit that is engendered by adversity – does, indeed, offer an example of creative destruction, the concept adapted from Karl Marx by the Austrian Joseph Schumpeter. Simplifying freely, it says that from the ruins of a failing economic order, something more positive will eventually emerge.

That is what Katrina seems to have brought about here. The transformation is not without its darker edges, however. The influx of Yurps (young urban rebuilding professionals) has not been universally welcomed. Brad Pitt's Make It Right homes project in the worst-afflicted Lower Ninth ward looks (from a distance) too shiny to be anything but a token, and my conference group can only view it from that distance because buses like ours have been banned from the Lower Ninth: residents were tired of being gawped at by disaster tourists.

In adjacent wards, many houses remain broken and untouched – impossible to say whether they're still lived in – since they emerged from the receding waters displaying the hieroglyphics left by national guard and army units belatedly checking for survivors and corpses. Only the little white churches speak of any kind of community life. Poor black families are still dirt poor, still badly housed, still at the bottom of the ladder of life chances, still at risk of casual murder in their own neighbourhoods. A city that cannot account for 100,000 of its citizens, seven years after they fled, can't be complacent about renewed prosperity.

But despite those caveats, what's happened here is an illustration of the human spirit at its irrational best. Regeneration is far from complete and far from all-inclusive, but it has moved at a pace which no pundit would have dared predict in late 2005. We are repeatedly told that music, food (the cuisine is terrific, unlike anywhere else in America) and the football team are what made residents love this city so much they refused to give up on it. What makes people happy in these seemingly trivial ways is what also makes them optimistic and determined. If only our British provincial cities, not hurricane-hit but drizzled on by dismal economics these past five years, could harness that kind of energy. If only a hurricane could sweep the City of London and let something more positive emerge. Visit the birthplace of Louis Armstrong and see for yourself; the Saints beat the Falcons by 31 to 27.

November 2012

— ✳ —

IT'S MINE, I SPEND IT

The most stylish fellow passenger in Delta Air Lines' business class cabin from Atlanta to Heathrow last week was a chap in shades and a hoodie with several kilos of bling slung round his neck. Enquiries in the galley identified him as '2 Chainz', a Georgia-born rapper formerly known as 'Tity Boi', whose real name is Tauheed Epps. I gathered he had invited the flight crew to call him Tad – and naturally I was keen to befriend him myself, but the Dracula's-coffin configuration of Delta's flatbeds made conversation impossible. So I was left trying to read what his thoughts might be on the issue of the 'fiscal cliff'.

That's the impending crisis in which the expiry of George W. Bush's tax cuts, combined with a federal spending squeeze also scheduled to begin in January, will cause a $600 billion shrinkage of the budget deficit that threatens to plunge the US economy, and possibly ours with it, straight back into recession unless a compromise is reached to soften the impact. Any self-respecting hip-hop artist is, of course, highly likely to have voted for Barack Obama (93 per cent of African-Americans did so) but Mr Epps's holding of portable precious metals and decision to seek fortune abroad – in his UK debut at the Electric Brixton alongside DJ Semtex, in case you missed it – suggest a pessimistic view of domestic economic prospects under the re-elected president. Judging by his lyrics ('It's mine, I spend it'), he's also no supporter of tax hikes for higher earners.

These opinions would align him with much of America's middle class, who wait to see whether Obama will be any more potent in his second term than he was in his first when it comes to arm-wrestling Congressional Republicans such as House Speaker John Boehner. The argument is all about symbolic tax rates and power struggles between the White House and Capitol Hill, much less about spending cuts or 'sequestration' – which if it happens in accordance with legislation already in place, will be broad, shallow and not in protected areas such as federal pensions and veterans' benefits. Brinkmanship will drag into the New Year until, in Washington's special way, the toughest decisions get kicked down the road again. But an extended stand-off combined with new tensions in the Middle East will depress markets and intensify the late-autumnal gloom – personified on this side of the pond by Sir Mervyn King's starkly pessimistic performance last week – that is dampening recovery hopes everywhere.

And that means investors will continue searching for safe havens – making rapper-style gold jewellery a prudent gift for any grandchild. In the mean time, if you're looking for something to raise your own pre-Christmas spirits, download 2 Chainz's 'Birthday Song'. 'All ah want for ma' birthday is a big booty hoe,' he chants, and in such challenging times who can really blame him?

November 2012

———✹———

On the Central Line

Crushed in crowded Underground
Assailed by irritating sound
Of youth who thinks his MP3
Beams him up and sets him free
Hip-hop heaven inside his head
Though his eyes are strangely dead
Music shared might make us calmer
But earphones are his body armour
And in this airless hostile space
We endure his drum and bass
Such insistent loud percussion
Ought to leave him with concussion
What a bloody awful din it is
I hope it gives him tinnitus

CHAPTER 7

French Leave

HAPPY MOTORING

M y friends and I have perfected a special kind of Tour de France. The formula is fixed, but it never fails to entertain us. To start, you need at least six people with several fast cars, and three texts. Never cross the Channel without Michelin's red-bound *Guide* and yellow-bound 1:200,000-scale road atlas. For spiritual guidance, take P. J. O'Rourke's peerless essay (in *Republican Party Reptile*), 'How to Drive Fast on Drugs While Getting Your Wing-Wang Squeezed and Not Spill Your Drink'.

True Englishmen respect the French for two things: their restaurants and their minor roads. Both are marvellously varied yet extraordinarily reliable. A perfect day can be had by selecting restaurants from the *Guide Michelin*, one for lunch and one for dinner, anywhere in France, so long as they are separated by a couple of hundred kilometres of yellow lines across the pages of the atlas. The yellow roads may be dead straight poplar avenues from one horizon to the next, or long series of hairpin bends – chasing rivers, climbing through dark forests, breasting great ridges of landscape, bisecting quiet towns of mellow stone.

The driving rules are simple. Don't challenge other cars to race through town centres unless they are French. Wear sunglasses. Stop at red lights if you see a police car. And, as P. J. O'Rourke says, never try it sober; it would be too frightening.

As for restaurants, being able to order in O-level French is much less vital than a mastery of the Michelin hieroglyphics which will help you pick the right spot in the first place. The umbrella means you can eat on the terrace and the green bench indicates a garden for your siesta. Experienced motorists learn to cherish the red Michelin-man-in-a-rocking-chair, meaning isolation and tranquillity, and the chicken's footprint for an exceptional view. The rare combination of these two is a guarantee of sporting, empty roads.

As a rule, you should never spend on dinner less than twice what you spent on lunch. Then, however disappointing the dinner, you will still be able to congratulate yourself on what a bargain lunch was.

Trying to translate the à la carte menu can be embarrassing. Simply order the longest set menu, telling the waiter that today is the birthday of the prettiest girl in the party and that a cake with candles would be a nice gesture as well. Always tackle a full cheeseboard from end to end.

Wine can be distressingly expensive. If you love fine wine, drink it. If you can't tell the difference, keep the wine list well away from anyone in the party who can.

Sleep is unnecessary on these trips, except perhaps in a meadow by a stream after lunch. If you have a taste for the pungent end of the cheeseboard and for those unlabelled, fruit-scented, cardiac-arresting *alcoöls*, sleep will be impossible anyway. The more you spend on dinner, therefore, the less you should spend on a bed for the night; in France even the cheapest hotel is rarely uncomfortable, and if you've had a proper dinner you really won't notice if it is.

So there you have it, everything you need to know. There is one more useful tip, but let me reach it by way of an anecdote. This May, the team which refined this approach to mobile gastronomy had its tenth anniversary trip. A lucky thirteen of us (including flown-in wives and one four-month-old baby) returned in splendour to Michel Guérard's heroic restaurant at Eugénie-les-Bains, a pink-painted temple to *cuisine nouvelle* and (for those who can't take the real thing any more) *cuisine minceur*.

It was impeccable; the aromatic mushroom-truffle ravioli lingers in the memory like a drug. But the place we found en route that same day, quite by chance, was something altogether different. It was the ultimate, end-of-the-rainbow expression of our ten-year quest for the perfect lunch.

On page 664 of the 1991 *Guide* (never travel with the current year's edition if you prefer to avoid anything too new) is a reference to the hamlet of Mauvezin-sur-Gupie, described as '*rattaché à Marmande*'. '*Rattaché à*' is good: it often means in the middle of nowhere. And so this place was, on a wooded knoll, in a garden full of curious hens, an old goat and a boxer dog called Clovis.

The hieroglyphics said 'book beforehand', but we just went along anyway. The bearded chef was busy eating his own lunch. It was quite impossible, he said, but if we could wait fifteen minutes he would see what he could rustle up. He rang for help from the village, dismissed our suggestion of something light ahead of the grand dinner to come, and produced one of the finest, longest, largest meals any of us had ever eaten.

In the intervals between courses, we lay on the lawn, watched the barbecue blaze, played with the dog, cooed at the baby. Occasionally, we paused to wonder whether the lonesome chef might have murdered his mother in the bizarre disco cellar full of stuffed birds below us. A table of talkative local *négociants* ate even more than we did.

The crown prince of our convoys is, nowadays, a father of four. Let us call him Andrew – conveniently enough, since that is what his long-suffering wife calls him. In the course of that particular lunch, he has cheerfully confessed, he drank the best part of three bottles of unpretentious, oak-scented Côtes de Duras *vin de table*. And he made only two remarks which anyone could later recall: 'I love big lunches', and 'These hire cars, the only way to drive them is to keep your foot absolutely flat to the floor.'

He proved the first claim and tested the second the moment we left the restaurant by embedding Hertz's neat little Peugeot straight in a ditch, where he remained at the wheel, eyes glazed, engine screaming, accelerator pressed to the board, until the rest of the party heaved him and his machine back on to the tarmac.

Whereupon, without a moment's hesitation, he set off to lead us for an hour and a half through the Landais pine forests at a pace which Peugeot would be proud and horrified to know their family saloons could attain. A marginally less well-fuelled Porsche had to struggle to keep Andrew in sight from behind. In the fullest tradition of the genre, villagers and livestock jumped to the scream of his tyres.

Also, perhaps, to the distant screams of its passengers. For the Landes is a region of long, straight roads, but it is in the nature of straight roads that there are bends at the end of them. And it is no reassurance to have discovered that a car can take some bends at terminal velocity if the driver simply doesn't register them at all. But then to brake, or even for the passengers to beg for mercy, would probably have been fatal.

The episode revealed to us the saintly tolerance of wives. And it confirmed one final point of guidance: sheer terror is marvellous for the digestion. As on every other evening of our tours, we fell on our dinner like wolves.

The Oldie, August 1992

——❊——

ON YOUR BIKE

At a dinner party in New York not long ago I was struggling to find common ground with my host's boss's girlfriend, an exquisite creature with a very short attention span. 'How do you, um, sort of, well, spend your day?' I essayed, hoping that hesitant delivery would redeem the lameness of the question by making me sound a bit like the actor Hugh Grant. 'I exercise,' she sighed, glancing at my spreading paunch. 'Do *you* exercise?'

'No,' was the not-so-hesitant and conversation-killing answer. Of course, I might have explained had she still been listening, I take a bit of exercise, in the comfortable English sense of walking my dog every day and skiing downhill very badly, in old and ill-matched ski clothes and always at the same resort, for one week per year. But the idea of exercise for its own sake – of going for the burn, or hitting the wall, or whatever other muscular sensations the hobbling survivors of the London Marathon are proud to recite – is abhorrent to me. The only 'fitness equipment' ever to enter my house – a weight-lifting contraption called a Soloflex – was rapidly converted into a very ugly towel-rail.

Despite these aversions, I confess that I have discovered a new passion which involves both expensive machinery and prodigious amounts of physical effort. But the machinery moves, and not just in circles: it goes from A to B; eventually it will arrive at Z and set off to return by a different route. Nor is the exercise, as it were, the point of the exercise: the point is the travelling, to which exertion is incidental, and the refuelling afterwards, to which exertion gives added zest. I have discovered the touring bicycle.

More particularly, I have discovered the pleasure of crossing France by pedal power. I am seven days and about 300 miles into a journey from Pegasus Bridge in Normandy to somewhere on the Mediterranean, a journey which will be completed, over the next year or so, in four- or five-day bursts whenever time permits. To be precise, my bicycling companion and I have reached the quiet porcelain-making town of Mehun-sur-Yèvre, close to the Cher and just south of Bourges. Another push in the autumn will take us over the hills into the Beaujolais region, and spring should find us in Provence.

This is not exactly a new idea. It has been done, and written about, many times before. But now is a good moment to suggest it, perhaps because it fits the lean spirit of the times, and not least because many other exercise-avoiders will be reading this while sitting like Mr Toad in Bank Holiday traffic jams, parping the horn and wishing themselves elsewhere, yearning for a more invigorating mode of travel.

The well-built, lightweight touring bicycle (about £500, made to measure) with twenty-one gears and a gel-pad saddle-cover to ease the pain, is absolutely it. For the reluctant nineties man, who used to be high-living eighties man, the bike is the perfect answer. Anyone who enjoyed the previous decade in full measure is more than likely to be in need of some muscle-toning by now, and may well be feeling the pinch in other respects. No longer – unless perhaps, you are a director of a privatised utility – is life just a matter of revving the motor, waving the credit card, and scanning the Abercrombie & Kent brochure for a flyaway holiday destination which trumps the yuppies next door ('Phuket, darling?' 'Yah!').

Two-wheeled touring is not only cheap, companionable and environmentally sound, but fashionably minimalist in terms of wardrobe and luggage. Nor – if conducted solely abroad – does it require you to associate yourself with the archetypal back-to-nature British cycling bore, or to endure the perils of British weather, traffic and hill-and-dale topography.

The French may not be everybody's cup of tea, but we sometimes forget, as we curse their truculent farmers and sneer at their posturing presidential candidates, what a glorious territory they have the good fortune to occupy. And in large stretches of it, there are remarkably few of them for the cyclist to contend with. You may pedal all day, for 50 or 60 miles, on the smallest minor roads (the white ones on Michelin large-scale maps) and be passed by no more than half a dozen cars. Encounters with the locals on the road or in village bars turn out to be much friendlier than you might at first expect, partly because most Frenchmen are themselves keen cyclists and partly because, if they do spot your nationality (helmets are a giveaway, the French would not be seen dead in them) they are inclined to assume that you must be harmlessly mad. Since we are stuck with them as European 'partners', we might as well know them better: this is the perfect non-confrontational way to do so.

A day's run of 50 miles also offers a satisfactory opportunity to get to know their landscape, which across most of the middle of France consists of long, gently sloping ridges dividing one river valley from the next, and great tracts of flat marshland and pine woods. Unlike British country lanes, many French byways are dead straight and miraculously pointed in the direction in which you want to travel. More miraculous still, at either end of them (with a certain amount of careful planning beforehand) you will find comfortable, family-run, bicycle-friendly, small hotels, with wonderful aromas wafting from their kitchens.

This, of course, is the other great advantage of the cycling tour – that it gives you an enormous appetite. The edge is so often taken off the pleasure of eating in France by the necessity of sitting inactive in a car all day in order to do so. But, for the non-athlete, five or six hours of steady pedalling burns an amazing amount of energy, ensuring that you will be ravenously ready for the full *menu gastronomique* with *surprise du chef* dessert. If the seventeen-stone-twelve army minister Nicholas Soames, now enduring the *Telegraph*'s diet challenge, took to bicycling instead, not only would he no longer need to observe that terrible 'no cheese' rule. On the contrary, he could adopt without shame an 'every cheese' rule, in which no misshapen *chèvre* or sweating *Époisses* is left untasted and a good night's sleep is still guaranteed afterwards.

Let us agree that exercise for its own sake is sheer hell. But let's face it, there comes a time for all of us when we had better start taking some in one form or another, and I think I have discovered the answer. With the zeal of the convert I urge you: on your bike!

Daily Telegraph, May 1995

— ✳ —

WORK IN PROGRESS

I am writing at a pavement table outside the Hôtel de France in Monpazier, a lovely *bastide* in the Dordogne, having come to chivvy the builders who are renovating an old watermill for me nearby. 'I'll be there Friday and expect to see progress' once had its effect, but this time it had none at all; ten weeks on-site, and they have achieved three weeks' work. They began by demolishing a bathroom and tipping the debris into the millstream. Next, someone – we politely agreed that it could not possibly be one of the workmen – nicked the stereo out of the house. 'Deep into Peter Mayle territory, then?' friends say, irritatingly, when I recount these frustrations. 'Why don't you write a hilarious book about it and make a million?' Because he's already written it long ago, twice over, and made the million, that's why. But still, the sun's shining, there's fresh asparagus for lunch, and there isn't a damn thing I can do. And, even if there's no music from the stolen stereo, I can calm myself by listening to the mill stream cascading gently over half a ton of gleaming broken porcelain.

March 2002

——— ✳ ———

A DOG IN THE DORDOGNE

Even the most seasoned traveller is gripped by fear as his passport is thumbed by border guards at some remote and hostile crossing point. I remember the moment on a Trans-Siberian train entering Russia from Mongolia, panic rising as the scowling scrutiny continued. Is the visa wrongly dated? Should I offer a bribe? But the tension of that encounter was as nothing compared to the torture I have imposed on myself this summer, taking my golden retriever Gregory to the Dordogne and back.

You probably think, if you have not encountered it, that the Defra Pet Travel Scheme which allows the English to holiday abroad without being parted from their faithful hounds is all about rabies, the rat-borne raging madness which would supposedly invade us if we did not have frontier defences. But rabies is the easy part. A couple of shots and a six-month wait, and your doggy is in the departure lounge.

No, the sting in the rear end on this one is *Echinococcus multilocularis*, the humble tapeworm. You probably also think – before I elaborate – that tapeworms are hardly an international threat and that this must be one of those French wheezes of the kind which enabled them some years ago to say they had no restrictions on imports of Japanese video players, so long as each one was processed through a warehouse in Poitiers, hundreds of miles from a port. But curiously – though they ban our beef and prefer our lamb grilled in the lorry – the French are relaxed about our dogs. At the Calais end of the Channel Tunnel they just wave them through, rather as they wave asylum seekers in the other direction.

If they're so worried about the bacteria in British cattle, you might think they would be concerned about what an omnivore like Gregory carries in his large intestine. Bureaucrats exist to interfere in other people's lives, but as any Eurocrat will tell you, the French are also masters of bureaucratic inaction. And in this case they just sit back and smile at the discomfort of English holidaymakers scrambling to fulfil Defra's *Echinococcus* instructions. In order for Gregory to re-enter Britain he has to have been treated by a French vet, between twenty-four and forty-eight hours beforehand, against tapeworm and ticks. The treatments must contain praziquantel and acaricide, and must be time-stamped on a French ministry form which Defra does not provide. What happens if your local vet runs out of forms, or your car breaks down at the forty-seventh hour? Defra's guidelines offer 'useful' French phrases which only make owners more nervous: '*Avez vous un lecteur des micropuces?*' (Have you got a microchip reader?) '*Mon animal ne reside pas en France. Il n'a donc pas besoin d'être tatoué.*' (My dog does not live in France, so he doesn't have to be tattooed.)

All this is to come when we set off for home. Gregory, it must be said, seems entirely relaxed about it: he probably thinks it would be cool to come back with a tattoo, like a teenager after a clubbing holiday in Faliraki. The tapeworms of the Dordogne are probably relieved that they will not have to face the microbes now polluting large parts of Britain's water supply. I shall spend the next three weeks worrying about that form. And officials at both sides of the border will offer that hard-eyed smirk which says: don't ever think you're a free citizen; we can always find another hoop to make you jump through.

Sunday Telegraph, August 2002

UN CAFÉ, S'IL VOUS PLAÎT

Like many of you, I will be spending Easter in France, where the government has just scrapped its controversial labour law reforms. I am particularly fond of Bergerac airport, which used to be a café with a hut attached handling fewer than fifty passengers a day. Now it handles 850, almost all British, happily accommodating them in slightly bigger huts that have not lost the original charm. Say what you like about low-cost airlines and global warming, but this swarm of British arrivals has done miracles for the local economy: not only have we bought the falling-down farmhouses and filled the restaurants, but the chamber of commerce boasts that we have also taken to starting new businesses. A few years ago French entrepreneurs were pouring through the Tunnel to 'Enterprise Britain' – well, at least as far as Ashford – to escape their own labour laws and taxes. Now there are 400 British-owned firms in the Dordogne alone, and I'm thinking of joining them by launching a cross-border bid for Bergerac's airport café . . .

April 2006

. . . I should have been more discreet about my plan. The airport's fire crew – small enough to fit into a Peugeot 206, but nevertheless essential – staged a patriotic walk-out so soon after our Easter edition came out that I can only assume they are online subscribers. That left me in mid-air over central France, because those seat-of-the-pants operators at Ryanair decided we should take off from Stansted anyway and revealed only at the last moment that we were, in fact, about to land at Limoges.

Oh well, at least the three-hour late-night bus to Bergerac gave me time to rethink my cross-border investment options . . .

May 2006

. . . I have been back to Bergerac, where I got very excited last year about the idea of launching a cross-border takeover bid for the booming airport café. I was worried at the time that this threatened incursion of Anglo-Saxon business methods was the reason for an otherwise unexplained wildcat strike by the airport fire crew. Now I'm worried that I have provoked a much more serious train of events. On this visit the café was plastered with huge posters declaring '*Non à l'expulsion!*' and referring in English to 'a huge political and financial conspiracy' which is about to terminate the livelihood of the café's staff. It turns out that, possibly prompted by me, the local airport authority has finally realised that the huge influx of British visitors on Ryanair and Flybe flights has turned this little business into a goldmine. The present concessionaire took it on in 1998 when the airport handled less than fifty passengers a day, the handsome barmaid told me. Now it handles almost twenty times that number, the sitting tenant is being forced out to make way for '*un ami*' of the airport's bosses. *Desolé, madame*: but it will serve the new tenant right if swingeing green aviation taxes cut the traffic in half next season. That will be my moment to step in with a rock-bottom offer and a promise to reinstall the *ancien régime*.

November 2006

— ✳ —

APRÈS SKI

I can't compete with the glamour of Taki's après-ski reports from Gstaad, but I can offer a few economic observations from Méribel and

169

its neighbouring French valleys. Notoriously mispronounced 'Mirabelle' by posh Brits, Méribel used to be SW3 on skis – but this year the Sloane voices were far outnumbered by the Irish, indicating that there's still some compensation for the pain of euro membership. In neighbouring Courchevel, gone are the Russians with their bodyguards, suitcases of cash and jet-loads of 'students and models' for female companionship. The resorts are by no means empty, however; many people seem to have decided to blow the redundo and go for it, one last time. It's expensive but it's worth it, and for £40 a head you can still enjoy one of the world's most stylish lunch spots: Courchevel's Restaurant Le Bel Air, under the command of dazzling Christophe Gormier, who greets me every year as though I might be Michael Winner. '*Alors, Christophe*,' I said, in best Mirabelle franglais, gesturing at the crowd on his terrace, '*Pas de credit crunch ici, je vois.*' He flashed me his George Clooney smile: the best entrepreneurs always survive.

February 2009

—✳—

STUPENDOUS SHOWING OFF

I remember a phrase from an obituary of Professor Richard Cobb, the eccentric historian of modern France who died in 1996. His idea of a holiday, it said, was 'to take a long time getting from St Etienne to Clermont-Ferrand'. I know exactly what he meant. There is a special pleasure in following the curves of almost empty secondary roads across the pages of the Michelin atlas: my own meandering last week took me to Millau, to see the viaduct over the Tarn designed by Norman Foster and engineered by the doyen of French bridge-builders, Michel Virlogeux. Opened in December 2004, this €400 million masterpiece of structural simplicity enables drivers to take a little less time getting from Clermont-Ferrand to Narbonne. But given the paucity of traffic on that route, other than at either end of the summer holidays, the project really had no economic justification at all. It is just a stupendous showing-off of what the French (with the help of a British architect) can do, and there's no wonder Jacques Chirac looks so smug in pictures of the opening ceremony. Still, great engineering has the power to boost the non-economic quantum of 'general wellbeing' – to lift the soul, in other words – and the draw of the viaduct has turned the town of Millau, once just a place to fill up on the way south, into a destination in itself. I recommend a stopover at the pleasantly faded Château de Creissels, with a view of the night-lit viaduct from its dining terrace. As the Michelin guide used to say, *vaut le détour*.

September 2010

———※———

AS OTHERS SEE US

A French friend told me, with passion, that he sees France being destroyed by the absence of respect for French cultural norms displayed by President Sarkozy and his clique, the rapid growth of an angry urban Muslim population, and *'la démocratie des imbeciles'*. But to a regular visitor like me, I responded, France is still the same courteous, well-ordered society that I've known for forty years, far more civilised than modern Britain – which made me think that, to foreign eyes, Britain is probably still the morally robust, gently eccentric, stiff-upper-lip place the world used to admire. Visitors this month find us snuggled under a cosy eiderdown of tradition: toasting the Ashes victory of our gentlemen cricketers, obsessing about the royal wedding, moaning about the weather.

Perhaps we should all just stop trying to be profound on the basis of superficial observation. If I want to understand modern France, I should keep a holiday home not in a timeless Dordogne village but in a Paris *banlieue* where they celebrate New Year's Eve by torching the vans of the riot police. And if the French want to understand modern Britain, they should tune into *The Archers*, where whingeing rebel single-mum Helen has been kept alive, and harmless, kind, middle-class Nigel has been hurled off the roof to a horrible death.

August 2011

LA FRANCE PROFONDE

Monetary Policy Committee member Adam Posen has been puzzling lately, as I have, over the contrast between dire UK GDP numbers and strong employment data. He would face the same conundrum if he joined me for a weekend of robust economic debate in the rural Dordogne. France has clocked up three consecutive quarters of zero growth, but that's not the way it looks in the village of St Pompon, where the long-derelict *épicerie* is being rebuilt, a new bistro thrives, the bar has had a facelift and the thronged Saturday-night *marché gourmand nocturne* rivals the Olympic closing ceremony for conviviality. The only dampeners are the Dutch, who are here in force but (I'm sorry to say, being distantly related to them) have the reputation of spending as little as possible. *The Spectator*, on the other hand, is doing its bit for trickledown: my own annual musical soirée was well received, though it was upstaged by Lord Sumption's opera company doing *Falstaff* at his chateau up the road,* while another books-page regular, Frederic Raphael, has been spotted holding court in the best local restaurant. And the sun shines gently, day after day.

August 2012

— ✳ —

---

* The historian and barrister Jonathan Sumption, now a judge of the Supreme Court, is a regular *Spectator* book reviewer.

THE FULL FISCAL BOWL

I'm still enjoying my sojourn in France, but sorry to report that the Parti Socialiste forgot to invite me to its summer school at La Rochelle, where ministers and party bosses gathered last weekend to discuss *'le ras-le-bol fiscal'* – the sense that voters have had more than a full bowl of François Hollande's tax hikes, which include a 75 per cent top rate of income tax. The meeting coincided with a warning from EU economic and monetary affairs commissioner Olli Rehn that the French tax burden (third highest in the OECD behind Denmark and Sweden, and set to rise again in 2014) has already reached a 'critical level' which is impeding growth, and that public spending cuts should henceforth be Hollande's clear priority. Underlining his point, France's jobless total rose again in July, to 3.3 million. Even Ségolène Royal, queen of the left and mother of Hollande's children, has been talking about a 'moratorium' on damaging tax rises. But the government's response was to shun Rehn's warning and announce a new carbon tax, to the joy of French green activists enjoying their own summer get-together at Marseilles.

I wasn't asked to that one either – but nevertheless I think it would be gracious of me to invite all these misguided ideologues to join me on Saturday night for the summer's last *marché gourmand nocturne* in my Dordogne village of St Pompon: a thriving model of small-scale free enterprise, community cohesion, minimal red tape and making the most of natural advantages, it's the lesson they need in how to maximise potential for economic recovery.

August 2013

———✳———

THERAPIE DE CHOC

This is my final despatch from France for this summer, and although I missed another top-level seaside meeting – it was 'Les Amis de Nicolas Sarkozy' at Arcachon, and I was secretly relieved not to be asked – I think someone in Paris must have read last week's column about how fed up the French are with tax rises. This week there was actually a cut: a one-year 25 per cent reduction in capital gains tax on sales of second homes and buy-to-let properties. I doubt it will halt the steady flow of capital towards South Kensington, however, given the huge number of bright young French people now choosing to make careers in London rather than Paris. As ministers return to work after the summer break, they should focus not on trying to provoke a short-term real estate bubble as a token of recovery but on the more fundamental issue of making their jobs market more competitive: the cost of French labour is €34 per hour compared to €30 in Germany and €20 in the UK and Spain. As a Francophile who genuinely wishes them well, I'd like to have made that point at one last summer gathering, at which François Hollande's cabinet painted their vision of 'La France 2025': full employment, social harmony, bubbling innovation, global influence. In response to such wishful thinking, I can only quote *Le Figaro* columnist Nicolas Baverez: without '*une therapie de choc*' to reform an unsustainable social and fiscal model, France is currently destined for 'the rank of peripheral nation, *spectatrice du monde de 2025*'.

September 2013

FROM ROPPONGI TO ROUEN

There is something sad about displaced works of art and bric-a-brac gathering dust in the obscurity of the world's junk shops.

Everything worth a glance there must once have mattered to its crafts-
man or artist, his subject or his patron, and might have an interesting
tale to tell if only we could discover it. This is the story of one lost object
and how it came back into the sunlight.

On the edge of the glittering night-life district of Roppongi, in
the shadow of one of Tokyo's thundering overhead expressways, there
is a cramped little antique shop called Ohyama Art. Or at least there
was in the mid eighties, when I lived nearby. The elderly Mr Ohyama
sat day after day watching television in his tatami-matted living space
adjoining a clutter of Korean chests, carved netsuke figures, hibachi
bowls, stone lanterns, wood-block prints and assorted paintings. Trade
was at best intermittent – apart from myself I never once saw anyone
buy anything – but like many Tokyo residents of his generation, he was
doubtless content in the knowledge that the land under his modest
building must have been worth a couple of million pounds.

The first time I went in to browse, an oil painting in the dimmest
recess of the shop caught my eye. For six months or more I watched to
see if it was still there. Eventually I asked Mr Ohyama the price. He
indicated 18 man (the unit of 10,000) yen. Bargaining is not prevalent
in Japan but for such slow-moving stock it seemed worth a try. I offered
11; we agreed at 13, then about £550.

The picture is of an orchard, with a small girl in the foreground.
Painted with a free, confident hand, it has a breezy feeling of warmth
and light. One fluid brush stroke created a distant paddock. It is signed
'Bordes'. The name looked French, the style, well, Impressionist or
thereabouts. The name-plate on the ornate gilt frame suggested that
it had once hung in a gallery or a grand collection. The Japanese taste
for such pictures is ubiquitous; in its recent life it had probably graced
some corporate presidential drawing-room. I thought perhaps I had
acquired a treasure.

It moved with me from Tokyo to Hong Kong and from there to
North Yorkshire. Familiar objects have a particular importance for
people who move from country to country – in a sense they are your
home, wherever you and they happen to be. The picture came to take

pride of place in the baggage of that itinerant phase, and I wanted very much to trace its identity. I suppose the detection would have been mundane to a professional researcher, but to me it became a slow-burning source of fascination.

I found, first, the one Bordes (Ernest, 1852–1914) who has ever exhibited at the Royal Academy. His most notable work was 'The Late Major General Sir Henry Colville KCMG', so it seemed unlikely to be him. The authoritative French dictionary of artists, *Benezit*, listed a Bordes de Lapierre, a Bordes-Guyon and, more promisingly, Léonard Bordes, a twentieth-century landscape painter of the Rouen school, so I wrote from Tokyo to the Musée des Beaux Arts there, presuming such an institution to exist. It does, and the curator, Jeanne-Marie David-Frank, wrote back.

Léonard Bordes, she said, was born in 1898 to a Parisian family of musicians – his pianist mother was a noted interpreter of César Franck and Léonard himself was for many years a cellist in the orchestra of the Théâtre Lyrique in Rouen, his only steady employment. But principally he was a painter gifted with a deep, often sombre, sense of place, particularly for the familiar scenes of Normandy ravaged by the Second World War. He rarely worked in a studio – '*Mon atelier, c'est la rue*', I found him quoted elsewhere. And he was truly prolific – completing thousands of canvases by the time of his death in 1969.

This last snippet reduced my expectation of a windfall. But better news came from a less academic source: Ben Kilpatrick, City trader turned Nightingale Lane art dealer, who came up with recent French auction prices for Bordes canvases. It was certainly worth twice what I had paid, maybe more.

Irrespective of the money angle, Bordes sounded a charismatic fellow. I continued the quest. Along the way I found out who the Rouen school were: a group of landscapists spanning the turn of the century, with strong influences of Impressionism, some later traces of Cubism. Alfred Lebourg was the first and grandest of them; Bordes was the last.

At last I went for a day to Rouen, first to the Musée. Lebourg hangs there beside Sisley and Monet; sadly the two Bordes canvases in the collection are in store. Its library was officially closed but a severe lady let me in to look at the press-cuttings files. Here were fifty years of exhibition reviews, many of them in ponderously over-egged prose from the pen of one Bernard Nebout of the *Paris Normandie* newspaper: '*seduisant pessimisme que tempére une attachante sensualité*' was the general theme, repeated down the years from 1926 to 1971.

The file ended with a 1989 retrospective in several Rouen galleries, and news of the publication of Dr Robert Évreux's full, illustrated biography. I set off to find the galleries. The first had no less than four works on display with the distinctive, sloping Bordes signature, including a memorable oil of hunters on a hillside at dusk, and a watercolour, which I eventually bought, of a church near Le Havre seen in the distance between wind-blown trees.

The prices of the oil paintings were surprisingly high: good news for my first picture, bad news for the idea of starting a collection. Another Bordes enthusiast happened to be there bantering with the proprietor; the painter was evidently a household name among Rouen art-fanciers. The profusion of his works had made him a stalwart for the local trade over several decades.

One more gallery; two more landscapes well beyond my price range. In several others I drew a blank. I set off to walk back to my hotel through the lovely mediaeval streets and alleys around the cathedral, and came by chance upon yet another art shop, with an unpromising display of prints in its window. But the name, Galerie de la Cour d'Albane, rang a bell from one of the yellowed cuttings at the library. I went in to enquire. Three women greeted me, one in her eighties, two of middle age.

This was, in effect, the Léonard Bordes appreciation society. They had all three been close friends of his family. The elderly lady, Madame Nocq, had run the artists' materials shop which supplied him with paint and brushes for many years, allowing him credit when he was short of cash, which was often. Her daughter, Madame Née, owns the gallery and deals on behalf of Bordes' two daughters (one of whom had been in the shop only the day before) in the collection left to them, including all the unsigned sketches. The third of the group, Mlle Menuisement, was the daughter of a gallery-owner who had promoted Bordes in the fifties and sixties. They were enchanted that someone had traced him all the way from Japan to their shop.

In the basement were more of his works.* Carried away by the warmth of the occasion, I bought yet another, a strikingly stylised water-colour of a gang of men with ladders, pollarding plane trees in the Place de 39e Régiment d'Infanterie. The composition looks down from the balcony of the artist's flat, his home for many years: he made numerous paintings of the same scene in different seasons. Afterwards I went to look at it, a grey brick building with an air of disappointment beside the grandiose stonework and half-timbered charm of much of Rouen. Coupled with portraits of him – thin-faced, sharp-eyed, always smoking – it gave a strong sense of a hand-to-mouth, bohemian life.

I promised to send the three ladies a photograph of the original painting. In due course it came back to me from Madame Née, signed on the back by both Bordes daughters. The elder of the two, Giselle, identified herself as the girl under the apple trees – aged eight, in the late summer of 1930. They had had no idea where the painting had been for the intervening sixty-one years.

So there it was, rescued from its Japanese twilight and restored, more or less, to its full significance – which, in truth, is not a lot. A family outing on a sunny day; a picture dashed off with the skill of a man who painted every day of his adult life; one cheerful afternoon in a career more often marked by melancholy. But the real pleasure is the simple one of knowing all this to be so, and, of course, of telling other people.

May 1993

---

* A few years later I went back to see the ladies in Rouen and persuaded them to lend me a carload of Bordes canvases; I brought them to Helmsley and hung them, with my own collection of his work, as a belated centenary exhibition in the French-themed 1999 Ryedale Festival.

STEAK FRITES

Steak Frites *is a café-theatre comedy about Brits in France. It was premiered in Helmsley in 2010 and toured to several other Yorkshire venues. It is set in a village bar-restaurant, Chez Henri. A middle-aged Englishwoman, Amanda, is having an unhappy motoring holiday with her boyfriend, Clive. At the next table in the café is Paul, an expatriate writer . . .*

PAUL: Take my advice, have the *menu du jour*. It's a taste of the *terroir*, terribly good in Henri's own special way. The steaks are excellent but the real speciality is his Île Flottante for dessert. You wouldn't think a brute like Henri could make anything so perfectly delicate. The proof of the pudding is in the eating, and I eat it every day. Doctor says my cholesterol's a medical miracle. Anyway, no one's ordered any of that stuff on the back since de Gaulle died. It'd probably kill you.

AMANDA: Oh, you're English, sorry. *(Scrutinises him.)* Well yes, of course you are, you couldn't be anything else. You look like . . .

PAUL: Roger Moore? Prince Andrew?

AMANDA: No, I was going to say you look like a writer, or a poet. Do you live here?

PAUL: Indeed I do, indeed I am. A writer in the sense that I write things, at least, if not in the sense that anyone pays to read them these days. But I can't complain. This place is the civilised Englishman's idea of heaven, *la France profonde*, good food, good manners, cheap wine, old stone, mellow sunshine, soft rain.

AMANDA: That's quite poetic already.

PAUL: Only thing that spoils it is all the tiresome Brits who insist on living here, not to mention the bloody Belgians. And don't get me started about the Dutch. Or the exchange rate. Not thinking of joining us are you? Lots of falling-down farmsteads for sale, bags of charm, dirt cheap to buy, cost you your life savings to put right.

AMANDA: Oh gosh, no – well not yet anyway. We're not meant to be here at all, actually, not in this village. Clive hasn't got the vaguest clue where we are and, to be honest, I don't really care. Anyway, we'll take your advice and have the set menu. Don't want anything else going wrong today.

PAUL: No, I can see that. Your husband doesn't look a happy bunny.

AMANDA: Not my husband actually . . .

PAUL: Whoops-a-daisy. Someone else's husband? Good for you, dear.

AMANDA: Oh gosh, no, I didn't mean that, I meant . . .

PAUL: Don't worry, our French friends are much more broad-minded than they look. Anything goes here, I can tell you. That's not the mayor's wife, for a start. And as for Larry and Harry over there, sometimes there's Gavin and Kevin from over the hill as well, quite a party. Then there's dear old Herman and . . .

AMANDA: You see, he thinks he's lost his . . . you know . . .

PAUL: Marbles? Mojo?

AMANDA: No . . . his mobile thingy, it's one of those fancy ones with the emails and stuff. He never leaves it alone. He's big in office furnishings, you see, and he's got an angry customer waiting for a lorry load in Sheffield or somewhere. Mr Singh. Big opening, lord lieutenant, curry buffet and everything. Nothing but boxes to sit on. The lorry's broken down on the M1.

PAUL: Oh dear. But it wouldn't do him much good round here anyway, the mobile thingy. You only get a signal when the express to Toulouse goes past, so they say. Next one's not till after two o'clock. To begin with everyone was clamouring to have one of those masts in the valley but then no one wanted it anywhere near their own house. So they brought a temporary one on a trailer and put it bang next to Larry and Harry's. The mayor said the radiation might straighten them out. But they made such a frightful fuss it had to be taken away again.

CLAUDINE: (*placing a gin and tonic on Paul's table, and waiting to take the order*) Don't listen to him, madame, he is a lot of talking through his . . .

PAUL: *Chapeau.* Hat. Panama, if you like.

CHAPTER 8

Yorkshire Life

MOMENT OF DESTINY

The idea that a casual act can change the course of personal fate has always been useful to film scriptwriters. If anyone ever makes a biopic about me – though I can't imagine why they would – it will have to begin with the moment, twenty years ago, when I bought a copy of *Country Life*.

It was 6 p.m. on Thursday, 29 June 1989. I was in Hong Kong's cramped old city-centre airport, Kai Tak, about to board a flight to Taipei, when I paused at the news stand. The magazine's cover caught my eye. I was not a regular reader. But after six years as an itinerant banker in Asia, I had developed an in-flight habit of fantasising about where I might buy a house when I came home: Scotland and Tuscany featured regularly, and sometimes my native Yorkshire. Shortly after take-off, the property ad that struck me with the force of a sudden bout of air turbulence was for 'a most impressive and unusual Grade II-listed country house standing in beautiful grounds and overlooking Helmsley Castle' in North Yorkshire.

With its classical single-storey frontage, it looked like a Georgian bungalow. Sunlight on the mellow stone of the gable end suggested elevated views. It wasn't big (three bedrooms plus 'extensive roof space for conversion') but it clearly wasn't small. It was in the lovely little market town where we used to spend family holidays. No price was given, but who cared: somehow I knew, right there over the South China Sea, it was the one for me.

On reaching the Ritz Hotel in Taipei (no relation to any other Ritz, believe me) I rang my parents in Surrey and urged them to contact the estate agent for particulars. Then and for months afterwards, they thought I had taken leave of my senses. Back in Hong Kong, I rang the agent myself and established that the sale would be by sealed tender on 14 July, and that the seller was Lord Feversham, whose mother had lived in the house. I was due in London that week, so arranged a flying visit.

As soon as I saw the house I knew I was right. Built as a school by the Lord Feversham of the 1820s, it sat handsomely in the view from the drive of his mansion, Duncombe Park. When it was converted to a house in the 1950s by the architect-baronet Sir Martyn Beckett (half-brother of the last Earl of Feversham), the schoolroom became a drawing-room with tall windows looking across the park. It was very special – and in an absolutely terrible state of repair. But again, who cared? I consulted my solicitor as to tactics in sealed tenders: bid an odd number that's a bit more than the guide price, he said. So I did, and Feversham chose me, though I was told later I may not have been the highest bidder; by the end of August, the house was mine.

And it has set my path ever since. Building work took three years, off and on, but I never regretted the project for a second; on the contrary, I longed to spend more time there. I gradually lost interest in the City job to which I returned, until the dramatic point in early 1992 when my employer completely lost interest in me. Instead I became a freelance journalist – just about the only occupation I could pursue from my new study, with its view of the church tower – and eventually a *Spectator* columnist. I helped build the local arts centre and became a keen amateur actor, as well as a town councillor and a churchwarden. I walked my dog every day across his lordship's parkland. I acquired not just a home that still startles me at the thought of my good luck every time I see it, but a curriculum vitae, a complete persona, that might never otherwise have been. And I found it in *Country Life*.

Country Life, *August 2009*

EVERYTHING IN A PIE

One of an incomplete series of Spectator *portraits of English counties*

Make your brass in the West Riding, farm in the East Riding, build your house in the North Riding. That was the old adage, and it captures part of the essence of what is called, for the time being, North Yorkshire.

That essence is one of prosperity generated by outsides and incomers – landowners, mediaeval monks, modern tourists – and of what economists might call a propensity to leisure: racing and shooting for the grandees; hiking, biking, steam trains, agricultural shows and trips to the seaside for the hoi polloi. This cheerful existence as a kind of giant theme park stands in striking contrast to the harshness of the living offered by the soil itself, in the upland stretches of the Pennine dales and the North York moors, which are the county's dominant features.

There are lowlands as well, in the rich vales of York and Mowbray and the marshy Vale of Pickering, but they are, frankly, boring. The villages of the region, high or low, tend to be elongated and quietly huddled. The real meeting-points of North Riding life – of dalesmen, sportsmen, trenchermen and elderly day-trippers looking for the toilets – are its small market towns: Masham, Leyburn and Richmond to the west, Thirsk in the middle, Helmsley, Kirkbymoorside, Pickering and Malton to the east.

It may seem an odd reflection, but to come upon one of these towns on market day is more like being in provincial France than modern-day England. It has something to do with the mellowness of the stone and the relaxed conversational ambience of the marketplace, but it also has to do with the quality of the food. Good and abundant eating, at plain prices, is something Yorkshiremen take very seriously indeed. Competition is particularly keen in charcuterie and baking – 'We like everything in a pie', as my allotment-keeping neighbour, Mr Basil Bean, once remarked over the hedge.

We also like dressed crabs and fresh kippers from Scarborough, blue Wensleydale (greatly superior to Stilton) or its white brother eaten with hard ginger parkin, new-fangled goats' cheeses from Farndale and Yorkshire curd tarts for tea. And in any of hundreds of comfortable pubs, the hungry farmhand can end the day with a chilli-filled Yorkshire pudding the size of a hub-cap or a well-fatted sirloin steak bigger than his flat hat, all washed down with Theakston's excellent bitter.

The farmhand's grandfather would have had to make do with a diet of fat bacon, potatoes and broth; his was a much harder life. In these same market-places, for centuries, workers came to the Martinmas hirings in November to take a 'fest' of a shilling from a farmer to signify a year's contract, which meant board, lodging and a paltry wage paid at the end. The system was supposed to have been abolished by the Agricultural Wages Act of 1924, but my old friend and gardener Ernest experienced it in the mid 1930s, earning £15 for the first year and £26 for the second.

A fine countryman and a walking compendium of folklore, Ernest Dowkes was the archetypal North Riding man. He died two years ago. 'Now then, Maa-tin,' he would greet me, before reciting the weather forecast of a local sage referred to mysteriously as 'him from Thirsk', or launching into a stream of anecdotes. I remember especially his story of a cantankerous acquaintance who fell into the stone-crushing machine at Hovingham quarry and was minced to a thousand pieces. 'By heck,' Ernest concluded phlegmatically, 'at least he won't have to pay t'Poll Tax.'

There are many reminders of the hardships of the pre-leisure age. Here in Helmsley, now famous as one of the most sophisticated shopping experiences north of Bond Street, the block of flats next to my gate was once the Union Workhouse. Its keeper was the maternal grandfather of Huddersfield-born Harold Wilson – hence, apparently, his choice of nearby Rievaulx for his lordly title.

Even at the middle level of the rural Yorkshire hierarchy – before the advent of bed-and-breakfast, caravan sites and goat's cheese enterprises – conditions were tough. Smallholders and craftsmen from the moorland dales had to go wherever they could to supplement their income, providing a pool of mobile labour for the rest of the county.

A hundred years ago, Job Todd of Hutton-le-Hole (an all-too-picturesque village now completely overwhelmed by tourists) would walk over the Hambleton Hills – pausing no doubt, as Wordsworth did on his wedding day, to absorb the huge view across to the Pennines from the top of Sutton Bank – to take work 'in the bottoms' of the Vale of York in the late spring. Then, lodging rough, he would make his way up Wensleydale to reach Chapel-le-Dale, still in Yorkshire but 90 miles from home and barely a dozen from Morecombe Bay, in time for haymaking in July. That done, he would take the train back from Ribblehead to Kirkbymoorside in time for harvest.

Others chose a different course and took ship from Whitby to Quebec for £3 10s in steerage, to make a new life in Canada or Cleveland, Ohio. Or they went to the industrial sweatshops of Middlesbrough, which accounted for a quarter of the population of the North Riding before it was hived off into a new county called Cleveland in 1974.

Middlesbrough, once renowned for building bridges for Sydney Harbour and the White Nile, is now better known as the north-east capital of motorised crime.*

Happy with our unbalanced, non-industrial economy, that city and its charmless hinterland is quite out of character with the rest of the Riding, except perhaps the ancient river port of Yarm, which looks very much like all the other North Riding market towns. Yarm has one pleasing incidental claim to fame: 170 years ago, five men met in the George and Dragon inn to plan the building of the Stockton to Darlington line, the world's first public railway.

Not far south of Yarm is Northallerton, county town of the so-called county of North Yorkshire. It is another handsome old marketplace astride what used to be the Great North Road, but now swamped by suburban villas and disguised for through traffic by a one-way system in which the only notable sight is the prison. Northallerton's Inland

---

* This remark attracted the headline 'Slur in Toffs' Magazine' in the *Middlesbrough Evening Gazette*, prompting me to withdraw my application to be the Conservative candidate for Middlesbrough Central in the 1997 general election.

Revenue men once policed the highest average per capita income of any tax office in the country, and that wealth is reflected in County Hall itself. A handsome complex of buildings in pseudo-Queen Anne style, it is big enough to be the seat of government for a medium-sized country. If it becomes redundant in the forthcoming local government reorganisation, it would be more than adequate for the European Central Bank.

Whatever the outcome of the Commissioners' work, it is hard to think of Northallerton as the heart rather than the head of the county, and, indeed, is difficult to pin that heart in one place. Northallerton was, as it happens, almost the exact geographical centre of the North Riding, midway between Filey Brigg on the coast and Mickle Fell (now in Cumbria), 2,585 feet up in the Pennines. But it stood between two regions of quite distinctive character.

The heart of the western side, consisting chiefly of Wensleydale and Swaledale, is easily identified as Richmond. With its military associations, its hilltop castle and its sloping, cobbled marketplace like a cold version of Siena, Richmond is the most dignified of all North Riding towns.

The eastern heart is the seat of the Lord Lieutenant, Sir Marcus Worsley, at Hovingham, in the lee of the Howardian Hills. The point about Hovingham is that it elegantly symbolises at the upper end of the spectrum the propensity to leisure which I claim as the spirit of North Riding, and which naturally infected the gentry first. Hovingham Hall was built around horses: its main entrance is an indoor riding school and it leads through the house on to one of England's prettiest cricket grounds.

Scarborough, the queen of the east coast, provides all the symbols we need at the other end of the leisure spectrum. Down on the seafront are the amusement arcades, Italian ice-cream parlours, hats that say 'Over Forty But Still Naughty' and irresistible bank holiday perfumes of fried onion and chip fat. Up at the Grand Hotel, once the biggest in Europe, now run by Butlins, elderly couples from West Yorkshire sip Happy Hour cocktails and wait for the ballroom dancing to begin.

Millions of leisure-seekers of every persuasion pass through the

North York Moors National Park each year. Teesside bikers scream round the bends across the Cleveland Hills past pedal-cyclists looking like butterflies in fluorescent Lycra. Caravan convoys crawl the A170 to the coast. Rich, Range-Rovered Americans arrive to shoot grouse. Busloads of oldies from the south complain about the café prices and ask the question the locals hate most: 'Is this Herriot Country?'

But miraculously, at five o'clock, they seem to evaporate into thin air, leaving some small portion of their wealth behind – and only occasionally, in the case of joy-riding burglars from Middlesbrough, taking some larger portion of our wealth away with them. Here in Helmsley, at least, we have the place to ourselves again by late afternoon. We can drive up to Rievaulx Moor to see the evening light in Bilsdale, or enjoy the peace of St Gregory's Minster at Kirkdale, or buy the best haddock and chips without queuing, or watch the end of the village cricket, or just go to the pub.

I sometimes worry that there might be a finer place in England to live, where the art of leisure has been developed to a higher state. But somehow I cannot imagine it.

June 1994

VILLAGE OF THE DEAD

It's hard to imagine a more pleasant spot to await the second coming than the parish cemetery of Terrington, on a ridge of the Howardian Hills in rural North Yorkshire. But the charm of the location for that purpose – and the possibility that it might be shared by large numbers of outsiders, especially folk of a duskier hue – has provoked debate of unprecedented ferocity. As a planning decision looms, the living community of Terrington – dubbed 'village of the dead' by the local paper – is tearing itself apart.

The existing graveyard, a quarter of a mile outside the village down a narrow farm lane, is perfectly peaceful. Surrounded by low stone walls and mature yews, it has distant views of the towers of York Minster to the south and the plateau of the North York Moors to the north. The historian Arnold Toynbee is its most distinguished occupant, and there are spaces available for another six decades' worth of Terrington parishioners, at the rate of about half a dozen per year, to join their parents and cousins. Among the surnames that recur on the weather-beaten headstones, there are a dozen Goodwills. It is a scion of the Goodwill dynasty, of which there are three branches in the village, who is the cause of the trouble. Robert Goodwill, thirty-eight-year-old fourth-generation farmer and Conservative parliamentary candidate,* owns the 8-acre field between the existing graveyard and the edge of the village itself. He wants to turn it into a commercial cemetery, the Mowthorpe Garden of Rest, which would eventually provide 1,700 graves. He has already built the car park, planted the hedges, and received a £3,000 training grant that (in an unfortunate choice of words) he says will enable the business to 'hit the ground running'. But the undead residents of Terrington, or some of them, are determined to stop him.

A graveyard, you may think, is about as inoffensive an enterprise as it is possible to propose. The dead make no noise. Their visitors tend to be distinctly subdued. Most of us walk past graveyards every day of our lives without the slightest shudder of distaste; indeed, we may often choose to walk through the graveyard as a haven of calm. In city centres, crowded cemeteries are having to reuse existing graves, and are too strapped for cash or vulnerable to vandalism to be properly maintained. In planning guidelines, graveyards are one of the few forms of development that are permissible on Green Belt land and in areas of outstanding natural beauty. 'Green' burial in a woodland setting, one of the options offered by Goodwill, is the only chic way for serious environmentalists to go. And everyone would probably agree that graveyards are more attractive as a use for spare farmland than, say, pig units, caravan sites or bungalows.

---

* Subsequently an MEP for Yorkshire and Humber, and now MP for Scarborough.

But among Terrington's Cemetery Action Group, led by retired GP, former magistrate, Neighbourhood Watch organiser and church-warden Peter Barber, reactions have been almost as strong as if young Goodwill had proposed to build an abattoir, a glue factory and a nightclub all on the same controversial site. There are certainly legitimate objections to the way in which the planning process has been handled so far, but there are also layers of subjective response which are a vivid illustration of that most potent of domestic political forces, pure parochial Nimbyism.

The Action Group's most rational objection is one of scale. With 1,700 graves (which Goodwill says will take up to fifty years to fill) the deceased would outnumber the live population by five to one, even if the burial site is barely visible except from the sports field and a few outlying cottages. Barber's group has put it about that another adjacent Goodwill field might be brought into play at some future date to create a necropolis of 7,000 departed souls, which would overwhelm the village entirely.

But whether catering for 1,700 or 7,000, it is argued, such an establishment would inevitably need a Chapel of Rest, toilets, tearooms, florists and wider roads. It might encourage the entrepreneurial Goodwill, or his successor, to open a crematorium as well. Among other side effects, the 'village of the dead' tag would be a disaster for the thriving local holiday cottage trade.

Cortège would follow cortège past nearby cottage gardens, and the children of the village, it has been seriously suggested, would need counselling for trauma and stress. In the *Yorkshire Evening Press*, the Terrington resident and architectural historian Professor Patrick Nuttgens, envisaging five or six funerals per day as opposed to Goodwill's figure of one a week or less, wrote: 'Why is the local authority deaf to all comments? Perhaps they should read Evelyn Waugh's devastating novel *The Loved One*. Perhaps Terrington will come to be known as Whispering Glades.'

Fear of an Americanised commercial enterprise is one aspect of the problem. If the project flourishes, the argument runs, it will surely expand; but if it fails it will become an untended eyesore. Goodwill has set up a trust for the perpetual upkeep of the site and is determined that its style should remain quietly attuned to its rural setting – but if he is smart, say his opponents, he may well sell out to some vertically integrated conglomerate of death, offering everything from neon-lit hearses to piped angelic choirs.

Most sinister of all is the question of who might come to Terrington to be buried. Several of the leading objectors are 'incomers' – Barber retired there from Warrington six years ago – but they are not at all happy with the idea that large numbers of other outsiders should make, as it were, a late arrival in their adopted village.

The cemetery will be open to burials of all faiths or none, and Goodwill (in partnership with a York undertaker) is believed to have been in touch with local authorities as far afield as Bradford, which has a large Muslim population. Dr Barber says that he himself has no particular problem with 'the coloureds', but others in the village apparently do. The idea of corpses in shrouds accompanied by wailing brown mourners is just too much for them to contemplate. In a vivid confusion of Eastern rituals, the prospect has been raised of hysterical widows hurling themselves on to burning pyres. One villager, trying to sound a little more tolerant than his neighbours, said, 'As far as I'm concerned, Muslims are just part of t'walk of life these days. But I suppose I'd rather have them here dead than alive.'

And what if Goodwill strikes a deal to handle pauper burials from nearby cities, or accepts gypsy funerals: what sort of criminal riff-raff would that bring into the village, stealing flowers from nearby gardens and casing the joint for a swift burglary on the way home? In the fraught atmosphere now pervading the village, no supposition is too extreme.

The district councillors of Ryedale failed completely to anticipate the strength of this emotional reaction. At its first presentation to the district's Northern Area planning sub-committee last December, the graveyard was approved (as the twenty-fifth of fifty-six items on the agenda) so swiftly that Terrington's own councillor, an elderly farmer called Bob Smith, did not have time to find the papers and express an opinion. John Richardson, editor of the local *Gazette & Herald*, sat in on the meeting. 'There were longer discussions on satellite dishes and illuminated signs,' he says. Told that there were indications of dissent from Terrington parish council, the chairman of the meeting remarked jokingly that perhaps they were just worried about competition for the existing cemetery, and waved the item through.

Since then, however, two well-attended parish meetings have voted overwhelmingly to seek to stop the scheme. Goodwill has been accused of 'concealment' of his true intentions in the wording of his application, which did not explicitly state that the Garden of Rest was to be a private, commercial venture, unconnected with the existing village graveyard. Recriminations have been flying between parish councillors, planning officials and Action Group members. There were ugly scenes in Terrington's only pub, the Bay Horse Inn. Faced with loud calls for revocation, the district council has conveniently discovered that proper notice procedures may not have been followed in the first place, and has called for Goodwill's application to be resubmitted.

If the application is rejected at this second hearing, Goodwill says that the district council 'will look very stupid indeed'. He will go to appeal, and if finally defeated, will have a strong case for compensation, running to thousands of pounds, for the cost of landscaping the site and marketing the project to date. This, say his opponents, places the district council in the farcical position of having to reconsider a matter in which the only new element is the fact that the council itself now has a financial axe to grind.

Looking out on to Terrington's main street from his converted farmhouse, Dr Barber says that the tide of opinion is running his way, and that 'we won't be having all those funeral processions passing by'. But people outside Terrington may think choice is a good thing in death just as in life, and that it is peculiarly parochial to oppose an entrepreneur who wants to offer us that choice in what is, in fact, a relatively unobtrusive way.

However far it may be from their original homes, many people would be pleased to be buried on the ridge of the Howardian Hills with a distant view of York Minster, rather than in some crumbling municipal cemetery. It is curious that we are free to buy retirement homes or rent holiday cottages there, but not to secure an eternal resting place.

April 1995

———✳———

THE HOUNDS OF HEAVEN

I took up beagling not as a political gesture but because my dog died. Having walked with him for twelve years, I found walking without him too sad, so I more or less stopped. Then I met a friend at a party – a state-school teacher who had once been a Marxist agitator in the local bacon factory – and heard a glowing account of the eccentricities of a day on the North York Moors with the Ampleforth Beagles. 'Lovely,' she said. 'It's like a big family outing. You just have to remember to keep saying Good Morning, because that's how they all greet each other, even though it's mid afternoon.'

In the long perspective of the history of hunting, it is later than that: it is two minutes to midnight. On Saturday 19 February next year, even this least bloodthirsty – and, frankly, least efficient – of blood sports will become a crime. By then, unless some legal wheeze defeats the Act* or an infusion of Ukrainian-style revolutionary spirit grips the gentle beagling crowd, we will all be saying Good Night – which is how beaglers bid each other farewell, even though it's still mid-afternoon.

But, I thought, better late than never – a sentiment which is apparently prevalent throughout the countryside this autumn: a foxhunting neighbour tells me that the Sinnington's early-season children's meet attracted record numbers, and that hunt tailors and horse dealers have

---

* The Hunting Act 2004 made illegal the hunting of hares (but not rabbits) with packs of hounds, unless the hare has already been 'wounded or shot'.

never been busier. Still, I approached my first beagling encounter, high on the moors at Levisham, north of Pickering, with trepidation. Was I fit enough to keep up? Was I dressed correctly? Besides this 'Good Morning' business, what other traps of etiquette were lying in wait?

Unhappy memories recurred of my last appearance on the fox-hunting field, twenty-something years ago: it was a day with the Exmoor Foxhounds – and I was not a success, socially, sartorially or by any measure of equestrian skill. To the extent that local hunting folk acknowledged my presence at all, they did so by sniggering at me for being a nervous visitor from London on a hired horse. Not one of them bothered to be friendly – except the legendary master, Captain Ronnie Wallace, who to his enormous credit (I really must have looked hopeless) bought me two big whiskies afterwards and urged me to try again.

Beaglers turned out to be a very different proposition. As to dress, almost anything goes: the master, the kennel huntsman and the whippers-in wear smart green coats and white britches, but everyone else is just dressed for a walk on the moors. Tweeds and waterproof gaiters prevail, but bright red anoraks are OK too, and I spotted one woman in a camelhair coat and sunglasses, for all the world as though the meet was taking place in Harvey Nichols. 'Good morning,' they all said; 'Good morning,' I replied, pleased to have jumped the first fence, and off we strode on to the moor in conversational groups, while the hounds searched ahead with bounding optimism for the scent of a hare.

You would have to be an optimist to be a beagle hound – and not only because a strong hare on open ground so easily outruns its pursuers. Any remote hope that the activity for which these hounds are bred will survive beyond February is diminished by the unavoidable lack of a serious 'pest control' justification. Lowland hares in large numbers are a nuisance to farmers, but it is a lot easier to shoot them; up on the moors, in relatively sparse numbers, they are not really a nuisance to anyone, and they have plenty of natural predators. And when the hounds face the final judgement, they will not be allowed to plead in mitigation that, statistically, they are not even very good at their job: in the whole of last season, the Master tells me precisely, the Ampleforth pack killed only 'nine and a half brace', roughly one in fourteen of all the hares they put up.

The Master, Major Ian Kibble, is an elegant, sharp-eyed man of around seventy who likes to quote Surtees and correct hunting solecisms. 'For God's sake don't call them dogs,' he tells me more than once, adding that all non-hound canines are known as 'cur dogs'. He hunts, he says, 'because I enjoy it'. He and his cohort took over the pack a decade ago from Ampleforth College, the Catholic public school, where for the previous forty years it had been run by a Benedictine monk, Father Walter Maxwell-Stewart; the hounds are still blessed annually, and a handful of boys from the school still take part.

They join an amiable cross-section of local life which includes, among my first sampling, a fish farmer, a paediatrician, a wine merchant, a sinologist, a prison officer, a retired schoolmaster and several small children. Newcomers and visitors from other packs are welcomed with unfeigned warmth. Anti-hunt protesters used to turn up occasionally too, but nowadays they devote their attention to high-profile fox hunts elsewhere.

My second meet is at a hill farm on Snilesworth Moor, one of the remotest places in England; the weatherbeaten old farmer beams with pleasure at having so much company. 'How are you, Wilf?' the Master asks. 'Fit as a lop,' says Wilf, leading us out of the filthy yard on to the hill. Being fit as a lop is (fortunately for me) not essential to the enjoyment. Since hares tend to run in circles around their territory, the technique is to stay high and walk at an angle to the direction of the pack, in the hope that the hunt will swing around you – though sometimes it dives deep into a dale and up the far side, at which point those who are fit as lops follow, while the less fit stay put until it comes back. The best viewing point is jokingly designated 'the talking hill', for idlers who prefer to stand and chat from the start.

But most of us spend the afternoon moving up, down and across the heather, trying to stay within earshot of the huntsman's horn and the voice of the pack. Despite periodic reprimands from the Master, we rarely stop chattering; because everyone has their own pace, and their own theory as to the best line to follow, conversations form and dissolve in random patterns. Discussion of moorland fungi swiftly gives way to amateur dramatics, international rugby, *Spectator* sex scandals, farming woes and stock market tips. Contempt for Tony Blair and his government crops up more frequently than most topics, but these days that is probably true everywhere from Sedgefield to Basra, not just on the hunting field.

And from time to time – twice in my five outings so far – somewhere in the distance a hare is killed, or as a hunting journal might say, 'hounds earned their just deserts'. Unlike many other creatures whose existence is interfered with to satisfy human urges – pigs destined for the local bacon factory, for example – the hare leads a free life and has thirteen chances out of fourteen of avoiding its fate. And unlike many other ways in which the hare might eventually die on the moors, this particular death, in the jaws of the leading hound, is almost always instantaneous. It is also the ultimate purpose of our outing, though the human participants rarely witness it at close quarters and do not celebrate it with pagan ceremonies.

Last Saturday, on a bleak northern spur of the moors called Glaisdale Rigg, I picked a bad line which took me out of sight and sound and I missed the moment of excitement when a hare made the fatal mistake of doubling back towards the pack. The sun went down and the cold crept under my coat; suddenly disconsolate, I decided to call it an early Good Night. As I drove along the ridge I found the hounds again, in fading light, streaming across the heather in full cry. The fittest beaglers were still with them. Ask them why they were there and they will say: for the fellowship, for the exercise, for the pleasure of watching hounds work; for the sport, if you like, but only incidentally for the kill. But soon it won't matter what they say, because it will all be gone.

December 2004

———✳———

DIVINE INTERVENTION

I f I had been at home in Helmsley on 19 June, I could have white-water rafted the River Rye that flows through the town. The fact that North Yorkshire, western Canada and parts of China have all recently experienced freak rainfall and flooding is widely taken as evidence of global warming. But it's worth pointing out that a cloudburst on a hot summer afternoon created an even more destructive torrent in Helmsley back in 1787 – and that there is another possible explanation for this year's weather event. It may have been my fault. As a town councillor, I launched a debate in May about whether we should build a new car park in an ancient meadow beside the Rye bridge. At a public meeting, a vociferous majority opposed the idea. Four weeks later a truly biblical scene came upon us: the sky turned black, the river foamed, the air filled with the bleating of sheep as they fought to escape the rising waters – and the meadow became a seething lake bestrewn with debris. I think we can safely say that God was voting against the car park.

June 2005

— ❊ —

CURRY AND VODKA

R egular readers already know Helmsley as a fertile source of eco-nomic parables – and here come a couple more, on the theme of globalisation. The first is the tale of a hill farmer who has gone for bold diversification: 2,000 acres of arable land in the highlands of Ethiopia. 'Wow,' I said, when he told me about hair-raising journeys from Addis Ababa to his remote farmstead along roads that are still being blasted out of the rock by Chinese engineers with convict work-gangs. 'That's brave.' 'Not really,' he responded. 'You should try farming in England these days. You have to be really brave to do that.' Ethiopia may have droughts and civil wars, he went on, but his new neighbours – devout Orthodox Christians – are helpful and welcoming and have one huge advantage: their lives are not made miserable by Defra.

My next vignette is an incident of inter-ethnic tension. I'm happy to report that no native Yorkshire folk were involved, however. A pub down the road was converted a couple of years ago into a curry house run by a team of cheerful Bangladeshis who commute daily from Bradford to this and other rural outposts. The flat above the restaurant was occupied by Polish construction workers, who are naturally inclined to homesickness. One evening, the upstairs Poles took to singing and dancing to cheer themselves up, driving diners out of the restaurant and enraging the downstairs Bangladeshis. Confrontation ensued, and six Poles were taken away in a police van. But no charges were brought and the flames of conflict were soon smothered under a blanket of social-services-speak: the local paper reports that 'amicable resolution was achieved thanks to a problem-solving multi-agency approach' – to be followed, I hope, by a banquet of curry, vodka and Yorkshire curd tart.

July 2008

---❋---

SAVE OUR LIBRARIES

What a curious double life I lead. Half the week I'm your disembodied commentator on the world of high finance – my anonymity protected, as I truffle for City gossip, by a portrait drawing that (I'm told) doesn't look like me at all. For the other half, I'm one of the north of England's most hyperactive citizens, blundering like Flashman from one battlefield of the cuts debate to the next.

Last week, for example, I was discussing library closures on Monday, policing reductions on Tuesday, the crunch in higher education on Wednesday, and doomsday scenarios for the arts on Thursday and

Friday. I can report that the real impact of all this on community life is becoming daily more apparent. But what is most interesting to observe is how the level of public acceptance varies with the degree of honesty displayed.

The Arts Council, for example, seems to have kept its client base well informed and to have created a decently transparent process that will lead, next month, to the painful announcement as to which arts companies have made it into the funded 'national portfolio', and which will be left to fend for themselves. Likewise our local police inspector, tasked with telling us that there is now a single constable and one uniformed 'community support officer' to cover our vast rural area, assured us that he is doing his best, reminded us that we have remarkably low crime levels, and left us feeling reasonably content.

Elsewhere, the approach is less frank. County councils have sought to present library closures, of which there could be more than 400, as an unavoidable *fait accompli*. But they have met a wall of protest and legal challenges. And their arithmetic is far from persuasive. In North Yorkshire, twenty-two libraries are under the axe unless communities come up with 'Big Society' solutions to keep them open. But the average running cost of these libraries last year was just £35,000 each, while the county employed 109 middle managers on salaries of £50,000 or more – including the very officers who have declared that cuts must fall on libraries in order to protect more essential items, namely themselves.

For the loss of just fifteen County Hall paper-pushers, in effect, our treasured network of libraries could be saved. Local government secretary Eric Pickles has been doing similar sums, and his beady eye is focusing on the bloated roll calls of high-salaried local government officers left behind by Labour. Meanwhile, fellow citizens, listen carefully to what you are being told, or not told. Where cuts make sense, accept the logic and move on. But where you suspect cuts are being rushed through to protect the empires and salaries of the cutters, give 'em hell.

February 2011

TEA BREAK

To the Spa at Scarborough, where Harold Wilson made his 'white heat of technology' speech to the 1963 Labour conference. I'm following in his footsteps to address a regional Women's Institute conference – a hall full of Yorkshirewomen so sensible and stout-hearted that I find myself wishing they would march south and form a rebel government. The only white heat generated this afternoon, however, is on the subject of tea and coffee. WIs in these parts have for many years enjoyed a happy informal relationship – free samples for their meetings in return for brand loyalty at the supermarket – with one of the county's most admired family-run businesses, Taylors of Harrogate.

Taylors is a genuinely ethical operator which has won a Queen's Award and a Business in the Community 'Example of Excellence' badge in recognition of its fair treatment of the tea and coffee growers in Africa, Asia and Latin America who are its direct suppliers. Its packaging also includes tokens to raise money for rainforest rescue. An ideal partner for the WI, you might think. The trouble is, Taylors' products do not carry the 'Fairtrade' mark which is endorsed by the London-based National Federation of WIs, pillar of political correctness that it has become in recent years.

Taylors point out politely that there are different ways to be ethical and that they pay growers of 'Yorkshire Tea' well above Fairtrade minimum prices. Critics point out that the preferred Fairtrade model, a co-operative at the end of a long supply chain, is (as Neil Collins wrote in *The Spectator* in 2008) 'a desperately inefficient way to help the poor'. But to no avail. To meet the National Federation's terms, Taylors would have had to sign a contract so demanding that they decided it wasn't worth the effort. The company rep is not even allowed on the conference platform to thank the assembly for past support, lest that should count as free advertising.

It all seems to me an absurdly heavy-handed interference in a pleasing example of capitalism and community in harmony, all the way from the tea-pickers of Rwanda to the tea-pourers of Scarborough.

The Yorkshire ladies think that too. Perhaps they should rebel against their own leaders.

April 2011

———— ❋ ————

ACTION NOT WORDS

I s there anything more irritating to the consumer than the worthless apology offered by a call-centre operator who is clearly not personally responsible for the fact that – to pick a random example – the roses your sent to Pippa Middleton every day last week were never delivered?* That disembodied voice in Glasgow or Bangalore has neither the power nor the incentive nor the corporate pride to ensure that the system failure behind the problem never happens again. She really ought to tell you straight: 'Look, mate, you and a load of other losers bought our super-cheap bouquet-a-day-for-Her-Royal-Hotness special, but we've only got funeral wreaths left, the van driver's been arrested as a terrorist suspect and we've lost your online order because the IT bloke's been on a bender since the wedding. So get over it.'

Barring such refreshing honesty, however, here's an example of how to get it right. Three weeks ago I sent a (correctly addressed) case of wine from London to my home in Yorkshire by DHL, the parcel service owned by the German post office, which promises to deliver, usually, within two working days and has a reputation for being sharper and more consumer-driven than our own Royal Mail. To my surprise, after four days I had had no delivery and no message; an operator apologised that the driver had failed to find my house, because the computer had scrambled my postcode, and had taken the parcel back to the Leeds

---

* This column was written shortly after the wedding of the Duke and Duchess of Cambridge, at which rear views of the bride's sister attracted worldwide admiration.

depot. Delivery was promised for Tuesday after Easter. When that didn't happen, the next operator apologised that a bottle had been broken but the repacked case would come on Wednesday. It didn't. On Thursday, a third operator apologised that she had no idea what was going on and was having trouble getting through to Leeds to find out.

But three hours later a shiny black car swept up my drive, and a cheerful chap called Wayne announced himself as DHL's health and safety manager for the north of England. 'Sorry you've had all this hassle,' he said. 'I happened to be in the office and overheard one end of the conversation. I told them, that's not bloody good enough, give me the parcel and I'll deliver it myself.' So he did. I hope they make him chief executive.

May 2011

— ✳ —

SHELF-STACKER BATES

Bates, Lord Grantham's lovelorn absentee valet, was discovered in this week's episode of *Downton Abbey* to be working at the 'Red Lion' in Kirkbymoorside – confirming my theory that I live bang in the middle of Julian Fellowes' imagined landscape. It also prompted thoughts both about economic change and about Ed Miliband's facile division of the corporate world into 'predators' and 'producers'. Kirkbymoorside is a Yorkshire market town 6 miles from my home in Helmsley, and has no pubs that look anything like the Cotswoldy inn glimpsed as the Red Lion. If Bates had come looking for work today, he would have had no luck at the real White Horse, which has become a pub-closure statistic and is for sale as 'retail units'; nor at the White Swan, which has become the Green Chilli curry house. But like so many twenty-first-century jobseekers he might have fared better at Tesco, which is planning to open a store beside the roundabout.

'Are the people of Kirkbymoorside happy to allow a corporate giant to suck the life out of the centre of their town?' asks an angry resident in the local *Gazette & Herald*. Tesco was expected to announce its worst UK sales figures for twenty years this week, but its store opening programme continues apace – and the dismal small-town blight of empty shops and closed pubs is in large measure due to the relentless march of giant supermarket 'predators'. Yet Tesco is also our biggest private-sector employer, a setter of high management and product-quality standards, and a flagship of British business abroad – while its discounted prices make it a bulwark against inflation for the hard-pressed shopper.

And here's another conundrum for Ed. If jobseeker Bates had got off the bus at Helmsley he could have applied to be manager of our new Oxfam shop, which will soon start ruthlessly cannibalising the trade of several long-established retailers in the town. Oxfam a predator? The economics of commerce are as complex as a Downton plot.

October 2011

— ❋ —

I'm a retriever

As a golden retriever
I'm an ardent believer
In a life devoted to pleasure

Comfortable snoozing
At times of my choosing
Is my definition of leisure

Though lust is frustrated
Since they had me castrated
I still feel the thrill of pursuit

Yorkshire Life

I may smell like a midden
Rarely do what I'm bidden
And I'm unhygienically hirsute

But my temperament's sunny
Unless you're a cat or a bunny
And I see in the dark like a loris

Yes I'm that lovable sinner
Who's just stolen your dinner
The canine equivalent of Boris

CHAPTER 9

Performing Arts

THE POWER OF AM-DRAM

What makes grown-up people want to cavort in their underwear in front of their neighbours, or crawl about impersonating furry animals? If it is not the demon drink, it can only be one thing: the powerful pull of amateur dramatics. It is a force which seizes the weekends and winter evenings of perfectly normal middle-class folk all over the country. And it has, belatedly, seized me.

Like most people, I did a bit of acting at school. But enthusiasm waned with a production of Peter Shaffer's *The Royal Hunt of the Sun* in which I played an Inca general, got up in a terrible smock: it was a deeply serious work, but the actors could barely make themselves heard over the torrents of laughter from the hall until the headmaster strode on stage and threatened to punish the entire audience. After that came *Charley's Aunt* (in which I would have been Mr Spettigue) but the show was so awful that the master in charge cancelled it at the dress rehearsal to spare himself further embarrassment.

At university I dabbled again, but only backstage. Out front were too many self-confident undergraduate Oliviers. Some of them have subsequently made it big on the professional stage – though others have long disappeared into careers at the bar or in advertising, and are perhaps now boring their own local amateur groups with heroic tales of *Coriolanus* or *A Streetcar Named Desire* at the Oxford Playhouse.

But in the back of my mind I always thought I might have another go. For the past six years I have been building and running a small arts centre in my home town of Helmsley in North Yorkshire – where my father, in his youth, was also a keen amateur actor, collecting admiring reviews in the local paper for his roles in town hall productions of *Gas Light* and *Laburnum Grove*. Drama had been dormant in Helmsley for a decade until we opened the arts centre in its first, rudimentary state. But just as nature abhors a vacuum, so wannabe actors appear from nowhere if you declare any building, however dilapidated or unlikely, to be a 'performance space'.

So it was in our case. Before we knew it we had a whole company, the 1812 Theatre Company – taking its name from the date of the building, a former Quaker meeting house – complete with president, committee and constitution. Almost immediately we encountered the divide that is the source of comic tension in drama groups everywhere, between the ham and the luvvie, between the resolutely amateur and the seriously semi-professional. The old-timers, successors of my father's group, declared (though some were very good comic actors) that they had only ever done it 'for a bit of a laugh'. The newcomers, including several college drama teachers, spoke of workshops and improvisations, the sort of self-revelatory loosening of the emotions which makes true amateurs want to curl up and die. There were rumours that we would have to stand in a circle in the dark pretending to be foetuses or raindrops or dying trees.

People become professional actors, I think, because they want to use such exercises to reach heightened levels of self-awareness and self-control which enable them to express character from the inside, in extreme or subliminal ways, unmediated by mechanical 'acting'. Alan Ayckbourn tells the story of Michael Gambon, having been asked by a director to 'do it a bit bigger, love', roaring like a crazed beast across the stage with a heavy table above his head, pinning a terrified actress to the wall with it and saying quietly, 'That big enough for you – love?'

Amateurs, on the other hand, work from the outside in, starting with funny voices and mannerisms and eventually arriving at some sort of characterisation, though rarely a big one. As with plumbing and conveyancing, professionals will never accept that amateurs can get it right; the unpaid have simply never been inducted into the magic circle. 'What irritates me most,' one theatrical grand dame imparted to me, 'is when you hear an audience coming out of an amateur show and saying how *good* it was.'

But true coarse actors don't know or care how the pros do it, and local audiences know they're not coming to see the Royal Shakespeare Company. The main weakness of amateur shows is the most elementary one of all, that the actors never learn their lines until the last week of rehearsal, if then. We are motivated less by the urge to explore our own psyches and paint the walls with raw emotion than by the opportunity for the unique social interaction which goes with a three-month rehearsal schedule for an amateur show: those currents of power, sex and intrigue which will all be safely earthed by the dropping of the final curtain.

Amateur directors do it, I suspect, for the opportunity it affords to exercise a kind of power that rarely comes along in normal life: mild-mannered chaps become short-fused temporary tyrants, bubbly girls become terrifying dominatrixes. In big productions, especially those with children in them, half the town seems to be dragooned into our unruly army, provoking outbursts of truly Napoleonic generalship. There is so much to be organised in such a short time, all of it with more or less unreliable volunteers. That includes the stage crew, who love big, complicated sets, with lots of scaffolding, wiring and ladders – the kind of thing their wives have long forbidden in the house. 'He's a real big-spanner man' is the highest compliment I've heard backstage. And everyone loves the gossip and sexual chemistry that goes with stage clinches and enforced proximity in small dressing rooms.

Am-dram is probably the most fun you can have without committing adultery, but that doesn't mean that you can't actually do the deed as well. In the first 1812 Theatre Company production I appeared in, James Robson's romantic comedy 'Falling Short', a married couple and their best friend played, respectively, husband, wife and mistress, only to reveal some time later (in the *News of the World* and the *Daily Mail*, in the course of Helmsley's notorious 'naughty vicar' scandal) that this was also precisely their arrangement in real life. The fact that most of the audience was aware of the possibility that this was so made it all the more titillating as an evening out.

But, returning to the boards for the first time since *Charley's Aunt* in 1971, I was preoccupied with my own part as a whisky-sodden Scottish publisher. I had the specs, the pipe and the accent ('your Dr Finlay impersonation', one of the serious drama types remarked with a curling lip), but did I have the character? It helped, oddly, to be told to act with my feet: smaller, prissier steps brought the literary fusspot closer to the surface.

On we went to *The Wind in the Willows*, a big production (lots of scaffolding, lots of children) to celebrate the reopening of our theatre after Lottery-funded rebuilding. Playing Mole requires rather less Zen Buddhist inner exploration, and rather more crawling around on the floor and not caring how stupid you look in a false nose and a velvet waistcoat.

'In yer element, eh?' growled our local grandee, Lord Feversham, looking me up and down as he arrived for his walk-on part as Toad's butler. 'All over the local paper again, I see.' But he enjoyed the curtain calls along with the rest of us. Everyone likes to step into the spotlight once in a while.

And what about the acting? Have we mastered the mysterious art yet? My next effort was Laurence the estate agent in *Abigail's Party*, Mike Leigh's savage assault on 1970s suburbia. It is wickedly funny, not a nice play: when it was first developed by Leigh through improvisation, the actors seem to have been working out their contempt for their own petty-bourgeois parents. The characters are unredeemed, and long discussions of their motivation made for uncomfortable rehearsals. 'Am I impotent?' I found myself asking the girl playing Beverly, the wife from hell. 'Bigger, Martin, bigger,' the director kept urging, though at least he didn't call me 'love'. 'This is as big as it gets,' was my feeble reply.

I hated the whole thing, really. I couldn't wait for my death scene every night. 'You sad bastard, Laurence,' I kept saying to myself. But I said it so often that in the end I did the job properly: I got a bit bigger, and I almost played him as a real person, or so one or two of the serious drama types told me. 'You were actually acting,' one of them said with undisguised astonishment.

Now and then in mid-performance, and watching it afterwards on video, I had a glimmer of what the difference might be. No doubt I shall be back on stage soon: though as a dedicated amateur I'll try not to let serious acting get in the way of a good show.

Daily Telegraph, *June 1998*

———— ✻ ————

SO MUCH FUN WE BUILT IT TWICE

It was Groundhog Day in Helmsley last week. We first opened an arts centre in the former Quaker meeting house of our small North Yorkshire market town back in 1993. We opened it again in 1996 after a remodelling paid for by a Lottery grant. And it was opened for a third time on Friday, having been rebuilt once more after a devastating fire last August. As its long-serving part-time director I even repeated the same speech, pointing out that the consolation of this unlooked-for moment of déjà vu was an opportunity to reinsert a paragraph of thanks to the architect, which I had forgotten last time.

Having finally uttered the full text, I told the audience, 'I hope I never have to make this speech again. So we've cancelled the fireworks and hidden the ashtrays.' And I concluded with my new slogan: 'Helmsley Arts Centre: so much fun we built it twice.'

But in reality, recovering from a catastrophic fire – even one in which no one was hurt and no one's home was destroyed – is a stressful experience. Readers of previous despatches from Helmsley may recall that our project was not one of those Lottery-funded mini-Domes of municipal egotism which now stand unloved in so many English cities. On the contrary, it is the cherished product of the imagination and effort of a group of diehard volunteers, each of whom feels a powerful sense of ownership. As one regional arts official said to me recently, it is 'extra-ordinary, especially in a place like Helmsley' which has a population of 1,500 plus a hinterland of scattered farming villages. On a miniature scale, it is a model of institution-building and active citizenship.

Not surprisingly emotions ran high and tears were shed, both in the aftermath of the fire and as the brass band and the primary school choir launched the reopening cabaret. Also on stage was the Helmsley fire brigade, heroes of the blaze. Invited to perform 'the full monty', they sensibly opted instead to be interviewed about the fire, somewhat in the style of *Tonight with Trevor McDonald*. Having been absent on the night – and awoken in a French hotel room by one of those early-morning phone calls which only ever signal death or disaster – I was gripped by Sub-officer Paterson's narrative. The fire had started, no one knows how, in a neighbour's semi-derelict shed, and travelled rapidly upwards into our eaves. The town postmaster, letting his dog out for a last run, had seen the flames and made the emergency call.

Paterson recalled how the fire exploded through the cupola of the arts centre as his fire-engine arrived on site minutes later. Having smashed his way in with a two-handed axe, he stood momentarily listening to the roar of the fire in the roof space above, until stage lanterns started crashing to the floor around him. His men saved the piano and the paintings, but by the time the last embers were extinguished the following afternoon, almost everything else – including the cast-iron 1950s cinema projector, every seat in the auditorium and the entire roof structure – had been ruined or destroyed.

What happened next was an example of what the much-misused word 'community' really means, and of just how insensitive large companies and arms of the state can be in dealing with people hit by misfortune. Locally, everyone wanted to help. Though the building was well insured, the contents were not ('That's always the way,' dozens of wise people subsequently told me) and we needed cash to replace them. First in line were the firemen, some of whose children take part in our youth theatre group; within a fortnight they had raised £750. The newsagent added £600 with a £1-a-go quiz sheet. The secondary school raised £525; the toy shop gave a giant teddy bear. Artists gave pictures to be auctioned, musicians performed for free. Owners of nearby stately homes offered venues for our orphaned programme. Several members of our audience quietly wrote four-figure personal cheques.

This wave of generosity encouraged us to press on, and there were morale-boosting highlights of the winter: a production of *The Magic Flute* in the eighteenth-century riding school of Hovingham Hall; an evening in a hotel bar with the poet Simon Armitage; a Christmas choral workshop in the church with Simon Halsey from the City of Birmingham Symphony Chorus. But all the time, out of sight of the audience, there was another layer of activity making huge demands on our resilience: the world of distant officialdom and corporate bureaucracy was not joining in the singing and giving. It was easy to see why those whose misfortunes are more devastating than ours – farmers whose healthy herds have been culled, families flooded out of their homes twice in eighteen months – believe that no one listens to the little people in a system that is loaded against them.

Try telling HM Revenue & Customs that your VAT return is delayed because your files are a sodden mess and your computer looks like a giant plastic Welsh rarebit. Try telling a British Gas call centre that your meter readings have been confused by the fire, that the final demand cannot possibly be correct, and that the threat of a police warrant to gain access to cut the gas off on the eve of reopening is an outrage. You may ring ten times and receive ten insincere apologies from different operators reading from the same script; but you can never speak to a manager, and you are more than likely to receive another copy of the same demand the next day.

Elsewhere, an Arts Council lady from London got in touch, in sympathetic tones, to find out what had happened. Does this mean the Council has some funds available to help arts venues stricken by acts of God? I asked. Gosh no, came the reply; we just wanted to check, 'for compliance', that what you built with your Lottery grant was properly insured. As for the insurers, they declined to renew our policy, leaving us scrambling for replacement cover with days to go before the brass band arrived.

Finally the bank where we have kept accounts in good order for the past decade started bouncing large cheques to our building contractors on the grounds that no customer categorised under 'clubs and societies' can ever go overdrawn, even for a day, even if it holds more than enough funds in a parallel account. When I asked the branch supervisor for the name of the manager who had taken this decision, throwing the most prominent charitable project in the district into serious financial embarrassment, she looked nonplussed. The decision came from 'Operational Support' in Leeds, she said; she did not know the name of the person in charge. I can't remember when I was last so enraged.

But it did not matter much in the end. We're back in business, and the life of our little institution has resumed as if it had never been taken away, perhaps strengthened by adversity. I'm even back on stage myself, rehearsing the furiously angry Mort in an amateur production of Neil Simon's *California Suite*. At least I can draw on recent experience to think myself into the part.

April 2001

— ❈ —

NOT STRICTLY PANTO

My friend Robin, a retired financier, is a fine comic actor but he'd be the first to admit he has a problem with lines. He bursts on to the stage in a huge grey wig and launches into an anarchic approximation of his part as the Magistrate at Calcutta in *Around the World in Eighty Days* – my adaption of Jules Verne's classic, and this year's Christmas show at Helmsley Arts Centre in Yorkshire.

Robin is off piste from start to finish, but with gusto and style. The sentences he imposes on Phileas Fogg and Passepartout (for the latter's failure to remove his hat and shoes in the pagoda on Malabar Hill, you may recall) are rarely the sentences, in either sense, that Verne or I wrote. They vary from one rehearsal to the next, and the other actors just have to follow as best they can. By the time the Magistrate leads them off in an unruly conga at the end of the scene, the director – that's me – is laughing so much it seems pointless to make them do it again.

This is amateur theatre at its most hilarious. The cast includes the vicar, the window cleaner and a lady who breeds pigs. Three generations of the same family form the backbone of the backstage crew. If you think I sound like Linda Snell, I can tell you that the real thing is vastly more entertaining as a pastime – almost narcotically so – than anything you've ever heard on *The Archers*.

Christmas shows in Ambridge or Helmsley are about the taking part, rather than the winning of drama awards. I'm a last-minute learner of lines myself, so I'm tolerant of actors clutching their books at the dress rehearsal. But in the end everyone wants to do the thing as well as they can – and don't think the pantomime genre is easy for amateurs, by the way, because it's not, as I found out as one of Cinderella's Ugly Sisters. Whacking doughballs into the audience with a giant wooden spoon while warbling Irving Berlin's 'There were never such devoted sisters' in drag struck me as a lot more difficult than Pinter or Chekhov, which just require a straight face and a high threshold of boredom.

My version of *Eighty Days* is not what you'd call strictly panto – and it has an elaborate narrative about the robbery of which Fogg is suspected and his bet at the Reform Club that he can circumnavigate the globe in time. But it has panto elements – plenty of 'It's behind you!' and audience singalong. And it will be playing to families with children who have never heard of Jules Verne and his nineteenth-century fantasy adventure: at best they might have seen Steve Coogan's atrocious 2004 film version.

So as well as telling a complicated story, the cast have to connect with an audience that may not be getting what it expected – and that includes many of their own nearest and dearest. In a small theatre, in a small town, the proximity of people you know in the front rows is hugely offputting for actors: I was once lowering my bulk gingerly on to a tiny folding stool at the front of the stage during a picnic scene in Ayckbourn's *Sisterly Feelings* when I heard my own mother, 5 feet away, hiss, 'He's not going to sit on that, is he?'

My cast will have to ignore whispering relatives, play off each other's mistakes, fill each other's silences, and all the while try to obey Noël Coward's basic instruction to all actors: 'Speak clearly and don't bump into the furniture.' It was always going to be a compromise between what the director first imagined and what's humanly possible on the basis of two rehearsals a week, a small budget, and the favours that can be called in from neighbours with handicraft skills. Ideas have to be jettisoned if they can't be done, and some of the best lines never get delivered at all.

But it's amazing what can be conjured up. We have dancing temple maidens and singing Reform Club members. A retired naval officer and his wife constructed a magnificent four-seater elephant and a retired colonel created a slide sequence of the transatlantic steamer *Henrietta* gradually disappearing when Fogg orders the woodwork to be fed into the furnaces to keep her speed up.

With a week to curtain up the scenery is wobbling, the actors are flagging and my temper is fraying. But against the odds, like Phileas Fogg and his companions, we shall reach our destination in the nick of time.

December 2011

AN INCIDENT WITH WILLARD

The best thing about being chairman of the local music festival is that so many interesting visitors come to drink or to stay in my house: last year's star guest was Willard White, the great Jamaican-born bass. He was excellent company, once we had recovered from an incident outside York Station in which a passing tourist – rebuked by Willard for lifting a boisterous child into the air, painfully, by one arm – shaped up to punch him. Fortunately, Willard is even more imposing in person than he is on stage in his Paul Robeson show. He took a step forwards and repeated, in an impossibly low growl, 'Be very careful with that arm.' The miscreant stepped back, fear in his eyes, while his wife tugged his sleeve and said, 'Leave it' – saving York from what would doubtless have been reported as a shameful racial incident.

March 2002

———✹———

PICNIC INTERVAL

A useful tip on dining at the expense of the corporate *crème de la crème*, acquired from a talkative stranger in the buffet car en route to York. His girlfriend, he said, wanted him to take her to Glyndebourne for her birthday; no tickets were available and he could not have afforded them anyway, but they dressed up and drove into the car park just before the interval, splashed out on a glass of champagne and mingled with plutocrats until the second half began. Our birthday couple then selected the most opulent unfinished picnic on the lawn, tucked into raspberries and cream, a full cheeseboard and a ripe Burgundy, and departed before the final curtain, leaving an anonymous note of thanks. That's what I call free enterprise.

September 2005

———✹———

VIRTUOUS PEASANTS

This year being the bicentenary of the death of Haydn, I spent the weekend in wig and tights, impersonating the great composer as the narrator of a concert performance of his opera *Philemon und Baucis* in our joyful Ryedale music festival. There aren't many jokes in this tale of virtue rewarded by the gods, but I got a laugh when I explained, in what I imagined to be an Austro-Hungarian accent, why our fine young soloists Daniel Turner and Louise Lloyd were about to double up both as the honest Phrygian peasants Philemon and Baucis and as their dead son and daughter-in-law, Aret and Narcissa, whom Jupiter brings back to life midway through the show. 'Vell, zis is not ze palace of Esterhaza,' I explained. 'Zis is your liddle festival in ze middle of ze economische crisis.' Here in Yorkshire, whether it's low-budget opera* or a picnic at the local agricultural show, we still know how to enjoy ourselves whatever ill-fortune the gods may send to punish the sins of our City cousins.

July 2009

—✳—

YOUR OWN, YOUR VERY OWN ...

I'm on stage this week, as Master of Ceremonies of the Christmas Olde Time Music Hall. This requires a recreation of the elaborate, alliterative verbosity of the late Leonard Sachs, who would have been 100 this year and whose weekly show from Leeds City Varieties, *The*

---

* Opera buffs will know that *Philemon und Baucis* was, in fact, written for marionettes with the singers offstage, but our festival could not afford to book the only puppet theatre company in Europe which performs it, hence my hammed-up Haydn impersonation instead.

Good Old Days, disappeared from our television screens in 1983 – though his persona remains engrained on the collective memory. The role also requires lively repartee with the audience. I've tried a variant of what I believe is an old Ralph Richardson gag: 'Ladies and gentlemen, is there a doctor in the house? Ah, thank you, doctor: tell me, what's your prescription for this show? Should we put it out of its misery, or give it another massive injection of laughing gas!' But I got the biggest cheer for introducing an extra item with: 'Ladies and gentlemen, is there a banker in the house? Ah, thank you, sir: have we got a bonus for you! And they can't tax you for it!' Believe me, it's all in the comic delivery.

December 2009

— ✳ —

DAZZLING DELUSION

I did not rush to see *Enron* when it first opened in London because I feared it might be another tiresome anti-capitalist rant in the mode of *Serious Money*, Caryl Churchill's verse play that castigated the boom-time bankers and traders (who perversely adopted it as cult entertainment) at the Royal Court back in 1987. But I finally caught up with Lucy Prebble's dramatisation of the rise and fall of the Texan energy giant at the Noël Coward Theatre last week, and found myself admiring it enormously, both for the dazzling theatricality of the staging and for the way Prebble tells her complex story in human rather than ideological terms. It's all about what went on inside the minds of Enron chairman Ken Lay, his chief executive Jeff Skilling and their finance wizard Andy Fastow, as they turned an old-style oil-and-gas business into a monstrous fabrication of hidden liabilities, false accounting, fake profits and high-flown corporate rhetoric that fooled everyone, themselves included, until the moment of its collapse in 2001.

'I decided there's no point in writing a drama where you condemn everybody and say, "Isn't making money bad",' Prebble told an interviewer. Curiously, as I left the theatre, I overheard a young banker type complaining to his girlfriend that the show was just another indiscriminate attack on everybody in the financial world. But City boys are over-sensitive these days, and he was quite wrong. As Lucy Prebble has also said, *Enron* is about 'the delusion that goes on in all of us'.

April 2010

— ✳ —

GRAND FINALE

To Garsington for the last performance by the opera company created by the banker Leonard Ingrams in his Oxfordshire garden. Five years after his death, the project is moving to a new site on the Getty estate at Wormsley in the Chilterns, a few miles away. It's a fine night – unlike past evenings here when rain swirled through the open side of the stage and the cognoscenti wore wellies under evening dress. A joyful performance of *The Marriage of Figaro*, and a final appearance on stage by Ingrams' widow Rosalind, provoke a standing ovation from a crowd which turns out to include, in separate parties, no less than four of my former City bosses. South Oxfordshire is densely populated with financiers, and there's an overpowering scent of wealth which some might find offensive in the mood of today – a scent that will now have to be distilled into £3 million-plus to pay for the proposed opera pavilion at Wormsley.

Does building a private opera house count as philanthropy? It's not quite the same as Warren Buffett giving $1.6 billion (as he did last week) to Bill and Melinda Gates's foundation for health projects in Africa. But speaking as a trustee of a music college and an opera company, both heavily state funded, I'm all for it: it will generate work for singers and orchestral players, and enthusiasm for the genre, which will help them and it survive the age of austerity. Henry Tate liked pictures, so he endowed a great gallery; if you like opera, build an opera house. Philanthropy works best if lots of people do it in different ways: if you're lucky enough or smart enough to have made money in the boom, put it to a use that interests you. The worst thing you can do now is just sit on it.

July 2010

—✳—

DOWN WITH THE RAPPERS

I've been down with the local rappers this week, and we've been giving each other a lot of respect. A teenage crew from a Scarborough hip-hop project came to take part in the Ryedale Festival Community Opera, *Odyssey* – I was playing Zeus, king of the Gods – and it was fascinating to watch them become absorbed in and uplifted by a musical project that was so far removed from their own apparently troubled life experience. If this sounds a bit like Gareth Malone's increasingly predictable singing-can-change-your-life reality television format, it was. But that doesn't diminish the potency of collective performance as a way of applying a little low-cost glue to the broken society. This kind of activity is generally funded by droplets of Arts Council money, plus local business sponsorship – but if it had been paid for solely by taxpayers of Ryedale District, *Odyssey* would have cost them just under a pound per household. Value for money? It's easy to picture a chorus of disgruntled Yorkshire citizens singing, 'What? You want us to pay for an assortment of eighty kids and misfits wafting around as sea-nymphs and ancient Greek sailors in the name of social inclusion? That can bloody well go for a start.' But my rapper friends and I think they'd be wrong.

July 2010

SAVAGE CUT

At Opera North, of which I'm a trustee, we're proud of this season's production of *Norma* with Annemarie Kremer in the title role. Audiences have been intrigued by director Christopher Alden's updating of Bellini's action from Roman-occupied Gaul to what appears to be rural nineteenth-century America, where a primitive sect is oppressed by top-hatted capitalists. But I wonder whether – appropriate to a show touring from Leeds to Nottingham, Salford and Newcastle – he also had in mind the passage in J. B. Priestley's *English Journey* (1933) about the City of London doing to the northern working classes 'what the black-moustached glossy gentleman in the old melodramas always did to the innocent maiden'. No doubt we're in for a wave of financial-crisis metaphors on the opera stage, but none more vivid than the moment when Roman-banker Flavio is castrated with a druid's sickle. That must be almost as painful as having your bonuses clawed back.

February 2012

———— ❋ ————

REFLECTIONS ON THE TYNE

Coming out of a sublime Opera North performance of *Fidelio* at the Sage Gateshead – in a heightened emotional state induced by the ecstatic finale, no doubt – I was moved by the sight of the Tyne at dusk. The Sage, the Baltic Centre and the Millennium Bridge (lit in changing colours) were all opened in the early years of the last decade, completing a transformation of Newcastle and Gateshead that can be traced from the opening of the Metrocentre retail park in 1986 via the revival of Newcastle United football club in the mid 1990s – both the work of Sir John Hall – to the erection of Antony Gormley's *Angel of the North* in 1998.

Sceptics will say much of the regeneration was state-funded folly, or morally worse, paid for by National Lottery scratchcards, and that it barely touched the deprivation beyond the showpieces. But that ignores a widespread revival of Geordie *joie de vivre* – at ten o'clock on a Saturday night you can hear waves of it drifting across the river – and the importance to the process of what Hall himself, a Northumbrian miner's son, once called 'capitalism with a conscience' rooted in regional pride. The name Sage has become so inseparable from the Foster-designed concert hall that most people have forgotten it belongs to a local software company, founded by Sunderland printer David Goldman and Newcastle student Graham Wylie, which became a global success and donated £6 million to complete the project.

These days – as seems to be confirmed by tales of the private-equity fortunes extracted from Southern Cross, the collapsing care homes group – we have a surfeit of capitalism without a conscience. Which cityscapes of 2030 will bring a tear to the eye as we give thanks to the moneymen of today for their generosity and vision?

June 2011

———✻———

AT LEAST THEY LAUGHED AT THE SNOW

As moments of tension go, waiting for the reaction of a first-night audience to your first play comes high of the scale. Nothing in my journalistic career compares, not even the morning the *Daily Telegraph* published an obituary I had written of a man who turned out not to be dead. 'Hello, I'm the author,' I whispered to the woman next to me as the lights went down. 'Just thought I'd warn you, in case I pass out.'

The play is called *Talent Night*. I described it in the publicity as 'a sharp-edged comedy about coming to terms with your own failings'. '... And your limitations as a writer,' I might have added. It's the story of a group of characters stuck in a remote Yorkshire pub in a blizzard. The landlady has advertised a talent contest in a desperate bid to drum up trade. But the only contestants who get through are an exotic dancer and a poet – followed by the protagonists in a Balkan peace negotiation, who are heading for a secret location nearby but are also caught by the snow.

Confusion ensues, out of which the cheerful publican conjures a settlement for the strife-torn Balkan republic and a romance with the failed British politician in charge of the peace talks, Sir Hector Clapham. The talent contest is won by the sexy Balkan lady president, Marja Slavica, and the handsome rebel leader, Colonel Hradko, former enemies who dance their way to a heart-warming finale. Put so briefly, it sounds like a pretty neat idea. I wrote the bones of it in one short burst, then added a gag a day for months afterwards. I took advice from an award-winning playwright, James Robson, who told me to add some younger characters: so I gave birth to the dancer and the poet. It gradually evolved into a rich theatrical cocktail incorporating an Abba dance number, a rap against American imperialism and a pantomime sing-along. If I could have worked in a headless ghost as well, I probably would have done.

That, of course, is the joy of playwriting. You dream up a set of characters and they dance across the stage of your imagination in perfect formation. You write a joke and no matter how many times you read it, it still makes you chuckle. But start rehearsing with an amateur company – especially if, like me, you have never written for the stage before – and the piece suddenly mutates into a lumbering, leaden-voiced monster. If all goes well it then mutates again, somewhere between the dress rehearsal and the last night of the run, into the show you first saw in your head.

Most first-time playwrights are saved this exquisite agony because their work never actually reaches the stage. In my case, however, *Talent Night* was almost guaranteed a world premiere because I had offered it to Helmsley Arts Centre, the venue which I have helped run for the past ten years, and its resident drama group. That made it an easy decision for my colleagues, but a heavy responsibility for me – all the more so because, in our small-town setting, the entire regular audience consists of my neighbours and acquaintances.

But the challenge of eventually facing an audience paled beside the immediate problem of making the play work in rehearsal. For the last half-hour all eleven characters are on stage, though only two or three are engaged in the central dialogue. That looked terribly untidy, while my exposition of the Balkan conflict turned out to be far too wordy. Happily, Dan Armour – a professional actor often seen in gritty television roles – offered to help direct. He produced wonders of stagecraft to tidy up the tableaux and make the most of the jokes.

The cast responded eagerly, the characters taking on lives of their own. Less happily for me, Dan was brutally frank about my writing. 'This bit's incredibly turgid,' he said of an admittedly lengthy exchange of accusations between the president and the rebel leader, 'but there's got to be a gag in it somewhere.'

As the opening night galloped towards us, Easter holidays intervened. For a vital fortnight, we could not assemble a full cast. In true am-dram tradition, several actors still had their books in their hands. Tempers frayed. I became haunted by the fear that 500 of my closest friends (we had almost sold out for the four-night run) were about to witness a humiliating flop.

But of course – also in true am-dram tradition – we pulled it together for the first night. Well, nearly. Some of the sound effects went AWOL; the poet missed one entrance altogether; and the politician dried up at the beginning of his longest speech, paused while the landlady ad-libbed suggestions as to how he might continue, then stormed to a big finish having omitted a page and a half of my text. By then, however, I was barely watching the stage: I was hypnotised by the audience's reactions.

The first scene involved falling snow – actually detergent foam – and drifts suggested by rumpled sheets of white material. I thought it looked great, but when the scene ended and the sheets were pulled off like the train of a wedding dress, the audience roared with laughter. From then until the interval, they barely uttered a sound. Only the words 'pork scratchings', 'spanking' and 'Hull' elicited a titter – though not from a somnolent party of church luncheon club ladies. In the bar at the interval the crowd seemed subdued, several complaining about the heat in the auditorium. As we returned to our seats for the second half, the woman next to me avoided my eye. 'If I pass out now, just leave me alone,' I thought, 'It'll be a welcome release.'

But fresh air and a drink had perked them up; they got almost all the jokes in the second half, and they sang the song at the end. The critic of the *Yorkshire Evening Press*, Robert Beaumont, declared it 'hugely enjoyable', and the audiences for the second and third night seemed to agree with him.

With one night to go, I was beginning to think I might be Ayckbourn's heir-apparent, only to be flattened again by a quiet Saturday audience and a selection of embarrassed comments over the next few days, from which I particularly treasure: 'What are you going to write next, Martin? Perhaps a comedy?' Perhaps indeed, but not with fake snow, or eleven people on stage at the same time. And I'll try it out first as far away as possible from my own home town.

April 2003

—✳—

TALENT NIGHT

Here's a short extract from Talent Night, *the play described in the preceding article – which was commissioned by a Sunday paper but never published, the arts editor having deployed one of those killer phrases used on such occasions: 'It's such a comfort to know I've got an excellent piece in reserve when I need it.'*

This is the moment when the politician Sir Hector Clapham decides to enter into the spirit of the pub talent contest by telling a joke much used by real politicians, and, indeed, by me, in after-dinner speeches...

KEN *(a cantankerous local)*: Stand-up, sit-down, dun't matter, bet you a fiver none of them can get a laugh out of me. Quizzes is what I like. Try me on presidents of t'United States ... I won every time at t'Fox and Hounds 'til they banned me ...

CLAPHAM *(sitting on a bar stool like a nightclub comedian)*: ... which reminds me of a funny story ...

KEN: Well, if he's going to start doing comedy, the bet's on. *He* definitely won't get a laugh out of me.

CLAPHAM: ...about a great banquet in the former imperial palace at Zbog in the old days, the era of President Slavic's unlamented predecessor, with all the leaders of the old communist bloc, President Brezhnev from Moscow, Erich Honecker from East Germany, President Ceaușescu from Romania and so on ...

MARJA SLAVICA: Is not so funny story.

COLONEL HRADKO: I think funny, maybe.

CLAPHAM *(picking up a fork from his paella plate)*: ... and in the middle of the banquet, Brezhnev happens to look along the vast table and see Honecker quietly picking up a fork and slipping it into his inside pocket. So he wonders why, and he picks up his own fork and looks at it and realises it's solid gold, priceless, the Imperial cutlery of the old Hapsburg emperors, and he thinks, 'I'll have some of that too.' So he moves the fork towards his pocket, but in doing so he accidentally taps his glass ... *(Taps glass, making a ringing sound.)* And because he's Brezhnev, the whole banquet of 500 people immediately falls silent and looks at him, expecting a speech. For a moment Brezhnev doesn't know what to do, but then he says: 'Tonight is a wonderful occasion. But tonight is not a night for speeches. No, tonight ... tonight is a night for magic. So magically I will make this fork disappear *(slips fork into his inside pocket)* and now I will make it reappear from the pocket of Comrade Honecker ...'

KEN *(huge guffaw, slapping crumpled fiver on the bar)*: Oh bugger, lost mi' bet.

HRADKO: Is extremely funny!

SLAVICA: Is quite funny ... maybe.

All the girls I should have married

Whatever happened to the Belgian fox
Whose pillow talk was lessons
In the language of my Flemish roots
But all I now recall is one short phrase
That asks the hour of day or night
'*Hoe laat is het?*': 'How late is it?'
And one day when I tried it out
She answered not 'It's half past four'
Or as I'd hoped, 'It's nooky time'
But grabbed her coat and from the door
Threw back: 'Too late – for you –
My German lover's outside in his Porsche'
And as she left taught one last word
Guttural, Flemish '*Vaarwal*': adieu

Whatever happened to Miss Takahashi
Who kept me company in Tokyo
For a year or so and took me once
To meet her uncle in distant suburban
Neon steakhouse cum wedding bower
Where couples had their pictures posed
And so did we, it's in my album still
Though uncle clearly thought I wasn't quite
Suitable as his sweet niece's Mr Right
'This fat foreigner' he growled in Japanese
He didn't know I knew, 'Must drink like a fish'
I worried too when I saw that photograph
Heard her plan to study English over here
Forgot to tell her I was moving to Hong Kong

Whatever happened to the English rose
The whole catalogue of roses, if I'm frank

Of ambitious, well-groomed graduate girls
Intent on serious, well-planned lives
With well-heeled, well-mannered men
Decent prospects, solid breeding stock
And if one by one those roses let me know
I had not passed that examination
I'd have to say, *je ne regrette rien*
The single life has ample compensation
I see them now, fine grandmothers-to-be
The way they sometimes glance at me
And hear again that little phrase: How late is it?
Too late to catch you next time round?

CHAPTER 10

Real Life

THE BACHELOR'S GUIDE

Bachelor living is an art. Even if you think of your own bachelorhood as a temporary twist of fate right up until the moment when your obituarist starts weighing the nuances of 'confirmed' and 'life-long', or if you are merely observing a short pause between third and fourth wives, it is an art worth mastering.

I have been studying it for a mere fifteen years (and on a purely temporary basis, of course), but I think I am beginning to grasp the essential rules. First, you should be completely comfortable at all times. Secondly, having reached that state, you should maintain it with a minimum of effort on your own part, on the principle that time spent on yourself is essentially time wasted.

Thirdly, you should fine-tune your presentation to the outside world in order to provoke just the right mixture of admiration and hospitable sympathy. You should not be so fastidious as to frighten people, not so chaotic as to encourage homely girls to want to mother you, not so set in your ways as to suggest that marriage is out of the question. You should display at least enough self-indulgence to let the world know that wifelessness has its compensations, but not so much as to reduce your life expectancy.

In short the third rule, as with Zen archery, is to make it look easy, but not too easy. Here, for those seeking this perfect balance, is the bachelor's alphabet.

A is for Accommodation, which has to be right before anything else. A proper bachelor home has lots of space, unlike the sort of quarters which might fit that outmoded description 'bachelor pad'. You need a library, with a log fire. You may want a room entirely filled with synthesiser keyboard equipment and bass woofers; another for hanging game; one for storing your collection of Napoleonic memorabilia, motor-cycle parts, model railways or (let's be broad-minded) cocktail dresses; yet another where you stop for a last whisky on the way to bed. Ex-army bachelors often like to have a room entirely devoted to shoe-cleaning, although the rest of us regard this as stretching the minimum-effort rule. As to bedrooms, remember that they don't need cleaning or heating until someone is about to occupy them, and the last thing you want is guests on camp-beds in the library: so have plenty.

B is for Blind Dates, not advisable for anyone over eighteen – although many desiccated singles secretly long to appear in the televised version.

C is for Clubland. The ideal club for bachelors is Pratt's, a basement with one long dining-table. The menu consists entirely of variants of mixed grill, all the staff are addressed as George, except the lady book-keeper who is addressed as Georgina, and leading nonagenarian bachelor Monsignor Alfred Gilbey is a regular diner.

D is for Dogs. Bachelors' dogs are eccentric, have their own armchairs, and lie around making terrible smells. The late chairman of Britoil, Sir Philip Shelbourne, a lifelong bachelor, kept a mongrel called Brit in his office, fed on a diet of expensive chocolates. Bachelors' dogs are also never more than semi-trained, except for comical tricks. I tried to teach mine to take videos back to the village hire-shop, but it has moved 6 miles away and the distance has so far defeated him.

E is for Entertaining. If you attempt it at home, keep it simple, keep the booze flowing and try for an element of surprise – one friend of mine with an oversized bath in the middle of his Docklands studio likes to throw guests into it before the cheese course. Another, an expatriate manager, realised belatedly that corporate convention required him to entertain visiting grandees to dinner at home. Sitting them down to a first course of ungarnished smoked salmon, he picked up the telephone and ordered the rest of the meal from Domino's Pizza. 'What *fun*,' the chairman's wife gushed. 'How terribly *clever* of you.'

F is for Furniture. Large, club-like, dog-friendly armchairs are essential. A useful DIY tip: if your last wife took all the rest with her, elegant, adaptable tables and desks can be made out of cases of claret and sheets of plate glass.

G is for Godchildren, who tend to accumulate. Most godfathers are hopeless at remembering birthdays. I am often told that the solution is to give all seven of mine presents on my own birthday, but easier still is just to wait until they are old enough to be given *Spectator* subscriptions.

H is for Housekeepers and cleaning ladies, who come in two types. There are those who work for the kind of married women who can't resist offering advice to bachelors: this category is invariably lazy, flirtatious, incompetent and prone to stealing teaspoons. Then there are those who actually work for bachelors: reliable, discreet, worldly wise and unfazed by burglar-alarm codes. I have proved this theory five times in a row, with five different nationalities. When I went to live in Kuala Lumpur in the mid eighties, the crone in the local shop recommended a Chinese maid who arrived dressed as though for an embassy reception. A married friend berated me severely: I was paying too much per hour, I would be seduced and robbed within days, I was a bachelor fool; just look at the trouble she herself had with the succession of village girls she employed, dishonest, stupid and frequently pregnant. But mine turned out to be impeccable and cooked delicious coconut curries into the bargain.

I is for Inspector Morse, a more appealing model of self-sufficient bachelorhood than the other obvious candidate, Sir Edward Heath.

J is for Jogging, out of the question.

K is for the Kitchen, where we want nothing too fancy. All bachelors should learn to cook, but not how to carve tomatoes into decorative roses. When cooking for yourself, a meal should (under Rule 2) take no longer to prepare than to eat – not easy to achieve except by frenzied stir-frying which can have unpredictable results. But the alternative, instant packaged food, is an admission of defeat. I once knew a hopeless fellow who lived on Bird's Eye Cook-In-The-Bag Cod in Prawn Sauce; perhaps even at this moment he is reheating a Tesco Chicken Tikka Masala with Onion Bhaji. As to kitchen equipment, a microwave is (shameful to admit) a lot more useful than an Aga, except for warming spaniels.

L is for Lodgers. The true bachelor relishes living on his own. He who fills his spare bedrooms with female lodgers is either crippled by Lloyd's losses or in desperate want of a wife. 'The trouble with girls,' one pompous lawyer told me, bragging about his spacious Knightsbridge mews house, 'is that they always leave their knickers in the bathroom.' 'I say!' A more modest chap in the party perked up, 'D'you mean on arrival?'

M is for Mail Order. Bachelors hate shopping, except for cheese and second-hand books (see Supermarkets). The solution to most problems (including, as it were, the ones best concealed in plain brown-paper covers) is mail order. A few plugs seem permissible here: all the clothing that does not come from your very cheap tailor in Hong Kong can be had from the Boden catalogue. Curtains can be obtained painlessly by post in thirty shades of velvet from a company called Econermine in Coningsby, Lincolnshire. Leather-bound albums from Lydden in Blandford Forum are an instant solution to every wedding present.

N is for Never, as in Somerset Maugham's dictum: 'Never do for yourself what you can pay another to do for you.' On this principle, you should never iron a shirt or sew on a button, although you should know how to do so effortlessly if the need arises, and never wash up. Never master anything more than the most basic 'programme' on your washing machine, and if weekend guests ask to make use of it, pretend not to know which room it is in. In similar vein, practise using the possessive pronoun in relation to occasional helpers and trades-people, as in 'my interior decorator', 'my Japanese gardener' and 'my Indian take-away chappie'.

O is for Oxbridge Dons, past masters of civilised bachelor living.

P is for most Popes, ditto.

Q is for Quiche, which we neither cook nor eat. We also never eat polyunsaturated margarine spread. We slap butter on everything, and plenty of salt.

R is for Recipe Books. Bachelors rarely follow recipes, but an occasional reference is useful. Delia Smith's *One is Fun!* is too embarrassingly titled to have on display in your kitchen. Jennifer Paterson's *Feast Days* is much more suitable, as are the slim volumes on fish-cookery and barbecue techniques by convivial television chef Keith Floyd. *The Gentleman Cook* (a compilation in aid of Distressed Gentlefolk) provides the definitive bachelor dish, submitted by a Mr Gurney of Norfolk: 'Take two pheasant legs, already cooked. Slash with sharp knife and spread with strong English mustard. Wrap in bacon and fry vigorously.'

S is for Supermarkets. The final ignominy is to be spotted leaving one of those late-night places with a single, telltale plastic carrier-bag which might as well say 'Lonesome Supper' in big letters on the side. The only way to deal with supermarkets is to go once a quarter to an out-of-town superstore and buy a huge quantity of basic requirements, steering your trolley against the general flow of traffic with a look of utter bemuse-ment on your face.

T is for Terracotta, tobacco pink, oxblood red and, in rare cases, matt black – the sort of colours bachelors like to paint their libraries.

U is for You, or rather me, me, me. Bachelorhood is a fundamentally selfish state, and would not be much fun if it wasn't.

V is for Venus, goddess of love, whose unpredictable call may interrupt the bachelor idyll at any moment. Beware.

W is for Will-making, an activity which offers may hours of harmless fun and mischief for bachelors without offspring.

X is for Ex-wives, of which some bachelors have several. I defer to Jeffrey Bernard on this one.

Y is for Yachts, racehorses, apartments in Val d'Isère, minor Post-Impressionists and all the other luxuries you can convince yourself that you might one day be able to buy with the money you might otherwise have spent on school fees.

Z is for the snooze in the library after a lunch of mustard-fried pheasant legs and claret, man and dog in their respective armchairs by the roaring fire, one of the simple consolations of bachelor life.

December 1993

———※———

TIME-TRAVELLING ON THE NORTHERN LINE

I'm standing on a hot platform at Tottenham Court Road, waiting for the relief of the momentary breeze that precedes an approaching train. I'm staring at a T-Mobile poster featuring people dressed as nuns at what looks like a karaoke party. And I'm thinking: do I really want to write another essay about the imagined pain of cuts to come, or the right way to regulate banks, or the prospects for growth in 2013–14? And more important, in a heatwave and a mood of post-World Cup gloom,* do you really want to read one? Then the air moves, the train rattles in, and I see that it's bound for the High Barnet terminus of the

---

* England had failed to reach the quarter-finals in South Africa.

Northern Line. And my mission for this week comes to me: I must find the Stone Parlour.

This will take a bit of explaining, but bear with me. Every family has a private vocabulary, and in mine a 'Stone Parlour' is a place of enforced contemplation. Thus if my dog Douglas misbehaves when we visit my mother – chases her cat up the stairs, for example – he is ordered into the Stone Parlour, which means he is shut in the porch until his hang-dog expression suggests that he's ready to repent of his sins.

The original Stone Parlour was a bare little cell reserved for precisely the same purpose at St Martha's Convent Junior School in Barnet, which I attended half a century ago, between the ages of four and six. It had a crucifix on the wall, perhaps a single wooden chair, and a window from which the solitary miscreant could see in the distance the playground from which he had been banished. Being a relatively diligent little chap, I was only occasionally incarcerated. But my naughty friend Bernard – who these days would have been diagnosed with a whole set of behavioural syndromes and dosed to the eyeballs on Ritalin, but who I like to imagine eventually made good as a Mercedes dealer on the North Circular, or perhaps a developer of buy-to-let flats – seemed to spend half his school life in there. I have a memory of his pale face at the window. I worried about him a lot.

And because we had been talking about it at home recently, and I had never set foot in Barnet since we moved away in 1961, I conceived a sudden urge to find out whether the Stone Parlour still exists. So instead of alighting at Euston, I stayed on the train all the way through leafy Finchley, Totteridge and Whetstone to the end of the line.

When we lived there, in a flat above Barclays Bank on the High Street, Barnet was a proud little Hertfordshire town; since 1965 its name has been attached to an outer London borough, its distinctive character blurred into a suburban sprawl from Edgware to Golders Green. But a stroll uphill past the parish church of St John the Baptist provides plenty of reminders of the town's history. This was the Great North Road, a day's ride and a steepish climb from the centre of London. It was also a great livestock market, where beasts were bought and sold before their final journey to city slaughterhouses. So it was a place where travellers paused; hence Dickens's observation, in *Oliver Twist*, that 'every other house in Barnet was a tavern, large or small'. Many are still there: the Olde Mitre, built in 1633; the imposing Victorian Red Lion, now sadly rebranded a 'Toby Carvery'; but not the Star, the ancient coaching inn in whose garage my father kept the absurdly magnificent 1932 Buick he bought on a whim. That one is long gone, replaced by a mini-supermarket.

Many other old premises along my walk had found modern purposes: I counted half a dozen charity shops, almost as many opticians, and some cheerful nail salons and 'smoothie bars'. But the Dutch-gabled Edwardian Post Office has yet to be turned into anything else; and the Barclays branch, a reassuringly dignified pre-war building, is still there and busy enough for me to slip unnoticed up the back stairs, where a sign said 'Local Business' – though no one seemed to be doing any – to the locked door of the flat, now empty offices. Through a porthole I could see the corridor where Bernard and I once made a pirate ship out of a folding table.

So on I went in search of the Stone Parlour: encouragingly, St Martha's Junior School was still shown on the town map. I walked back past the church into historic Wood Street – diverting briefly into a park where, in Red Indian costume, I won a prize in a road-safety themed fancy dress competition, wearing a card round my neck saying 'I'd rather be hit by a tomahawk than a Humber Hawk.' How my father was proud of that line.

And here at last, set back in a little garden, was the convent and school built in 1914 for the French order of Sisters of St Martha. 'Couvent St Marthe Montmartre' says the stone frontage – but the statue of the Virgin has gone from the garden, and I'm too late. The gates are chained, and an estate agent's sign proclaims 'St Martha's Court', a development of luxury one- and two-bedroomed apartments 'suitable for investment', about to go on sale. The school closed last summer, I discover, victim of a decreasing pupil roll and the adverse economic climate.

But I wasn't giving up. I went round the back into Union Street and found an open gate into the schoolyard, which must have been sold separately and is yet to be redeveloped. The classroom where Sister Mary Joseph filled my five-year-old head with the theology of limbo and purgatory had been rebuilt, but otherwise the place was just as I remembered, except for a stout new fence separating it from the old convent.* Peering over the top, I picked out what I thought was the window of the Stone Parlour, now perhaps the designer kitchen of one of those desirable apartments. No Bernard peered back – but who knows, perhaps he's the developer of St Martha's Court. That would certainly be a form of revenge.

Ah well, I'm glad I made the journey. As I wrote about the banking crisis, institutions and places that seemed so permanent in our earlier lives rarely prove to be so, but very often find interesting new destinies. Normal service will resume next week, when I shall no doubt nominate some City sinners for a spell in my imaginary Stone Parlour.

July 2010

— ✳ —

THE TROUBLE WITH BEARDS

'And while you're at it, Martin, why not shave that beard off?' quipped 'Dick Turpin', gossip columnist of the *Yorkshire Evening Press*, commiserating in print for my near-misses in Tory selection contests for two promising parliamentary seats. The accompanying photograph was pinned up in my local Conservative office, with the offending whiskers carefully Tippexed out to reinforce the message.

---

* Some months after this piece appeared, I received a charming letter from a nun in St Martha's Convent at Rottingdean near Brighton, telling me that the sisters from Barnet had moved there some years ago and that a visitor had shown them my column about the Stone Parlour, which they had enjoyed. The letter ended 'Bless you.'

The political disadvantage of facial hair is a well-known phenomenon: American research shows that, other things being equal, a bearded candidate has a 5 per cent disadvantage against a clean-shaven opponent. Image-makers have this week been advising Labour men to reach for their razors to improve their television approval ratings.

Tony Blair's party still accommodates more than thirty bearded MPs, led by the dense front-bench thicket of Dobson, Cook and Blunkett, and on this issue – as with every other abandonment of rough-cut Old Labour integrity in favour of smooth New Labour electability – there is bound to be resistance. But among Tory selection committees the length and breadth of the country, there is virtual unanimity: beards are not us. Frankly, you might as well turn up for the interview in eye shadow and fishnet stockings. Though I hesitate to blame my own non-selection entirely on my beard (as Turpin also pointed out, I am in need of a 'doe-eyed, Sloaney bride' as well as a good shave), it certainly seems to be a factor.

It may have been a freak that the beard and I were allowed on to Central Office's approved list of potential candidates in the first place. But it happened that the MP who grilled me for that purpose was one of the few hirsute men previously to have slipped through the net – Robert Jones, who is now a junior environment minister despite a particularly elaborate set of facial topiary.

Since leaping that first hurdle, however, things have not gone well. Some of the constituency associations that have declined to interview me may well have been put off by my saturnine mugshot. But in two seats I have actually come within sight of winning, and I can only wonder whether a last-minute swipe with a disposable Gillette in the cloakroom (or even a dramatic waving of the razor in mid-speech, with a suitable sound-bite like 'Whiskers are optional, principles are not!') might have turned a crucial handful of votes in my favour.

I shall never know. In York, I came a close second to the clean-cut, sharp-chinned Simon Mallett. In the rock-solid Tory heartland of the Vale of York, out of a field of more than 150 applicants, the only man to beat me was the clean-cut, sharp-chinned David Ruffley, political adviser to Kenneth Clarke. The eventual winner was the even cleaner-cut (and in this respect naturally advantaged) Anne McIntosh.

'Looks like Clement Freud', was one disapproving comment overheard at the Vale of York meeting. 'Looks like some sort of intellectual', was another, even more damning. 'Looks absolutely horrible', I was told at another recent event by a lady member who had not seen the growth before, 'What on earth have you done to yourself?'

It is well known that Margaret Thatcher disapproved of beards and most Tories of her age group (who make up the bulk of constituency activists) would be proud to think that they uphold her views on this as on many others matters. The advice passed on at second hand from one of her senior ministers was: 'Remember that no one is prejudiced against not having a beard.' Except Sikhs and ayatollahs, I suppose one might riposte, but there are not many of those in rural Conservative associations.

What's the problem about beards? The anti-beardists of Middle England see in them an attempt to hide something unpleasant or inadequate about the wearer's personality; they are symbols of shiftiness and vanity; they are an aggressive – literally in-your-face – statement of non-conformity. Ironically, I find I am capable of passing such sweeping judgements myself, if I think about Frank Dobson or Gerry Adams, whereas I think my own beard has no significant purpose at all, other than perhaps to add a touch of style and gravitas.

Confronted by all-party agreement that facial hair is a dangerous thing, we beardies are in danger of becoming political pariahs. But I am not about to co-operate in the decommissioning of my goatee. After all, the image-makers' advice is not followed so slavishly that any politician with a really devious streak in him is almost bound to be clean-shaven, so beards could eventually come to symbolise straightforwardness and integrity.

Take, for example, Hartlepool MP Peter Mandelson, the Machiavelli of Tony Blair's inner circle. 'He's gone from a beard to a moustache to nothing at all,' a BBC commentator pointed out this week. 'He's saying: "Look, I've got nothing to hide."' Oh yes? Well, Hartlepool

Conservatives have just started looking for a candidate to fight him. My advice is to emphasise straightforwardness and integrity and go for the first ever all-beard Tory shortlist.

Daily Telegraph, *October 1995*

———— ✳ ————

A MAN FOR THE NINETIES

There is no species on earth more vicious than the adolescent public schoolboy. At Glenalmond in Perthshire we were nasty to each other all day long.

We were intolerant of dullness or eccentricity, of stupidity or cleverness, of physical peculiarities or weaknesses of personal hygiene, or anything out of the ordinary about each other's parents – intolerant of almost any characteristic at all, in fact, except for a kind of brutal laddishness which was our idea of how to be cool. On balance I enjoyed the place: it toughened me and got me to Oxford. But five years there did not make me a gentleman, and at least as long a stretch of real life outside was required to rub off the sharp edges. Rediscovering classmates from those days can, therefore, be a disturbing experience: we're all grown-ups now, but somewhere inside us the horrid schoolboy lives for ever.

All of this is by way of a preamble to my encounter with Adair Turner, recently appointed director-general of the Confederation of British Industry and, at thirty-nine, youthful recruit to the squadron of soundbite pundits who will talk Britain into the next century.* We shall see more of Turner in a few days' time, at the CBI's annual conference in Birmingham. Thereafter, I predict, we will hear from him *ad nauseam*

---

* Now Lord Turner of Ecchinswell, he went on to be chairman of the Financial Services Authority, among many other public appointments.

on the hottest potato of the second half of the decade, the question of British participation in a single European currency. 'Our businessmen want it' is one half of the argument; Euro-sceptics provide the other. One of Adair Turner's tasks is to tell us what our businessmen really want.

But to me, Turner will always be the fellow who sat next to me at school and beat me in every exam. We were on civil terms most of the time, but not really friends. A scholarship boy whose father was a local government officer in Argyll, he worked harder than anyone else in our year, quietly absorbing hefty volumes of history the rest of us barely skimmed, filling notebook after notebook with perfectly regular, rather childlike handwriting. He was never 'one of the lads', but my oafish chums could not categorise him as a 'vegetable', since he was far cleverer than all of them; nor as a 'pseud', since (unlike me) he did not indulge in superficial intellectual flash. So, on the whole, they left him alone. At sixteen he was a university-level swot who scored A in everything, but took a minimal part in the rest of school life.

He was not an actor, a musician, a Marxist, a Leonard Cohen fan, a smoker, a football hooligan, a shoplifter, a chaser of kitchenmaids or a hoarder of pornography. I think he wrote poetry, but he never showed it to anybody, and I remember him being an ardent Conservative when, around the time of the 1970 election, I thought I might be a socialist.

After the barbarities of school life, Cambridge must have been a great relief to Turner. He took a First, was chairman of the Conservatives and president of the Union. From there he joined the Chase Manhattan Bank in London, scoring such astonishingly high marks on the credit-training course that they put him in charge of it the following year.

At that point, in the late seventies, I caught up with him once for lunch in the City. From a rather weedy youth, he had grown taller and stronger, but the loping gait and discomfiting seriousness of manner were instantly recognisable. Another seventeen years on, a few days ago, I called on him at the CBI. This time he seemed almost to have evolved into a completely different person, grey but somehow better-looking – as can happen to clean-living people in early middle age – more polished and jovial, approaching the suave. But, I wanted to know, was the solitary bookworm still there inside.

In the third-of-a-working-lifetime between these two meetings, Turner had moved from Chase to BP's planning department, and thence to McKinsey, the ubiquitous management consultancy. He left the Conservatives and was briefly active in the SDP, shifting rightwards again in the high-Thatcher era. The past five years were spent advising privatised banks in Eastern Europe, and composing himself for his entry into the public arena – something which, he has told other interviewers, has long been on his personal agenda. I followed his career at a distance, convinced that significant past acquaintances always crop up again in the end.

So it came as no surprise to find him appointed to a post of national prominence. Indeed, it is an entertaining irony that it should turn out to be the only job of that kind for which I have ever applied myself. In a whimsical moment in 1991 I answered a CBI recruitment ad in the *Financial Times*. On that occasion the successful candidate was Howard Davies, who is now deputy governor of the Bank of England. But I still treasure a letter from Mr Norman of Norman, Broadbent, head hunters, saying that he could see I had 'much to offer', and would be in touch again shortly. I still haven't heard from him: could it be a clerical error that they eventually appointed the boy who sat next to me, rather than me?

We lunched briskly, without much small talk, in Turner's Centre Point office, on sandwiches and mineral water – a lunch fit for Nineties' Man. For that is what Turner has evolved into, or perhaps was always waiting to be. He is, in fact, a perfect Blairite lapsed-Tory pragmatist, and on the big issue, the single currency, he sounds at first like *Private Eye*'s Rev. J. C. Flannel, who once declared: 'In a very real sense I am both for and against the bomb': 'We want to be at the table, thoroughly engaged in Europe . . .' Turner begins – but this is more than even-handed waffle. Expanded at length, it is as clear an analysis of the subject as I have yet heard. Turner's intellect is just the sort of finely tuned instrument we need to interpret this hugely complex question.

'Macro-economics is my hobby,' he says. 'I like looking at monetary statistics.'

And deep in his eyes the scholarship swot is still there, just as the cynical teenage mischief-maker is, I guess, still in me. When we finally came around to the subject of school (I had always assumed that he was rather unhappy there), he seemed to have acquired rosier-tinted memories than mine. He has even accepted an invitation to address next year's prize-giving – news which provoked an unexpected pang of jealousy.

But, on reflection, I can see that he is the perfect man for that job as well. The 'lads' and the 'pseuds', the chancers, the rogues, the jokers and the radicals, had their time in the 1980s – and a fair mess they made of it. Now is the age of greying suaveness, of the carefully reasoned middle way, of the sober, studious types we chose to ignore when life looked easier. Good luck, Adair, old chap, your era has arrived.

Sunday Telegraph, *1995*

———✳———

I AM 39, GOING ON 40

I can pinpoint the precise moment when I first started worrying about my age. It was slightly less than six months ago, at the halfway mark between my thirty-ninth and fortieth birthdays.

Feelings of uneasiness were provoked by the arrival of an otherwise delightful twenty-three-year-old houseguest who used the word 'like' in every sentence (as in, 'So I'm like, "Wow, this is, like, really amazing …"'), delivered in alien rhythms and flattened tones. It was the voice of youth, the voice of video games and *The Big Breakfast*, and it just did not sound like my generation at all: as distant from our early 1970s received English as our own speech is from the mannerisms of 1950s film actors, or as the present Prince of Wales's broadcast voice differs from that of Edward VIII. Suddenly I felt the ice-cold slipstream of time blowing, as it were, straight up my trouser-leg.

As the dreaded fortieth came closer and closer, uneasiness turned to mild panic, not knowing whether to celebrate or repine, to laugh or to cry. Of course, birthdays are artificial milestones which hindsight rapidly diminishes into insignificance. The young make a fuss about reaching twenty-one – I remember being monumentally sick in the college squash court, though not, I think, directly provoked by fear of getting old. Fashionable metropolitan thrusters make a fuss about reaching thirty, in a self-admiring, still-cool kind of way.

But forty really is a big one, the equivalent of the last stage of the *Gladiators'* televised assault course, in which contestants sprint up a steep walkway moving against them and hurl themselves through a stretched sheet of black paper. On the far side of that sheet is middle age, wisdom, closed options, the ripening career, the settled family life, the golf club and the personal pension plan. Forty is the barrier beyond which you cannot seriously consider yourself young any more.

Other people may politely reassure you that you can and you are, but such blandishments are notoriously untrustworthy. Everyone thinks forty-one-year-old Tony Blair is still young, even though he is eleven weeks older than Graham Gooch,* who everyone thinks is as old as the hills. But what, I wonder, does Blair think of himself, as he checks his hairline in the mirror? And more importantly, should I be reinvigorated by the thought of being even younger than him, or worried by the thought of being almost as old as someone who is almost prime minister? Should I be relieved that I can never be as old as Gooch, or plunged into gloom by the realisation that, until death us do part, I am a full two-and-a-half years older than Mike Gatting? Should I simply abandon this fruitless, solipsistic line of analysis and check myself into a health farm for a month's grapefruit juice, monkey glands and

---

* The former England cricket captain had recently retired from Test cricket but continued playing for Essex until 1997. Mike Gatting, also mentioned here, was another former England captain.

Mongolian tone-chanting, as a birthday present designed to preserve the vestiges of youth – what Joseph Conrad called 'the heat of life in the handful of dust' – for as long as I can?

But perhaps my concern is unnecessary and ill-mannered, given that the average *Spectator* reader is, so the publisher tells me, forty-seven years old. Several people with whom I have raised this subject have resorted to the cliché that life begins at forty, or rather, in a tentative tone, 'Well, they do say that life begins at forty', no one so far quizzed being willing to affirm this dictum wholeheartedly from their own experience, or to identify who 'they' are. And there are plenty of interesting examples. Conrad himself was a sailor until he was thirty-eight. Lord Hanson made the first acquisition of what was to become the Hanson Trust conglomerate when he was forty-one. Nigel Lawson first entered the House of Commons when he was forty-two. And I have always like the example of Rossini, although I'm not quite certain which side of the argument it supports: he stopped composing operas when he was thirty-seven, and devoted the last four decades of his life to cheerful gormandising.

Underlying all this, you may discern a certain residual worry about achievement, or lack of it. At forty, you may be no more than two-fifths of the way into a really distinguished career, or you may be in the first flush of an interesting second one. On the other hand, though you may not yet know it, you could just as easily have peaked at thirty-nine and be within ten years of ignominious early retirement.

As an undergraduate, I used to argue extensively with a man on my staircase (indeed, I was probably hectoring him on this very point shortly before bringing somebody's squash match to such an abrupt halt on that dimly remembered evening) that to make the life ahead of us worthwhile, it had to be approached as a serious career assault course and a race against time – not unlike *Gladiators*, as it later turned out. I poured scorn on his view, much influenced by Jethro Tull lyrics and other stimulants, that life would just happen to you in a kaleidoscopic collage of experience out of which some useful meaning might or might not eventually make itself apparent. Current undergraduates may care to confirm, by inserting the word 'like' in three or four places in each of the last two sentences and substituting Take That, whoever they may be, for Jethro Tull, that the identical debate is still engaging them today.

I am told that at my college neighbour's recent fortieth birthday party, I made a long impromptu speech to the effect that he, now a raging careerist in the American advertising business, may have been right after all and I may have been wrong. I suppose that must be the mellow reflectiveness of middle age creeping in. It may also have been the influence of Anthony Powell, and his proposition in *A Dance to the Music of Time*, reassuring to anyone worried by the passage of years, that continuous achievement for its own sake is all right for the likes of Kenneth Widmerpool, but that what is really fascinating is the way in which patterns of life form, dissolve and reform in new configurations, driven by the interaction of chance and human nature.

Critics have long disputed the validity of Powell's use of coincidental meetings to deploy symbolic characters 'round whom the past and future have a way of assembling'. But I have to report that, as the sand piles up at the bottom of life's egg-timer, the world comes more and more to fit the Powell model. The plain fact is that almost everyone becomes more interesting as they grow older, and that those who become less so have a fortunate habit of fading into their own domestic obscurity – except at old boys' dinners, where they seem to congregate en masse.

All the others, the men who were once no more than unreliable beer-drinking companions in Oxford cellars and dim Fulham bars, your best pal in the lower sixth, the old girlfriend you should have married, the colleagues from your first job. The people encountered in Greek campsites or on Greyhound buses in 1973, the people you cannot remember at all but who claim to remember you, have grown up to be extraordinary people. They are colonels and Queen's Counsel, advisers to Bolivia and experts in the steel industry, film-makers, chefs, deckhands, organic farmers, prime-ministers-in-waiting, bad guitarists and suspected fraudsters. They have long CVs, forthright spouses and, in some cases, polite children. They disappear for years but somehow you always seem to know what they have been doing.

The age-band of social life becomes wider and wider, as old and new acquaintances appear in odd combinations and comic circumstances, not always as felicitously composed as Powell's set-pieces, but satisfying enough to make us all say, time after time, 'Well, come to think of it, I don't really feel a day older than the day we first met . . .' And there are very few loose ends: one of these days, the anaesthetist in the heart-transplant theatre or the cellmate at Ford Open Prison or the buffer next to me on the House of Lords bench will lean over and mutter, 'I know you. You're the drunken buffoon who cost me the college squash championship in '76. Still got the dry-cleaning bill somewhere . . .'

You may also have discerned by now that at last I am beginning to think more positively about reaching forty. I think perhaps it was the effect of a conference in California a few days ago – much worse for the body but better for the mind than a month at a health farm – with a cast of dozens all a short distance either side of forty, strangers to begin with but swiftly connected by personal echoes going back ten or twenty years and, I have no doubt, destined to reconnect in entertaining semi-random patterns for many years to come.

It was the rejuvenation cure I had been looking for. The hair may recede, the neck may thicken, but as the discotheque blasted out 'Shout' from the soundtrack of *National Lampoon's Animal House*, I suddenly realised that some vital part of all of us never ages at all.

Life does not begin or end at forty, I have decided, it just goes round in subtly changing patterns, mostly changing for the better. But can it always be so? Mr and Mrs Average Reader, you have my sympathy: I mean, like, imagine the horror of reaching fifty . . .

December 1994

— ❋ —

CAN I BE YOUR MR WONDERFUL?

Surely the biggest news this week, bigger even than the Budget, is the Duchess of York's announcement that she may never find Mr Right. 'Any man who took me on would have to take on an awful lot, really,' she laments in *Hello!*, going on to list all the baggage of media scrutiny, royal children and 'mad' family (the Fergusons, not the other lot) which she thinks any sensible chap would find overwhelmingly offputting. 'It would be nice to have someone who loved me so much it didn't matter. There must be someone out there who's nuts!'

There is, Fergie, never despair. But I think you may be rattling the wrong cages in the masculine zoo. In your preferred world of princelings, euro-counts and racing drivers, you may well have exhausted all the possibilities. Those perma-tanned playboys can afford trophy girlfriends fifteen years younger than you, who come with no baggage except a few little items from the Janet Reger catalogue. When it comes to competing on that Riviera catwalk, you may be right to admit you're too much of a handful these days.

But there is another kind of man for whom you could be the fulfilment of the wildest dream: the shy, shabby, over-forty British bachelor. There are thousands of them out there, sitting quietly in their anoraks in pub corners and libraries, waiting to be rescued. The late Inspector Morse was a fine example. Indeed, some might say I am not a bad model myself, having once written an A to Z of bachelorhood in *The Spectator* which included: 'V is for Venus, goddess of love, whose unpredictable call may interrupt the bachelor idyll at any moment. Beware.' And I happen to have been playing an even better example on stage last week, in an amateur production of James Robson's comedy *Mr Wonderful*, about a woman of Fergie's age searching in vain for her perfect partner.

The point about shy bachelors is that (provided they are interested in women at all) they are not generally on the lookout for shy spinsters: that combination often doesn't work, because neither party is brave enough to pull the pyjama cord and jump. What such men secretly want is 'a woman of the world' (as Fergie was often called when she became engaged to Prince Andrew), not just in the hope of a vigorous refresher course on the sofa, but as a matter of deep psychological yearning. They have often stayed single into middle age for the very reason that in their youth they were too susceptible to falling in love with troublesome women, who treated them wrong or were too vampish to take home to mother. A certain type of once-bitten-twice-shy bachelor finds himself perpetually drawn to the Fergie archetype.

My stage character, Eric Box, owner of a northern DIY emporium, with Brylcreemed hair and a neat set of biros clipped in his pocket, was such a man. In a brief encounter arranged by a dating agency, he held forth about the merits and uses (for DIY purposes) of 'the solitary screw ... I don't suppose a woman like you gives much thought to the common or garden screw, Norma, let along the solitary screw.' You can see why Norma didn't stay for a second drink, but then perhaps she was too shy; a more worldly woman might have been intrigued to find out what Eric really packed in his tool box.

And from Eric's point of view, the idea of romance with a tigress like Fergie, rather than a mouse like Norma, would have all the allure of trading in his bicycle-clips for a classic E-Type Jaguar: rich upholstery, sleek polish, the promise of throbbing performance under the bonnet; unreliable, but in an exciting way. Inside every lonesome Eric is the Randy Andy he once might have been, waiting for a Fergie to get his motor running again.

And he's not going to worry about how much luggage she brings along. He's ... but why am I still talking about Eric here? Those potent E-Type images have stirred forgotten yearnings. Yoohoo, Fergie, I'm the one in the corner with the biros in the pocket and the rose in the anorak buttonhole: let me tell you about my hobby ...

Evening Standard, *April 2002*

—✳—

THE MUSIC OF TIME

I t was a great pleasure to hear a new serialisation (by Michael Butt) of Anthony Powell's *A Dance to the Music of Time* on Radio 4 recently. For his devotees, Powell has never gone out of fashion, because life is full of moments when the past and the present connect in unexpected patterns – the essential plot device of the *Dance* novels. The *Spectator's* summer party is perpetually fertile in this respect. Last year's, with its oppressive presence of Brown henchmen in getting-to-know-you mode, provided a perfect Powellian exchange with a writer who doesn't get up to town much. Writer, pointing into the throng: 'Who's that tall bloke in a suit?' Me: 'Newish cabinet minister. Very much on the up, I hear.' 'Really? Used to sell him drugs at university. Always wondered how he'd end up.'

July 2008

—— ❉ ——

RETURN TO BRUSSELS

I t's twenty-five years since I lived in Brussels, and the building in which I once managed a portfolio of loans to dodgy Latin America state borrowers has long since been taken over by a Catholic overseas aid charity: I hope they scatter their funds more sensibly than we did. Otherwise – apart from the billion-euro follies of the tarted-up Berlaymont and the monstrous European Parliament building – the city seems hardly to have changed at all. It's a far more civilised place than British Brussels-bashers habitually credit: taxi drivers are polite, eurocrats still tuck into a decent lunch however low their morale, and even the dingier parts of town have, for me, a certain nostalgic charm.

Wandering the *quartier* behind the Berlaymont between meetings, I found myself drawn in an Anthony Powellish sort of way to a dingy side street called rue John Waterloo Wilson – scene of a *liaison dangereuse* which briefly distracted me from my loan-officer duties all those years ago. I did not ring the doorbell of that third-floor bedsit to see whether the ghost of my youth was still there, but I wondered again, as I had done even in the depth of romantic trauma, who the blazes John Waterloo Wilson was. Google has nothing to offer on the subject, but if any kind reader can tell me, I might finally achieve what psychoanalysts call 'closure' . . .

September 2005

. . . Interesting news from rue John Waterloo Wilson, the Brussels back street whose name has been engraved on my heart these past twenty-five years. Two kind readers answered my appeal for information – and it was a relief that neither of them turned out to be the *femme fatale* who drew me to that mysterious address in the first place. But one of them did lead me to a conversation with a great-great-great-grandson of John Waterloo Wilson himself, who I now know made his money in the nineteenth-century equivalent of launderettes, bequeathed twenty-sixth paintings to the Musée de Bruxelles in 1878, and had a school of linguistic studies named after him. He sounds like a model *Spectator* reader, and it is a healing experience to have made his acquaintance at last.

November 2005

—❋—

FAMOUS BELGIANS

Call me sentimental, but I'm sorry to see Belgium on the brink of divorce. My Flemish ancestors came to England some decades before Belgium declared itself independent of the Netherlands in 1830 – they were silk weavers who took advantage of an early local-government enterprise scheme, offering migrant craftsmen freedom from taxes in the city of Norwich. But still I feel a certain affection for the stolid, damp, unlovely country where I lived in the early 1980s, and which is now enmired in mutual antipathy and political stalemate between its Flemish- and French-speaking communities.

Perhaps there's still time for the two sides to reunite in irritation at the fact that the British media uses any story about Belgium as an excuse to revive that old party game, 'Name a Famous Belgian'. René Magritte, the cyclist Eddy Merckx and the singer Jacques Brel are popular answers, but let me throw in a couple more. The first was suggested by an affronted Belgian to whom I undiplomatically outlined the game: he nominated Georges Nagelmackers, a nineteenth-century banker from Liège who made a giant contribution to civilised travel by introducing the railway sleeping-car, or wagon-lit; he also founded the Orient Express from Paris to Constantinople and the Nord-Express to St Petersburg. The second was a lawyer who made his name defending outspoken journalists and went on to be a founder member of Belgium's revolutionary government, its representative in London and its prime minister, for eight months, in 1845. His name was Baron Sylvain Van de Weyer, and I'd love to claim him as a cousin if only I could trace the remotest connection.

October 2007

———— ✳ ————

DEATH DUTIES

This column generally strives for jocularity, but sometimes life just isn't funny. My sister Linda, a gifted artist and teacher, died in November, aged only fifty-five. Grief and anger being adjacent emotions, I embarked on the task of putting her affairs in order in the expectation that unfeeling bureaucracy would drive me repeatedly to rage. But someone somewhere has been running courses on how to deal with the bereaved on the telephone: so far the process has really been quite therapeutic. Utility companies, local government departments, benefits offices, have without exception been helpful and sympathetic. One bank fell at the first fence – its call centre operative offering duff information and no condolences – but made sufficient amends to avoid being named and shamed. I especially warmed to Miss Agoo, the registrar of deaths at Lambeth Town Hall in Brixton, where I had braced myself for a gruesome experience. She was dignified and kind, with beautiful handwriting, and she lent me her fountain pen to sign the certificate in the great book; when I complimented her on it, she said simply 'We're registrars. We like pens.'

I cannot, however, speak for the dignity or kindness of the gentlemen of HM Revenue & Customs, who sit silent in their counting house waiting to receive a cheque equivalent to several years' growth in value of my sister's very modest south London house. The word is that taxmen these days are under orders aggressively to pursue every last pound of inheritance tax – and anyone who thinks IHT at 40 per cent is not going to be a major electoral issue next time round should contemplate the potential six-figure fine it now represents for every suburban family. Just take a look at form IHT 200, which demands to know the value of every chattel, down to 'garden equipment, tools etc'. That old mower might fetch twenty-five quid in a car boot sale? That'll be another tenner for Gordon then.

January 2007

———❋———

THE VISITORS' BOOK

S ir Roy Strong's eyes widened;* his nostrils twitched; his pen hovered as though the horror of what confronted him had momentarily robbed him of the power to write.

---

* Sir Roy is the former director of the National Portrait Gallery and the Victoria and Albert Museum.

The offending object was the visitors' book of Helmsley Arts Centre in North Yorkshire, where he had just given an eloquent talk about his life, and where I happen to be the part-time director. I sensed the problem immediately: every celebrity signatory on the open page had committed the heinous solecism of adding some witticism or phrase of thanks, instead of doing what toffs do, which is simply to sign and add the shortest possible indication of their address. The hard-left punk poet Attila the Stockbroker, for example, had scrawled 'ROCKIN' GIG'. Most troubling of all, the undoubted über-toff John Julius Norwich – a viscount, no less – had written '2nd time, gluttons for punishment that you are!'

That exclamation mark must have been especially painful: with a sigh of profound regret for the crumbling of another pillar of the social order, the great aesthete, gardener and museum director slowly inscribed his name – but not, of course, his knightly title – adding, after a considered pause, 'Herefordshire'. 'Quite right too,' said a *Spectator* colleague of the toff persuasion on whom I tested this anecdote. 'We don't want comments. And we don't want postcodes either.'

In castles and country houses of the old-fashioned kind from Bodmin to the Black Isle the visitors' book is a goatskin-bound, gold-tooled artefact of almost biblical sanctity. Its plain pages (no naff little grid of boxes for Date, Name, Address and Comments, like a seaside B&B) record a solemn procession of names and geographical identifiers. If the house happens to be a holiday home – a shooting lodge or an Alpine chalet – even the host signs each time he stays, just as the true gentleman, I'm told, will enter himself neatly in the Game Book before retiring to the billiard room to blow his brains out.

No wonder, then, that a scene like an H. M. Bateman cartoon awaits the ill-tutored guest who dares deface the visitors' book (or should that be 'guest book', as the top people's stationer Smythson of Bond Street has it?) with a saucy limerick or a smiley face. But I think the toffs have got it wrong. No toff myself, I have a sneaking respect for their arcane rituals; on this one, however, I think they're simply missing the fun. It's time they joined the Norwich-Atilla revolution.

In Helmsley, besides the arts centre book, I keep one at home which now runs to more than 700 signatures and accompanying remarks – it came from Harrods, I notice, and the binding is still in good order after eighteen years of use. The catalogue of names is an entertainment in itself (as is the progress over the years of my godchildren's handwriting) but the comments add all sorts of pleasing memory-triggers. If you'll forgive a bit of name-dropping, the jazzman Kenny Ball wrote 'Cheese, wine, good drunken conversation, what more could one ask'; the composer Sir Richard Rodney Bennett, a three-times visitor, said 'It was magic'; and mayor-to-be Boris, on what may well have been his first ever outing to speak to a local Conservative association way back in January 1995, encapsulated our blizzard-hit drive from York to Helmsley – in which I made him lie spread-eagled on the bonnet of the car to give us traction over the hills – with the single word 'Epic!'

And why not take the free-form visitors' book a step further? In a remote cottage on a West Highland sea loch at Hogmanay, I was offered a beautiful, floral-cloth-bound scrapbook, with big, creamy pages of handmade paper, in which guests were expected to write or sketch full accounts of their visits. In my hideaway in France, I have come up with a new formula: asking each guest to write down a recipe. This seems to work well, on the basis that on French holidays food is a perpetual talking point anyway and even non-cooks like cooking with fresh ingredients bought from the market and limitless quantities of local wine to encourage them.

The prize-winning entries so far are the opera director Stefan Janski's fruity lamb casserole, into which he seems to have thrown the entire fruit bowl, and my octogenarian uncle Desmond's rich lemon cream pot. If I ever persuade a publisher to turn this into a coffee-table foodie book (I foresee an award-winning television series to go with it, by the way), we'll have to test all the recipes pretty rigorously to see whether they produce anything edible at all. But as a record of long, happy, hilarious lunches blurring into dinners, it could hardly be bettered.

And it provides a perfect get-out for that agonising social dilemma (perhaps Sir Roy has suffered this one too) when a guest comes into the kitchen and says, 'If you've got some garlic, Tabasco, maple syrup, mustard and Marmite, I'll make you a jar of my famous salad dressing.' All you have to say is, 'Oh no, please don't go to all that trouble. But *do* write the recipe in the visitors' book.'

October 2007

—✳—

WHAT'S YOUR IDEAL JOB?

At a twenty-first birthday party full of bright, well-scrubbed final-year students and new graduates, I go round the room asking them all whether they've found jobs, or if not what their ideal job would be. The ones in the first category are mostly going into the City, on graduate training schemes at firms such as Goldman Sachs and Lloyds – another small indication (despite Lloyds' recently announced plan to shed 15,000 staff) of returning normality after the crash. The no-jobbers all come up with fluffy answers such as 'food writer', 'film critic' and 'sports marketing'. 'Aha,' I respond, avuncular but stern, 'That's the problem with the youth of today – no one wants to be a railway engineer or a biotech entrepreneur or a farmer. Who d'you think's going to produce the essentials of economic life and growth for the next generation?' They all look a bit embarrassed – but then I remember how I answered the 'ideal job' question myself in an interview to get into Oxford thirty-eight years ago: what could have been fluffier than 'I want to write for *The Spectator*'?

July 2011

—✳—

DIALLING 999

For the first time in my life I had to call an ambulance, because my mother was suffering from chest pains. It was a fascinating episode: so much so that my mother, when she was feeling a little better, accused me of actually enjoying it. The reality of Monday morning in a south London A&E department – within twenty-five minutes of the 999 call, she was in the Recovery Room at St George's, Tooting – may lack the intensity of *ER* and offer no hint of the tangle of doomed doctor-nurse-paramedic relationships that afflicts *Holby City*, but it gives you plenty to think about.

Recent news stories have suggested that NHS blunders cause 2,000 needless deaths annually, and that the service is heading for crisis over its new £6 billion computer system to add to a continuing crisis of funding shortfalls. St George's itself was reported to be £24 million in the red last year. But at ground level – to the observer hanging around A&E for a day – it is reassuringly robust. It is also surprisingly homely: the 999 operator addressed me as 'my love' and the big, brisk, Afro-Caribbean woman driving the ambulance called me 'sweetheart'. A nurse took the trouble to move a couple of male patients out of an alcove of the medical assessment ward because, she said, 'My mum wouldn't like being surrounded by blokes in here either.'

The only features that deserved criticism were the baffling pay-as-you-go bedside phone and television provided by Patientline plc of Slough – in which I shall not rush to buy shares – and the stewed food. 'Vile,' my mother declared, feeling a little better still and despatching me to a nearby kiosk for fresh fruit and sandwiches.

But if it felt homely, it also felt foreign. At a time when there is so much debate about the influx of half a million Polish workers into Britain, we forget how heavily the health service relies for its workforce on previous waves of immigration and temporary visitors. In the course of my mother's brief emergency, she encountered doctors from (I'm guessing, since it seemed impolite to interrupt and ask) South Africa, India, Hong Kong and Egypt; nurses and paramedics from Singapore, the Philippines, Barbados and Cyprus. We should be glad that they all want to train and work in the NHS, because without them it could not function; just as we should be gratified that so many Poles see Britain as a land of opportunity. And if there's a concern about overcrowding – I mused, watching a multi-ethnic throng at the main entrance of St George's, which when you think about it is nicely symbolic – let's remember that migration works both ways. One in five Britons wants to leave the country because they consider themselves over-taxed, according to a survey this week – and half a million have already moved to France, many in the hope of finding a better health service. On this experience, I'd say they were misguided.

September 2006

— ✳ —

FROM MY HOSPITAL BED

I blamed the pheasant casserole, but I did it an injustice. Its only contribution to the drama behind my disappearance in mid December was a residue of lead shot in the small intestine that briefly confused the radiologist. The real villain revealed by the scan was my appendix, which had taken on the raging, bull-necked appearance of Ed Balls faced with a set of improving growth figures.

And so it was that I spent a week in the Friarage at Northallerton, a small 'district general hospital' that has survived every NHS restructuring to date and is cherished by citizens of rural North Yorkshire. For someone who hasn't been hospitalised since 1957, this was the Full Monty: the ambulance in the night, the agonised wait in A&E, the sudden euphoria of morphine; and when the crisis had passed, the stultifying routine of life on the ward, waiting for the relief of the next visiting hour or doctors' round or tea trolley or troublesome patient. But at least it gave me time to think – not just about the state of the NHS, but about the ailments of the nation in 2014 and beyond.

Of course, I shouldn't leap to generalisations on the basis of a single skirmish with the NHS. But I'll say this: given limitless demand as longevity rises, inevitable scarcities and bottlenecks of resources, bureaucratic risk-aversion driven by fear of the *Daily Mail*, and voters' reluctance to pay more tax for anything, including their own healthcare, it's a miracle this giant contraption is as robust as it is. Could it be more efficient? Of course it could, in every corner. It took sixty hours after admission – and a clearly foolish threat to discharge myself – before they finally wheeled me past a scanner appeal poster and fed me into the space-age machine that settled the diagnosis. Staff levels sometimes looked lavish, at other times skeletal. There was no means of knowing who was in charge. As for keeping track of the patient, I kept thinking, 'Why don't they buy some software from Travelodge or DHL or Ocado, instead of all this scribbled paperwork and duplication?'

But I couldn't accuse anyone, from consultant surgeon to catering assistant, of not trying their best within an imperfect system, or not caring. I eavesdropped through the curtain on a young nurse – near the end of a twelve-hour forty-minute shift, in which the forty-minute lunch break is unpaid – gently comforting a patient whose spirits had crumpled after he woke from a bowel operation to find himself with a temporary stoma bag. It was done with real empathy, and it made me think that the ethos of the NHS is good even if the nuts and bolts are loose.

And in the end, the 'patient experience' is far more about ethos than about management structures whose prime objective is cost elimination. What's needed here is not Whitehall-driven top-down re-engineering, destabilising networks and pitting one entrenched interest group against another – but bottom-up *kaizen*, the Japanese factory-floor philosophy of continuous improvement.

And then there are the patients. All life is here, even in small-town Northallerton, and my first observation is that if you want a non-judgemental argument in favour of tax breaks for married couples, take a look at a busy NHS ward at visiting time. It seemed to me that every older patient had a spouse or a sensible grown-up daughter at the bedside, bringing news of grandchildren and fussing over arrangements to be made at home. But all the younger men had broken relationships, and some seemed troubled by the 'next of kin' question.

One likeable lad gave us the whole soap opera between mouthfuls of crisps and painkillers: 'I'm not with mi'girlfriend any more, I just went off on one and walked out. But I love mi'daughter to bits, she's two, I'm getting a new tattoo when I get out of here, whole back, angels wings, just for her. I rang and said can I have a council house, I've nowhere to go, and the bloke said no you can't, we need them all for t'Romanians. It's like this Polish bloke at work, he got a council house for his brother who hasn't even left Poland yet, no bother, it's their human rights apparently. I'm telling you, I'm the biggest UKIP supporter there is, it's the only hope for this country. So I'm living with mi'grandad . . .'

You don't have to project far – many would argue we're already there – to a time when this breakdown of traditional family structures translates into spiralling demand for state welfare that voters will be even more reluctant to pay for, and that acts as a brake on growth as well as a catalyst for inequality. The talkative lad was worrying about all that too: 'I'm putting aside money for mi'daughter now, when I can, I mean, otherwise how's she ever going to get to university, this economy's never getting any better . . .'

I tried to reassure him on that last point, having got the gist of George Osborne's autumn statement on my iPhone (never ask for the television to be switched on in a hospital ward, you end up staring at hours of silent snooker). 'Growth's up 0.8 per cent in the last three months,' I pointed out eagerly, 'factory output up 4 per cent, job vacancies rising at their fastest for fifteen years; of course, we should worry that export demand from the eurozone looks weak . . .' The pills seemed to have put him to sleep, which was lucky because I was about to add '. . . and I'm afraid your chances of buying a house, which is the best way you can secure your daughter's future even if you don't get back with her mother, will get worse as property prices race ahead of earnings. . .'

Even without his angel wings he looked beatific as he snoozed: like the nurse behind the curtain, like most of us really, he was just an ordinary human trying to do the right thing in an imperfect world. I guess that's my theme for 2014.

January 2014

———— ✳ ————

Funeral instructions

There must be brass bands
The best in the district
Marching in front
And marching behind
The cortège a sandwich
Of uniformed bandsmen
Fat ones with tubas
Small ones on cornets
Hymn tunes and jazz tunes
A touch of New Orleans
A half-mile procession
Of trumpets and mourners
And bass drums and buglers
And neighbours and strangers
And golden retrievers
And singers in costume
For scenes from the opera
Outside the Town Hall
An all-girl orchestra
In beautiful ballgowns
Act II, *Don Giovanni*
The knock at the door
The statue who calls me
To repent for my sins
Offers his cold hand
And drags me to hell

You may think that's odd
As a funeral prologue
But it's a tidy reminder
That nobody's perfect
Least of all me
Before we process
Brass to the fore again
Through the church porch
For a magnificent requiem
By Mozart or Fauré
Or Berlioz – I don't know
Which I prefer of them
I love every one of them
Even Brahms's in German
So the choice is for you
My friends, my executors
My final stage managers
And if there's a eulogy
Let it be funny

And short and poetic
But unsentimental
And let the last moment
Be 'Beim Schlafengehen'
The third of the four
Of Strauss's Last Songs
If you can't afford
The great Jessye Norman
Or she passed on before
Just play her recording
As I did for my father
And again for my sister
And wait for the moment
The unbearable moment

At four minutes forty
The high notes sustained
That signal I'm certain
The soul has departed

And after the last chord
Let there be silence
Long as you can bear
Until a brass fanfare
From far in the distance
In a garden of sunlight
Announces the bar
And the buffet are open
Let the feasting begin
The telling of stories
The laughing and drinking
Of whisky and rosé
And Pimms and champagne
The plateau of cheeses
The plateau of gateaux
The cracking of walnuts
The fragrant cigars
And even the reeling
Though I never enjoyed it
But if it's your cup of tea
Then reel one for me
Till midnight's stroke
When fireworks explode
Launch my ashes aloft
In a volley of rockets
And leave my solicitor
To pick up the bill

Index